THE GOSPEL ACCORDING TO JAMES AND OTHER PLAYS

THE GOSPEL ACCORDING TO

JAMES

AND OTHER PLAYS

Charles R. Smith

OHIO UNIVERSITY PRESS · ATHENS

Ohio University Press, Athens, Ohio 45701
ohioswallow.com
© 2012 by Charles R. Smith
All rights reserved

Printed in the United States of America
Ohio University Press books are printed on acid-free paper ⊗ ™

20 19 18 17 16 15 14 13 12   5 4 3 2 1

Library of Congress Cataloging-in-Publication Data
Smith, Charles, 1955–
The gospel according to James and other plays / Charles R. Smith.
   p. cm.
ISBN 978-0-8214-2005-8 (pb : acid-free paper) — ISBN 978-0-8214-4421-4
(electronic)
I. Title.
PS3569.M5152G67 2012
812'.54—dc23

2012027990

CONTENTS

ACKNOWLEDGMENTS

I would like to thank a number of people who have been instrumental in the development of the plays in this collection, including managing director of The Acting Company Margot Harley; my artistic namesake, Chuck Smith; my Victory Gardens family, including Dennis Začek, Marcelle McVay, and Sandy Shinner, for their singular dedication to the voice and vision of the writer; artistic director of Indiana Repertory Theatre Janet Allen for allowing *The Gospel According to James* to develop in its own time; André De Shields for his work on the development of *The Gospel According to James* and the refinement of *Knock Me a Kiss*; Shelley Delaney for her work on the development of *Free Man of Color* and the refinement of *Knock Me a Kiss*; my colleague Erik Ramsey for his support and creative eye; and my wife, Lisa Quinn, who always tells me what I need to hear whether I want to hear it or not.

INTRODUCTION

THE GOSPEL ACCORDING TO JAMES is based on a double lynching that happened on August 8, 1930, in Marion, Indiana. The title character of the play, James Cameron, is based on the real-life James Cameron who, at the age of sixteen, narrowly escaped the lynching that took the lives of his two friends, Abram Smith and Tommy Shipp. James Cameron died in 2006 at the age of ninety-two after devoting his life to various causes focusing on civil rights and calling attention to the scourge of lynching in America. Although Mr. Cameron was the founder of multiple chapters of the NAACP as well as founder of America's Black Holocaust Museum in Milwaukee, Wisconsin, he will primarily be remembered as the only man known to have survived a lynching in America.

Janet Allen, artistic director of the Indiana Repertory Theatre, commissioned *The Gospel According to James* in 2005 after we received a Joyce Award for the research and development of a play based on the 1930 Marion lynchings. After receiving the commission, I spent two years researching James Cameron, his story, and the events surrounding the lynchings before deciding what I wanted the play to be *about*.

From the beginning of my research, I realized that not everyone believed James Cameron's version of the events of August 8, 1930, and for good reason. Parts of his story had huge holes and other parts were simply implausible. As I continued to research James Cameron's story, its veracity, for me, became almost irrelevant. I realized that the facts were far less important than the truth, and the truth that buttressed James Cameron's version of the events that night is vital, relevant, and undeniable. While some parts of his story may not stand up to close inspection, I understood that he told his story the way he remembered it. He told it the way he needed to tell it, and that was his right because it was his story, his truth, his gospel, and that's what the play, *The Gospel According to James,* became. It is a play about individual memory and vision, a play about an individual interpretation of events. However, it isn't James Cameron's memory, vision, or interpretation of events that drives the play. *The Gospel According to James* is my vision, my interpretation of James Cameron's interpretation, and while there is a character in the play named James Cameron, that character is not, and does not pretend to be, the man who once walked this earth. Theater must do more than simply try to realistically recreate or represent people and events on stage. Theater must be transformative in nature. It must at least attempt to articulate things that cannot be articulated in any other way.

Some scholars and critics have characterized four of the five plays in this collection as historical plays. Such genre-based definitions are often useful for a general understanding of the work. However, for a more comprehensive understanding, that characterization could prove counterproductive because it suggests that the engine, the soul, the raison d'être of these plays resides in the historical events on which the plays are based, when in reality, the historical events on which the plays in this collection are based are merely the devices, the vehicles in which we ride to arrive at a different, more contemporary destination.

JELLY BELLY is the only play in this collection that has not been characterized as a historical play. However, it is the only play in this collection with a plot that closely follows actual events. Three of the four other plays represented here, *Knock Me a Kiss, Free Man of Color,* and *The Gospel According to James,* were each based on a few salient facts that had captured my imagination. Beginning with those facts, I researched the time period of each story, and that research informed, but did not generate, my imagining of what could have happened. My imagining was based on a very subjective, personal, and individual point of view without even a perfunctory nod towards objectivity. All of the themes, 90 percent of the characters, and perhaps 70 percent of the plot of these plays was the result of that imagining. *Jelly Belly,* on the other hand, is the only play in this collection whose plot, characters, story, and theme were largely based on an actual event that I experienced firsthand. That makes the only play in this collection not considered to be historical in nature, *Jelly Belly,* even more historical than the others.

I met the man on whom I based the character Jelly Belly in August 1982. I had finished my first year of graduate school at the University of Iowa and had stopped to visit with my brother before heading back to school. That night, I sat on the porch of my brother's house, drank beer, and listened while Jelly Belly expounded on his system of values used to assess human life in terms of cartons of cigarettes and time spent in jail. According to Jelly Belly, killing an uneducated black man would probably get you probation. If you killed an uneducated white man, you would probably get five to ten years. An educated white man would land you ten to twenty, and a white woman with a family would probably get you the death penalty.

What surprised me was not the fact that Jelly Belly had very calmly and openly admitted to murdering several people on different occasions, some of whom had been his friends, but that each time he had been convicted, he had spent no more than six months in jail.

I decided at first that Jelly Belly was an aberration, a freak of society who had slipped through the cracks of justice. But as the night wore on, I came to understand that Jelly Belly was no more of an aberration than I was, and that his system of values could not exist without a concrete foundation for those values. I understood that his system of values was not his own, that he had inherited it from a system much older than himself; that he was not the perpetrator of the unending cycle of violence, but a perpetuator.

The thought of writing a play based on that night did not occur to me until months later when the literary manager of a theater phoned me regarding another one of my plays. He said they liked the play but couldn't produce it and wanted to know if I had a one-act they could consider. Unfortunately, I did not have a one-act, so I did what any young, hungry playwright would do. I lied. I told him I had a play and would put it in the mail to him on Monday. This was on a Friday, so I hung up the phone and went to work believing that my entire embryonic career as a writer depended upon my writing a play over the weekend and getting it to the theater by Monday. I finished the play Sunday night, FedExed it Monday morning, and received my rejection notice a couple of weeks later in the guise of a poorly duplicated form letter.

The play was produced a year later by Penumbra Theatre in St. Paul, Minnesota, and, of course, has been produced since. And while my impetus for writing the play came from a phone call and a chance encounter on my brother's porch one night in August, I couldn't tell you whether the character Jelly Belly bears any resemblance to the man I met that night. If I had to hazard a guess, I would guess not. However, what does exist is a clear and unmistakable resemblance between the character in the play and my impression of who he was. This makes the play less a retelling of the events of that night and more my impression of, or my comment on, those events. As with James Cameron in *The Gospel According to James,* my goal was not to try to reproduce the man but to use my impression of the man, combined with my view of the world, to arrive at a more contemporary, more personal destination.

Jelly Belly is one of the first plays I wrote that helped me understand who I was as a writer. As head of the Professional Playwriting Program at Ohio University, I've spent considerable time and energy over the years developing a program that I wish had been available when I was in graduate school. As head of that program, and in solidarity with the writers in the program, I also thought it was important to include a play in this collection that I wrote when I was in graduate school.

PUDD'NHEAD WILSON is a stage adaptation of the Mark Twain novel of the same name. The play was commissioned and produced in 2002 by The Acting Company in New York as part of a five-year project named The American Century. The purpose of the project was to develop new works for the stage based on works of American literature. *Pudd'nhead Wilson* was the second commission in that series.

When Richard Corley, the associate producing director of The Acting Company, approached me about the project, I was unfamiliar with Mark Twain, had not read *Pudd'nhead Wilson,* and had attempted only one other stage adaptation—that of Jean Toomer's *Cain,* which was commissioned and produced by Victory Gardens Theater a few years earlier with dubious results. One of my mentors, the late Darwin Turner, was a Toomer scholar, and my desire to tackle the stage adaptation of Toomer's *Cane* was propelled by my need to prove my worthiness to him as a playwright and as an artist. With the adaptation of Twain's *Pudd'nhead Wilson,* I had nothing to prove. With nothing to prove and nothing at stake, I read *Pudd'nhead Wilson* with no preset agenda.

Reading Twain's *Pudd'nhead Wilson,* I was immediately struck by the wry humor, its timelessness, and its sophistication. Set in the charming but fictional Missouri town of Dawson's Landing in the first half of the nineteenth century, the story is about two babies, one slave, one free, who are switched at birth. The child born a slave grows up believing he is white and free. The white child born free grows up living life as a slave.

On first glance, the novel is a powerful commentary on slavery and perceptions of race. Dawson's Landing is an idyllic place, and the characters who live there could have stepped straight out of a Norman Rockwell painting if it were not for their free and easy use of the word "nigger" when referring to a member of the slave population. This is a disconcerting juxtaposition, to be sure, so unsettling that even today some politicians and educators regularly embark on crusades to ban Twain because of his use of the word "nigger." Others try to sanitize Twain, to expunge the offending word in order to make his work more appropriate for young audiences. But to remove the word "nigger" from the work of Mark Twain is to attempt to rewrite and sanitize a loathsome part of American history. The word "nigger" is offensive, as well it should be. But the word is not nearly as offensive as the social, cultural, and political climate that gave rise to the word and everything it represented. We should not be offended by the word "nigger." We should be offended by our actions or, in most cases, our inaction to stop the development of a social climate that bred the physical, emotional, cultural, and economic genocide and violence that accompanied the word. Any attempt to excise the word "nigger" from the English language is an attempt to excise the history that comes with it, and that history should not be changed, smoothed over, sanitized, whitewashed, or revised in any way whatsoever. It is a difficult subject to address. And it should be. But it is a part of who we are as a nation. It is part of our past and, whether we want to acknowledge it or not, part of who we are today. And Twain knew what he was doing when he liberally sprinkled the word "nigger" around the idyllic town of Dawson's Landing. It's called irony.

Some aspects of the stage adaptation of *Pudd'nhead Wilson* afforded me the opportunity to explore some very contemporary ideas of the perceptions of race in this country, as well as take the story even further in the direction in which I think Twain was moving. For example, while the audiences who read *Pudd'nead Wilson* in its original serial form in 1893 appeared to have had no problem digesting the word "nigger," they might have had a problem digesting the idea that a respected, upstanding, white member of Dawson's Landing, Judge Driscoll, could be the father of a slave.

Twain establishes that the two babies who were switched at birth were the exact same age. One was born to Mrs. Percy Driscoll, the wife of Judge Driscoll, and the other was born to the slave Roxy. Both babies looked exactly alike, so much so that only Roxy, the mother of the slave baby, could tell them apart. However, Twain then goes on to tell us that the father of Roxy's baby, who later became Tom, was a mysterious Colonel Cecil Burleigh Essex who is mentioned only once in the story.

Making Judge Driscoll the father of both children in the adaptation, for me, was as natural as taking a breath. It seemed to be the clear implication of the story. While Twain assigned a different father to Tom in chapter 1, thereby avoiding the explicit idea that the respected Judge Driscoll raped a slave girl and thereby fathered a slave, the rest of the novel unabashedly supports the idea. This implication, combined with today's widespread acknowledgment that sexual congress between master and slave was commonplace, made the change easy and one on which I think Twain would have smiled. However, other aspects of the adaptation were a bit more problematic.

In the novel, the two children, Tom and Valet de Chambre or Chambers, appear to be physically identical in every respect. However, one was white and the other was a very light-skinned slave. While this was not an issue in the world of the novel, it presented an interesting dilemma when it came to the stage. It suggested that I was going to have to cast two actors who physically resembled each other. Adding this restriction would make the play almost impossible to produce, and even if we could find two actors who physically resembled each other, I knew that I could not cast a white actor in the role of Tom. While some plays could be cast colorblind without changing or distorting the meaning of the play, colorblind casting in plays where race is a central theme would be foolish and irresponsible. In this particular case, casting a white actor in the role of Tom would radically change the meaning of the story, turning it into a tragedy of a white man whose life was destroyed when he discovered that he was black. This is not what Twain intended and certainly not the story I wanted to tell in my adaptation.

The solution was to embrace the perceived differences between the two characters and cast two actors who appeared to have been drawn from opposite ends of the physical and racial spectrum. As a result, the script calls for a white actor in the role of Chambers, who is born to privilege but, after being switched at birth, spends most of his life as a black slave. The script calls for a dark-skinned African American actor in the role of Tom, who is born a slave but, after being switched at birth, grows up in a white household, spending his life in privilege as a white slave owner. In the world of the play, Tom grows up believing he is white. He thinks he is white; all the other characters in the play believe he is white; therefore, when the other characters look at him, all they can see is someone white, even though we the audience see something different. Likewise, even though a white actor is playing someone who, in the play, is thought to be an African American slave, he believes himself to be a slave; he acts like a slave; therefore, when the other characters look at him, all they can see is a slave.

This theatricality is supported by the casting of the visiting Italian Twins as well. Even though none of the characters in the play can distinguish one twin from the other, the script requires that a black actor play one twin, and a white actor play the other. This reinforces one of the main themes of the play: that what we consider to be race is not the result of some set of definable predetermined biological markers but the result of a manufactured social construct. This idea was most recently demonstrated on a national level when during the 2008 presidential campaign, the nation viewed Barack Obama as a biracial example of a postracial world. After the election, he was no longer considered to be biracial. He simply became black. Of course, his ancestry did not change. What changed was the nation's perception of him.

KNOCK ME A KISS is about Yolande Du Bois, the daughter of W. E. B. Du Bois. The impetus for this play came when I was doing research for an earlier play, *Black Star Line,* which was about the messianic Jamaican leader and entrepreneur Marcus Garvey and his back-to-Africa movement. Research into *Black Star Line* included a journey into the life of W. E. B. Du Bois, whose political feud with Garvey during the early 1900s was well publicized. While researching the life of Du Bois and reading his work, I found his attitude toward his daughter to be curious. At times he seemed to be hypercritical of her, and at other times he seemed to be dismissive. When I was in rehearsals for *Black Star Line,* I mentioned this to the director, Tazewell Thompson, who was surprised that I was not familiar with what he considered to be a well-known story.

The facts on which I based *Knock Me a Kiss* are that on April 9, 1928, Countee Cullen was married to Yolande Du Bois, the daughter of W. E. B. Du Bois. Two months later, Countee Cullen sailed to Paris with the best man from the wedding, Harold Jackman, leaving Yolande, his bride, behind. Yolande was granted a divorce from Countee on December 9, 1929.

In his essay, "So the Girl Marries," the elder Du Bois wrote, "It was not the mere marriage of a maiden. It was not simply the wedding of a fine young poet. It was the symbolic march of young and black America.

John Newton Templeton delivered a speech on a provocative topic about which he felt passionate. And that was the play I had planned to write.

During my research, I discovered that President Wilson of Ohio University was an ordained Presbyterian minister. I also discovered that Reverend Robert Finley, also an ordained Presbyterian minister, founded the ACS. In addition to this, the Presbyterian Church, like the Quakers, ardently supported the ACS. They were joined in their support by many American slave owners who viewed the ACS's goal of transporting free men of color to Liberia as a convenient way of quelling discontent and maintaining superiority and control over the enslaved population.

This means that my original assumption that John Newton Templeton was somehow an iconoclast was uninformed and misguided. He was admitted to Ohio University not through a progressive humanitarian act of altruism, but in a carefully calculated act of opportunism. And although it's sad to say, when reading "The Claims of Liberia" in the light of this new information, it appears as if John Newton Templeton capitulated. It appears as if he did exactly what was expected of him. These were not the ingredients of any play that I was interested in writing.

Whenever I've been engaged in research and make a discovery that is contrary to a direction in which I've been moving, my wife teases me by saying, "So what? You've never let the facts stop you before." And she's right, to a degree. I've always been more interested in a fundamental truth of the story than I am in the facts.

For example, in the play *Knock Me a Kiss*, Yolande Du Bois confronts Countee Cullen and makes the decision to end their marriage before Countee sails to Paris. Historically, this confrontation happened after Countee had sailed to Paris and after Yolande had joined him there, but I considered that distinction to be irrelevant to the story I wanted to tell, and to what I wanted to communicate by telling that story. However, the information I discovered during my research for *Free Man of Color* was not irrelevant. That information was more than factual. It spoke directly to the fundamental truth of the story, and I had no choice but to try to incorporate it into the texture of the play. The only question was how to incorporate it while continuing to tell the story that I was interested in telling.

I believe that John Newton Templeton was admitted to Ohio University under false pretenses. When I tried to imagine what that must have been like, I started to think about my own experiences in the Chicago public school system and immediately saw what I imagined to be an undeniable parallel. John Newton Templeton was admitted under false pretenses, and I believe that I, like many of my classmates in elementary school in Chicago, was also admitted to those classrooms under false pretenses. We were there, ostensibly, to be educated, but instead we received training or indoctrination. Instead of being given the freedom to develop our own ideas, we were given the ideas of others, then called on to mindlessly repeat someone else's principles, doctrines, and conclusions. Instead of being given tools and the means by which we could conduct our own intellectual inquiry, we were given the answers and then asked to repeat those answers and believe them without thought or question. Education, or at least, I believe, true education, is teaching a student how to think. Indoctrination is teaching a student what to think.

I imagined that John Newton Templeton's time as an ex-slave in the early 1800s at Ohio University was similar to my early "education" in the Chicago public school system. This imagining is what helped me take information that initially appeared to be problematic and turn it into the core, the engine, the central theme of the play.

Occasionally the subject of my time in the Chicago school system comes up in conversation and I tell people of my Kafkaesque journey through the bureaucracy and my struggle to avoid the brutal and sometimes sadistic, but well-meaning, civil servants who called themselves teachers. The people who hear my story always listen with their mouths agape, and inevitably they always ask the same question: "Why don't you write a play about that?" And I always mumble some lame excuse about not having enough time when deep down inside, I know that I have written a play about it. I have written a play about that and many other traumatic, puzzling, and often amusing events in my life. I wrote about it in *Free Man of Color* and *Knock Me a Kiss*, in *Pudd'nhead Wilson*, and in *The Gospel According to James*, as well as in *Jelly Belly*, *Freefall*, *Les Trois Dumas*, *The Sutherland*, and all my other plays.

It does not matter if the play is set in Chicago in 1982, in Harlem in 1930, or in France in 1825. The settings are merely the devices, the vehicles we use to travel to destinations that are always contemporary and personal.

JELLY BELLY

PRODUCTION HISTORY

An early draft of *Jelly Belly* titled *Jelly Belly Don't Mess with Nobody* was awarded the 1985 Cornerstone National Playwriting Award and was produced by Penumbra Theatre Company in St. Paul, Minnesota, in 1986. The production was directed by James A. Williams, with set and lighting design by Scott Peters.

Bruce	Marion McClinton
Mike	Abdul Salaam El Razzac
Kenny	Walter Pridgen
Jelly Belly	Latifu

The current incarnation of *Jelly Belly* received its world premiere production at Victory Gardens Theater in Chicago on January 21, 1989. It was directed by Dennis Začek, artistic director, with set design by Linda L. Lane, costume design by Glenn Billings, lighting design by Larry Schoeneman, and sound design by Galen G. Ramsey. Doug (Frosty the Snowman) Thompson was the production stage manager. Marcelle McVay was the managing director.

Barbara	Diane White
Mike	Charles Glenn
Bruce	Donald Douglass
Kenny	Oscar Jordan
Jelly Belly	A. C. Smith

Jelly Belly was produced Off Broadway by Chicago's Victory Gardens Theater and the New Federal Theatre in New York in 1990. It received the NBC New Voices Award, the Theodore Ward Prize for African American Playwriting, and an Audelco Award nomination for new work. The play was produced by Woodie King Jr., and was directed by Dennis Začek, with set and lighting design by Richard Harmon, costume design by Judy Dearing, and sound design by Jacqui Casto. Jesse Wooden Jr. was the production stage manager.

Barbara	Gina Torres
Mike	Weyman Thompson
Bruce	Donald Douglass
Kenny	Ramon Melindez Moses
Jelly Belly	A. C. Smith

A. C. Smith as Jelly Belly and Donald Douglass as Bruce in the Victory Gardens Theater production of *Jelly Belly. Photo by Jennifer Girard.*

Oscar Jordan as Kenny and Donald Douglass as Bruce in the Victory Gardens Theater production of *Jelly Belly. Photo by Jennifer Girard.*

Charles Glenn as Mike and Diane White as Barbara in the Victory Gardens Theater production of *Jelly Belly*. *Photo by Jennifer Girard*.

Characters

Barbara — Sometimes known as MISS MIKE. She is a young woman in her early twenties who has been around the block a few times.

Mike — Married to MISS MIKE. He's a construction worker in his midtwenties who's doing the best he can.

Bruce — A junkie in the true sense of the word. He's not addicted to one drug but to a myriad of drugs: Phenobarbital, Seconal, Nembutal, Tuinal, alcohol, but his drug of choice is angel dust. BRUCE moves almost like a dancer. He leans, dips, and turns, but never falls. Although his dress is a bit outdated, he is immaculate—except for the dirty collar and the rip in his pants at the knee. BRUCE has seen better times and may see better times again in the morning, but tonight he's having problems. BRUCE is cool and very smooth. He is not a dirty fall-down drunk.

Kenny — A friend to MIKE, KENNY is an innocent, amazed by the smallest wonders of the world.

Jelly Belly — Just a regular guy with a large belly that shakes like jelly.

Time: 1980

Place: South side of Chicago

Jelly Belly is to be performed without intermission.

JELLY BELLY

A play in one act

The setting is the high porch of an old, narrow, two-story, wood frame house on a block in a neighborhood where dozens of other narrow, two-story, wood frame houses exactly like the first line the street. There is very little room at the top of the porch, forcing anyone sitting in front of the house to sit on the steps.

The other houses, which are only suggested, are too close together, creating a feeling of territorial claustrophobia. Everyone remains only on their own tiny tract of sidewalk or porch, careful not to stop or stand in front of anyone else's sidewalk or porch unless invited to do so.

It is nighttime, summer. Children are playing and music can be heard off in the distance. As the lights come up, BARBARA is sitting at the top of the stairs drinking a beer. After a moment, something out of the corner of her eye catches her attention.

BARBARA: Hey, boy. You. I'm talking to you. No, not you, the other one. The little nappy-headed boy. Don't try and act like you don't know who I'm talking to. What you doing messing with that car? I said, what you doing messing with the door on that car?

> *Beat.*

Do I look like a fool to you? Boy, you know good and goddamn well that ain't your car. You ain't old enough to pee straight, how you gonna be old enough to drive an automobile? Why don't you gone on away from here and leave that car alone? You don't live around here.

> *Beat.*

What? Wait a minute, ain't you that little Patterson boy? Your momma Evon Patterson? Don't try to lie to me, I know who you are. I know your momma, knew her from back when before she got pregnant with you. What? I'll tell you one thing, if I got to come down off this porch, I will kick your little ass. I'll beat your ass, take you home, and then your momma will beat your ass.

That's right. Now take your little butt on home and leave people's property alone. That's right, go ahead.

> *Beat.*

Goddamn juvenile delinquent.

> *MIKE enters from the house.*

MIKE: Who you out here talking to?

BARBARA: Little hard-headed hoodlum from across the way.

MIKE: No Kenny yet?

BARBARA: Not yet.

MIKE: Want another beer?

> *MIKE hands BARBARA a beer.*

BARBARA: Mikie asleep?

MIKE: Went straight out.

BARBARA: That was quick.

MIKE: He was tired.

BARBARA: Him? Shit, what about me?

MIKE: He kept talking about school, man it was funny. You know what he calls it?

BARBARA: Don't tell me, let me guess. Kenny's Garden.

MIKE: Don't you think that was funny?

BARBARA: Yeah, well, we almost didn't make it to Kenny's Garden. Little boy wore me out. First he started with the questions. "Is Kenny's Garden real big, Mommie? Mommie, will there be other kids there? How come Kenny's Garden is inside, Mommie? Mommie, will they have bathrooms there?" When we got there, he looked around and didn't see no Kenny. That's when he folded his arms, nodded his head, looked up at me and said, "Thank you, Mother. I'm ready to go home now." I tried to explain to him, no, Mikie, this is Kindergarten, remember? You have to stay. But he wasn't having none of that.

MIKE: Did he cry?

BARBARA: At first.

MIKE: Man.

BARBARA: Until I told him that if he wanted to be like his daddy, he couldn't cry.

MIKE: I wish you wouldn't tell him that.

BARBARA: Whatever works.

MIKE: Look at that.

BARBARA: What?

MIKE: There. That little boy messing with that car.

BARBARA: That's that little Patterson boy.

MIKE: Hey, boy!

BARBARA: Little delinquent.

MIKE: What you doing messing with that car?

BARBARA: Juvenile delinquent.

MIKE: You better get away from that car!

BARBARA: I done told him once.

MIKE: Somebody ought to talk to that boy's momma.

BARBARA: And what you think that's gonna do?

MIKE: It'll do something.

BARBARA: That woman don't care about that boy. If she did, he wouldn't be out here.

MIKE: Go on home, boy! Go watch TV or something. Go ahead!

> MIKE and BARBARA watch the boy leave.

Damn shame.

BARBARA: That boy is sliding on a slippery road to hell.

MIKE: I'm gonna call Kenny.

BARBARA: For what?

MIKE: See what happened.

BARBARA: Will you stop worrying about Kenny? Kenny's going to have to learn how to take care of himself. Now sit down for a minute. Chill out.

> MIKE sits.

I called my father today.

MIKE: For what?

BARBARA: Just to talk.

MIKE: Shit.

BARBARA: Mike . . .

MIKE: I wish you wouldn't have done that.

BARBARA: He's my father.

MIKE: Yeah.

BARBARA: I'm allowed to talk to my father, ain't I?

MIKE: Depends.

BARBARA: On what?

MIKE: On what you two talked about.

BARBARA: We didn't talk about nothing. We just talked.

MIKE: Yeah, okay, just talked.

BARBARA: If you don't want to go back, you don't have to.

MIKE: Right.

BARBARA: You could find another job.

MIKE: Where?

BARBARA: Anywhere. There are places out there that would hire you in a heartbeat.

MIKE: Everybody's cutting back.

BARBARA: But you got experience.

MIKE: Everybody's got experience.

BARBARA: You don't have to take this shit from them, Mike. With all of the construction going on in this town, you could find a job paying twice what you're making now.

MIKE: Where?

BARBARA: Anywhere.

MIKE: I already looked. There was nothing in the newspaper. I went down to the unemployment office, but there was a line. I can't see myself standing in line all day.

BARBARA: Then I'll get a job.

MIKE: You?

BARBARA: Damn right. Me.

MIKE: Doing what? Working with your father?

BARBARA: I don't have to. I can do other things.

MIKE: Work as a receptionist.

BARBARA: They call it administrative management, baby. Director of Interoffice Communications.

MIKE: Receptionist.

BARBARA: Receptionists make lots of money.

MIKE: Yeah, like your last job.

BARBARA: That's not quite what I had in mind.

MIKE: Call her. I'm sure she'll be glad to have you back.

BARBARA: That bitch was crazy, Mike.

MIKE: Tell me about it.

BARBARA: Come rubbing up on me telling me how I can increase my cash flow.

MIKE: You should've told her something.

BARBARA: I did. Told her she didn't have nearly enough cash to be getting into my flow.

MIKE: So call her. Yeah, that'll be nice. You call up the dyke and I'll quit my job and stay home with the kid.

BARBARA: I'm serious, Mike. You don't have to go back. If worse came to worse, I could always go to work for my father.

MIKE: See? That's what I thought.

BARBARA: Come on, Mike ...

MIKE: That's exactly what he wants. For you to go to work for him. His little girl. No. Absolutely not.

BARBARA: So I can go someplace else.

MIKE: Why you so set on getting a job? You don't have to go to work. Not unless you really want to. I mean, if that's what you want to do, say so. It's fine, by all means, go right ahead. But you told me you wanted to stay home with Mikie. And I mean, hell, we're doing all right. We got a little money in the bank, we don't owe nobody nothing. We are three steps ahead of everybody else who are two blocks behind. I mean, we're not doing that bad, Barbara.

BARBARA: I just want to make sure you don't have to do anything you don't wanna do.

MIKE: You ain't got to worry about that. I'm going back tomorrow and act like nothing ever happened. I'm going to be all smiles, handshakes, and grins, cause right now, that's exactly what I wanna do and exactly where I need to be. But the day is going to come when I won't need them anymore. I'm going to be my own boss, get my own company, and that's the day I'm going to walk into that office and tell them to kiss my black ass. But until that happens, I can not quit, I will not quit, it's going to take a lot more than this to knock me down.

BARBARA: Does this mean I have to stay home now?

MIKE: Not if you don't want. You can go back to work for the dyke if you want.

BARBARA: Well, you know . . . she and I did have a certain rapport.

MIKE: So call her.

BARBARA: You don't mind?

MIKE: Course not.

BARBARA: You sure?

MIKE: Positive. You just have to find you someplace else to live, cause you sure the hell ain't staying here.

BARBARA: Boy!

> BARBARA slaps MIKE about the head. MIKE tries to duck, then freezes.

MIKE: Wait.

BARBARA: What?

> BARBARA freezes.

MIKE: Shit.

BARBARA: What?

MIKE: Look.

> BARBARA looks.

BARBARA: Shit.

> BRUCE enters. He is blasted out of his mind. He walks slowly and smoothly, leaning to the side. Taking three steps forward and two back, he moves across the stage, past the point where MIKE and BARBARA are sitting.

MIKE: Good. He didn't stop.

BRUCE stops. He starts to take three steps backward and one forward until he is once again standing in front of the porch.

Damn.

BRUCE slowly melts at the foot of the steps and lapses into a stupor.

BARBARA: You know what this means, don't you?

MIKE: What?

BARBARA: Jelly Belly's out.

MIKE: No.

BARBARA: Why else would Bruce be here?

MIKE: It hasn't been that long.

BARBARA: Six months.

MIKE: No.

BARBARA: I'm telling you, Jelly Belly is out and is here, somewhere near.

MIKE: Bruce.

Beat.

Hey, Bruce!

Beat.

BRUCE!

BRUCE wakes, looks around, and looks back at MIKE.

BRUCE: Yo, Mike. Brother man, what you doing here?

MIKE: I live here, Bruce.

BRUCE: What?

BRUCE looks around, then back at MIKE.

That's right. Glad to see you're on top of things, Brother man. Right on.

BRUCE starts to lapse back into a stupor.

MIKE: Bruce.

Beat.

Hey, Bruce!

Beat.

BRUCE!

BRUCE: Yo, Mike. Brother man.

MIKE: What you want, Bruce? What you doing here? You looking for somebody?

BRUCE: Naw, Mike. I'm just . . . you know . . .

MIKE: No, I don't know. What do you want? You don't live around here.

BRUCE: You know, Mike, say like . . . I know that. But what happen was, see . . . I come to check you out, Mike. Yeah. I come to see what was happening.

BARBARA: There ain't nothing happening.

BRUCE: Well, you know, that's cool too.

> *BRUCE starts to nod off again.*

MIKE: Bruce!

BRUCE: Goddamn, man. What you want?

MIKE: I want to know what you're doing in front of my house.

BRUCE: I just told you. Damn.

> *Beat.*

Didn't I just tell you?

MIKE: You ain't told me nothing.

BRUCE: I just told somebody.

BARBARA: You ain't been around here in six months, Bruce. What're you doing around here now?

BRUCE: Hello, Miss Mike.

BARBARA: I asked you a question.

BRUCE: You did?

MIKE: What you doing here, Bruce?

BRUCE: I wanted to stop by and check you out, Mike. You and your fine lady. Why don't you let me have one of them beers, Miss Mike.

BARBARA: Ain't no more.

BRUCE: Why don't you let me have a swallow of the one you got then?

> *BARBARA drains the can, then shakes it.*

BARBARA: It's empty. Nothing left but some spit. You want that?

BRUCE: Let me check it out.

> BRUCE *takes the can, turns it up, drains it, then looks at the can.*

That was all right.

MIKE: There's nobody here and nothing to get high on.

BRUCE: You don't want me in front of your house or something? All you got to do is say so. If you don't want me here, just say so and I'll leave. Shit. I can take a hint.

MIKE: I don't want you in front of my house.

BRUCE: You ain't got to be subtle with me, Mike. I can pick up on the nuances.

MIKE: Then leave. Good-bye. So long. See you on the rebound.

BRUCE: I mean, shit man. You know? I ain't got to hang out around here. I can find someplace else to go. It don't matter to me, Mike. You know why? Cause I got . . . a strong mind.

BARBARA: Here we go.

MIKE: What'd you want to do?

BARBARA: What can we do?

MIKE: We can go in the house.

BRUCE: Man . . . I was walking down the street and the mutherfuckin police came up to me and said, "Bruce, we ought to lock your monkey-ass up." And you know what I told them? I told them, "Go ahead, mutherfucker. You can't hurt me by putting me in jail. You won't hurt me one bit. Cause I got a strong mind." Mutherfucker got out of his car and knocked me down, Mike. Kicked me in the head and shit. Said, "Are you hurt now?" And you know what I told him? I told him, "Naw man, you still ain't hurt me. You ain't killed me so you ain't hurt me. I still got my life." You know what I mean, Mike?

MIKE: Yeah, Bruce.

BRUCE: See, you can be in jail, or you can be on the street, or you can be in a mansion with lots of money and a woman and shit, but if you got a strong mind, it's all the same, Mike. It's all the same.

BARBARA: Let's go in the house.

KENNY (*From offstage*): Mike! Hey, Mike! Mike!

KENNY enters carrying a roll of blueprints under his arm.

Jelly Belly's out! He's down the street, Mike. He's on his way down here.

BARBARA: I told you.

KENNY: What you doing around here, Bruce! Get away from here! Go back out on the boulevard or something!

BRUCE: I'm waiting on Jelly Belly.

KENNY: Well, go someplace else and wait, cause we're going in the house, ain't that right, Mike? Jelly Belly can come, but won't nobody be here.

MIKE: I'll be here, Kenny.

KENNY: But Jelly Belly's coming.

MIKE: So?

KENNY: So, let's go in the house, Mike.

MIKE: I'm not running from Jelly Belly.

KENNY: We're not running, Mike. We're just going in the house.

MIKE: Remember what I told you, Kenny?

KENNY: Yeah, Mike, I remember.

MIKE: Jelly Belly's a man, Kenny. Just like you and me. You don't have to be afraid of him. Now, you finish up the blueprints?

KENNY: Finished.

> *MIKE takes the blueprints from KENNY, opens them, then begins to examine them.*

BARBARA: You get it right this time, Kenny?

KENNY: Think so. Been working on it all day. Worked on it during my lunch break at work, and worked on it after I got home from work. You know, Mike . . . it gets dark out here nowadays.

> *KENNY looks up to the sky.*

It's dark out here now. You might go blind, Mike, trying to see, it's so dark out here.

MIKE: We're not going in the house, Kenny.

KENNY: Okay, Mike. That's cool. No problem. Any beer?

BARBARA: Fresh out.

MIKE: You wanna go get some?

KENNY: Don't want no beer that bad. Jelly Belly's out. What happened to you at work today, Mike?

MIKE: Nothing.

KENNY: You wasn't there.

MIKE: I told you I wasn't coming.

KENNY: You said you were going to be late, Mike. That's what you said.

MIKE: I said I might take a sick day and that's what I did. I took a sick day. You fix all the problems with the foundation?

KENNY: Yeah, Mike. It was easy.

MIKE: Good.

KENNY: So you were sick today, Mike? Is that what happened?

MIKE: Ain't that what I said?

KENNY: You said you took a sick day. You didn't say you was sick.

MIKE: Well, I was sick, okay?

BARBARA: He had the stomach flu, Kenny. A twenty-four hour bug. He had to get it out of his system.

KENNY: I had the stomach flu once. Throwing up and stuff. Diarrhea. It was something. You had that, Mike?

MIKE: Yeah. Stomach flu.

KENNY: That's bad.

MIKE: Yeah, bad. Come here, Kenny, look. You don't need collar beams and the ceiling joists.

KENNY: Yes I do, Mike.

MIKE: Look. The ceiling joists will give you all the support you need. See?

KENNY: Yeah, Mike, I see that.

MIKE: See where the tension is?

KENNY: But suppose I wanted to finish the attic? Suppose I wanted to put an extra room up there?

MIKE: Then you would add collar beams.

KENNY: How?

MIKE: You clamp them onto the ridge boards, Kenny.

KENNY: But you won't be able to get to the ridge boards. See? See what I mean? Look. You'd have to tear up the whole roof just to get to the ridge boards.

MIKE: I didn't see that.

KENNY: So I figure, you put in the collar beams now. That way, you have a good, strong roof. Tornado comes, hurricane, you got nothing to worry about. You know that house we pass on the way to work? The one that got the caved-in roof? I went in there, Mike. I went inside and looked around. And you know what? No collar beams.

MIKE: I like this, Kenny. This is good.

KENNY: On the way to work this morning, I showed Mr. Perkins and you know what he said? He laughed. He said I was stupid to try to do something like this.

MIKE: Well, Perkins don't know what he's talking about.

KENNY: Mike? I don't want to ride with Perkins no more.

MIKE: You won't have to.

KENNY: One time was enough for me.

MIKE: I'll come and get you in the morning.

KENNY: You're not going to be sick tomorrow?

MIKE: Nope.

KENNY: You and me, we can ride together again?

MIKE: Just be ready when I come and get you.

KENNY: I'll be ready, Mike. Five o'clock in the morning, right?

MIKE: Right.

KENNY: Just like always, right, Mike?

MIKE: That's right. Just like always.

KENNY: So can we go in the house now?

MIKE: What did I tell you?

KENNY: Okay, Mike.

BARBARA: I'm with Kenny. The man gives me the creeps.

MIKE: You want to go in? Go ahead. Ain't nobody stopping you.

BARBARA: You want something to eat, Kenny?

KENNY: No, ma'am. I already ate. Momma cooked lots of food tonight. Cooked it all on that old stove. You know what I'm going to do? I'm gonna get my momma a new stove. New house, new stove. Yeah. New refrigerator too. She cooked beans and rice, pork chops. I ate so much, I couldn't move. Couldn't work on the blueprints. Couldn't do nothing but lay there and look at TV.

BARBARA: Got a big pan of lasagna in the house.

KENNY: Lasagna?

BARBARA: That's right. Even got a loaf of french bread. I could put some garlic and butter on it . . .

KENNY: You got any of that cheese in a can?

BARBARA: Parmesan cheese?

KENNY: Yeah. You got any of that?

BARBARA: Sorry.

KENNY: Don't matter. Hey, Mike, let's go in and eat some lasagna. Then we can play Monopoly. I'll be the shoe.

MIKE: No.

KENNY: Then you be the shoe.

MIKE: I'm not playing Monopoly, Kenny.

BARBARA: Come on, Mike. Let's go in.

MIKE: We got business to finish.

BARBARA: Finish it later. Let's keep tonight to ourselves.

MIKE: I'm not putting it off.

BARBARA: You wasn't here when that woman came by. I ain't never seen nothing like that before. She couldn't stop shaking, couldn't sit down. She would jump every time the phone would ring or a car drove by. It scared me, Mike.

MIKE: So go in. You don't have to stay.

KENNY: Come on, Barbara. Let's go eat.

MIKE: You are staying out here.

KENNY: Okay, Mike. I'll stay.

MIKE: You got the money?

KENNY: Yeah, Mike, I got it.

MIKE: When he gets here, I want you to give it to him, okay? Just give him the money and it'll be all over.

KENNY: But what should I tell him, Mike? What should I say about what happened?

MIKE: Don't say anything. Just give him the money and shut up.

KENNY: But what if he asks?

MIKE: He ain't going to ask. And don't you go volunteering any information either.

BARBARA: Yeah, Kenny. Just give him the money and keep quiet.

MIKE: You're a grown man, Kenny. You don't have to answer to nobody.

KENNY: Okay, Mike. Just like at work, right?

MIKE: That's right.

KENNY: You know what happened to me today? The foreman came up to me while I was eating my lunch and said, "Kenny, I want you to go dig out that septic tank." And you know what I told him? I told him, "I'm eating my lunch right now. You wait until I get through eating my lunch and then I'll go dig it out."

MIKE: Good for you.

KENNY: Cause I'm a man,

MIKE: That's right.

KENNY: And they got to respect me, right?

MIKE: Right.

KENNY: But they won't respect me if I don't stand up for what's mine. I got to stand up and be a man and can't let nobody push me around or let nobody tell me what to do, cause if I don't, I'll get used, right, Mike? They'll use me and I'll never have a life of my own.

MIKE: Yeah, Kenny, now shut up. Okay?

KENNY: I'm sorry, Mike.

MIKE: And don't start apologizing.

KENNY: I piss you off or something, Mike? I don't want to piss you off.

MIKE: No, Kenny, you haven't pissed me off.

KENNY: You're still not feeling too good, are you, Mike?

MIKE: No, Kenny, I'm not.

KENNY: Mike's not feeling too good, Bruce, so get away from here!

Go on! Leave him alone! Go home or something.

BRUCE: Fuck you, Kenny. You always jacking off at the mouth. Jackety, jackety, jackety, jackety, jack. You worse than an old ho, always bumping your gums.

BARBARA: I'm going in. I'll see you when you get through.

BARBARA exits into the house.

KENNY: You better watch who you talking to, boy. I'll rearrange your face for you.

MIKE: Cool it, Kenny.

KENNY: I'll send you to the moon.

BRUCE: You ain't going to do shit, but talk, cause that's all you know how to do. You worse than a mutherfuckin politician, I swear.

MIKE: Leave him alone, Kenny.

BRUCE: Yak, yak, yak.

MIKE: Just ignore him.

BRUCE: Mutherfucker get tired of hearing you yak all the time. In my ass like a goddamn hemorrhoid.

KENNY: You just better be glad Mike is out here. That's all I can say. Junkie mutherfucker.

MIKE: No need for all of that, Kenny. Don't let him get you upset. Look at him. You're better than he is. Don't let him pull you down to his level.

KENNY: You ain't nothing, Bruce. Get away from me.

KENNY pushes BRUCE to the side as JELLY BELLY enters.

JELLY: Mike! Brother man!

BRUCE: This is what I'm talking about.

JELLY: What's happening? Jelly Belly's here and it is time to roll.

BRUCE: Jelly!

JELLY (*Indicating BRUCE*): I don't believe this shit. Somebody tell me I'm dreaming. Mutherfucker's got a nose like a bloodhound. Get out of my way boy!

BRUCE: I'm sorry, Jelly. I was just standing here.

JELLY: Well, go stand someplace else. You make me sick. I don't want you around me and Mike don't want you around him either, do you, Mike?

MIKE: He's not bothering me.

KENNY: Well, he's bothering me! Go back out on the boulevard, Bruce! Hang out with the Puerto Ricans or something.

JELLY: That's right, boy. Your presence is bringing down the value of the neighborhood. Go on! Get away from here!

> BRUCE *stumbles to the edge of the space and instead of falling flat on his face as it appears he will do, he softly glides to rest and lapses into a stupor.*

JELLY (*Cont'd*): Sorry mutherfucker. So, Brother Mike. Tell me about it. What's been happening? How you been? What you been doing?

MIKE: Working.

JELLY: Same ole Mike.

KENNY: I've been working too, Jelly.

JELLY: You?

KENNY: That's right.

JELLY: Doing what?

KENNY: Construction. Mike got me a job with him. I've been working with Mike.

JELLY: I don't know how. You ain't smart enough to do shit but get high and steal.

KENNY: I don't like it when people call me dumb, Jelly Belly.

JELLY: You never minded it before.

KENNY: That was then and this is now.

JELLY: Time don't change ignorance.

KENNY: I'm telling you, Jelly, I don't like it!

MIKE: He's just playing with you, Kenny.

JELLY: Yeah, boy. You know I'm just playing with you.

KENNY: Well, I don't like it when people play with me like that. I got a job now. Ain't that right, Mike?

MIKE: Yeah, Kenny.

KENNY: Me and Mike, we go to work at five o'clock in the morning and work until five, six, sometimes seven o'clock at night.

JELLY: I'm impressed.

KENNY: I'm learning how to build houses, Jelly Belly. See, look.

> KENNY hands JELLY the blueprints.

I did these myself, didn't I, Mike?

MIKE: With no help from no one.

JELLY (*Pushing the blueprints away*): Please, boy. I'm not in the mood for this shit.

KENNY: I'm working labor right now, but one day, I'm going to be an apprentice, right, Mike? Mike's teaching me how to do everything. Carpentry work and bricklaying. Me and Mike, we're going to start our own construction company, right, Mike?

MIKE: Yeah, Kenny, now will you please shut up?

KENNY: Mike's not feeling too well.

MIKE: I would feel better if you would stop running off at the mouth.

KENNY: Mike was supposed to get promoted at work but they gave the job to this college boy instead.

MIKE: It's no big deal, Kenny.

JELLY: Is that the reason you're all long in the face?

MIKE: It ain't nothing, Jelly.

JELLY: Sounds to me like you can use a little pick-me-up. A little something to help clear your mind. Help you think.

MIKE: What you got?

JELLY: What you want? I got rock, powder, dust. I got whatever you need to help ease your troubled soul.

MIKE: You know I don't mess with that rock.

JELLY: As well you shouldn't. Crack is a drug for fools, used by fools to make them even more foolish. Angel dust, on the other hand, is a working man's drug. The thinking man's drug. Here you are, Mike.

> JELLY offers MIKE a small foil.

Treat your nose to heaven. This here is some ace, number one, primo mad dog dust. Untouched by human feet.

MIKE: No thanks.

KENNY: Mike's been working his job and doing the job of the supervisor for almost a year and they didn't even pay him extra for it, did they, Mike? They didn't pay you one dime extra, did they?

MIKE: No, Kenny, they didn't.

KENNY: And yesterday they bring in this college boy and give him the job they should've gave Mike.

MIKE: The boy is educated for the job.

KENNY: No he ain't, Mike. You got to show him everything. You got to show him how to run a theodolite and how to check foundations. You even got to show him how to read a blueprint.

MIKE: It's no big deal.

KENNY: Then how come I saw you cry?

MIKE: You didn't see me cry.

KENNY: Yes I did, Mike. Right after they introduced you to that boy and told you that he was going to be your boss. I saw you walking away and you had tears in your eyes.

MIKE: You didn't see a goddamn thing.

KENNY: Okay, Mike. Don't get pissed at me.

MIKE: It's a job, Kenny. A simple fuckin job. What the hell I look like crying over some goddamn job?

KENNY: I'm sorry, Mike. I thought I saw a tear in your eye and I felt bad. I felt real bad.

MIKE: Well, you didn't see nothing, okay?

KENNY: Okay, Mike. Just don't get pissed at me.

JELLY: If I've told you once, I've told you a hundred times, you play by the rules, Mike, you get fucked every time.

MIKE: Yeah, Jelly, I don't need to be lectured, okay? You say you got some dust?

JELLY: Of course I got dust. I always got dust.

MIKE: So what the hell are you waiting for? Break it out.

KENNY: You're not going to toot no dust, are you, Mike?

MIKE: Just leave me alone, Kenny.

KENNY: But what about the morning, Mike? We got to go to work in the morning.

MIKE: I ain't got to do nothing but pay taxes and die.

KENNY: You got to go to work in the morning.

JELLY: Leave him alone, Kenny. Can't you see that the man has a lot on his mind?

JELLY hands MIKE a small foil.

He knows he has to go to work in the morning. And from what I hear, you have to go to work in the morning too, don't you?

KENNY: Yeah, Jelly, me and Mike, we work together.

JELLY: That's good, Kenny. Real good. Bet you work hard too, don't you?

KENNY: Yeah, Jelly, I work real hard, cause construction ain't easy. You have to be strong if you want to build something, ain't that right, Mike? You got to know how to take some wood and some nails and bricks and build a whole house. I watch them brick layers working and you know what they do? They'll start with one brick, Jelly. Just one little, red, brick. And I'll ask myself, I'll say, "Now what are they going to do with one brick?" And I watch them lay it down on the ground, put a little cement on it and then they go get another brick and lay it right next to the first one. Next thing you know, you're not looking at one or two bricks laying on the ground. You're looking at a brick wall, Jelly Belly. A whole brick wall. And that's how they do it. Using one brick at a time. Did you know that?

JELLY: No, Kenny, I didn't.

KENNY: I didn't either. But I just learned it. Ain't that right, Mike?

MIKE: That's right.

KENNY: You see, Jelly Belly, it takes patience to build something like that. And that's what Mike's teaching me right now. Patience. And I'm learning too, ain't I, Mike?

MIKE, who has been concentrating on the foil, has it open, and with one finger covering one nostril, he places the other nostril to the foil and makes a long, distinct snorting sound. This sound arouses BRUCE who, with his eyes closed, slowly sits up as if being drawn by some unseen force. The sound stops, Bruce freezes. MIKE switches nostrils

*and makes another long, distinct snorting sound. Following suit,
BRUCE starts to lean in the direction of the sound. The sound stops,
Bruce freezes, smiles, and lapses back into a stupor.*

JELLY: Look at that boy. Got built-in radar. Could sniff out a bag of dope a mile away. Hey, Bruce!

Beat.

Bruce!

Beat.

BRUCE!

BRUCE: (*Coming out of his stupor*): Yo, Brother Jelly, Brother man.

JELLY: Where are you, Bruce? Do you know where you're at?

BRUCE looks around and contemplates his answer.

BRUCE: I'm right here, Jelly Belly.

JELLY: No, you're not.

BRUCE: I'm not?

JELLY: Naw, boy. You're lost. That's where you're at.

BRUCE: Lost!

BRUCE has a brief moment of concern, then slips back into his stupor.

JELLY: Sorry son of a bitch. Don't give a shit about how he looks or what people think about him. Got no pride at all. But he's happy. If there's one thing that Bruce is, it's happy. Ain't that right, Bruce? Bruce!

BRUCE: What!

JELLY: Ain't that right?

BRUCE: Ain't what right, Jelly?

JELLY: Ain't you happy?

BRUCE: Yeah, Jelly, I'm real happy. Cause I got a strong mind.

JELLY: Why don't you take you and your strong mind for a walk out on the highway somewhere.

MIKE: Man, Jelly, it just don't make no sense. I've been working that job for eight years now. I ain't missed a day of work in five of those eight years. Now I don't plan on being there all my life, it's no secret, I'll tell anybody who wants to know, one day I plan to move on. But goddamn, man. They should at least give me what I deserve, what's rightfully mine. But what do they do? They bring in this college boy, give him the job they should've gave me and if that ain't bad enough, they've got the nerve to ask me to train him.

JELLY: Don't do it. Quit.

MIKE: Can't quit. Not now.

JELLY: Money ain't no problem, Mike, if that's what you're concerned about. You and me can hook up and make so much cash that our only problem will be how to spend it without the Feds finding out.

MIKE: Naw, Jelly. This one I'm going to do according to the rules cause I'm going to make it. You can bet on that. I'm going to end up on top. And when I do, you can bet, I will have no trouble sleeping cause I'll know I did it right. By the book. No tricks, no short cuts, just good hard work.

JELLY: And patience, right, Mike?

MIKE: That's right. Good hard work and patience.

JELLY: So what the fuck are you crying about? If you didn't like the goddamn job, you'd quit. Money ain't no problem. But apparently you like getting fucked over so shut your goddamn mouth and quit your complaining cause you ain't getting no sympathy here.

KENNY: Let's go in the house, Mike. We ain't got to stay out here.

JELLY: And you, shut up. Go drink a beer or something.

KENNY: Ain't no beer.

JELLY: I'll get you some beer if that's what you want. You want some beer, I'll get you some beer.

MIKE: I'll go to the store. I could use the walk.

JELLY: Bruce can go to the store. Hey, Bruce! You sorry mutherfucker, you! Bruce!

BRUCE: Brother Jelly, Brother man.

JELLY: It's party time.

BRUCE: That's what I'm talking about.

JELLY: Go to the store and get some beer.

BRUCE: I ain't got no money, Jelly Belly.

JELLY: I know you ain't got no money, boy. Here. Go down on the boulevard and get some beer.

BRUCE: What kind?

JELLY: Whatever Kenny wants. And Bruce? Bruce! Look at what I'm giving you, Bruce. You see it?

BRUCE: Yeah, Jelly, I see it.

JELLY: What is it?

BRUCE: It's a twenty-dollar bill.

JELLY: Now put it in your pocket so you don't lose it. Bruce! Put the money in your pocket, Bruce. What kind of beer you want, Kenny?

KENNY: I don't want any beer.

BRUCE: I'll get a case.

JELLY: And bring back my change, Bruce. Bruce! You hear me, Bruce!

BRUCE: I hear you, Jelly.

JELLY: What did I say?

BRUCE: You said bring back my change.

JELLY: Not your change, mutherfucker! My change! Bring back my change!

MIKE: Hold it down.

BRUCE: I can hear you, Jelly Belly. Goddamn, man. You ain't got to shout.

JELLY: Don't forget, Bruce. You forget my change, I'll have your ass. You understand me?

BRUCE: Brother Jelly, brother man. Cool out. Don't you realize who you're talking to? This is Bruce. I'm your boy. Remember?

JELLY: That's the very thing that's got me worried.

  BRUCE exits.

MIKE: He's getting better. He's not as bad as he was.

JELLY: The boy is like God, Mike. Always was and always will be the same. I have to admit that I was happy to see him. But after six months, I was happy to see a dog walk down the street.

MIKE: I can imagine.

JELLY: I saw the little Paterson boy out, still fuckin with them cars. And seeing you and Kenny . . . I'll tell you, Mike. It's just like old times. Just like nothing's ever happened. You want another toot of this dust?

MIKE: Not now. Maybe later.

JELLY: Kenny?

KENNY: No thanks, Jelly.

JELLY: Where's Barbara? She ought to be out here.

MIKE: She probably sleep.

JELLY: It's still early. Liquor store ain't even closed yet.

MIKE: You know Barbara.

JELLY: How about my sister, Mike? You seen my sister?

MIKE: I ain't seen her.

JELLY: Come on, Mike. I know my sister and your ole lady's tight. I know she had to come by here some time or another.

MIKE: What I tell you?

KENNY: She probably left town, huh, Jelly Belly?

JELLY: What?

KENNY: She probably didn't want to stick around. She probably packed up and left.

JELLY: Let me tell you one mutherfuckin thing. Blood is thicker than mud, you understand that? Me and my sister been together since day one.

KENNY: Okay, Jelly. I was just talking.

JELLY: You ought keep your fuckin mouth shut if you don't know know what the hell you talking about. You dim-witted son of a bitch, you.

MIKE: Leave him alone, Jelly. He said he was sorry.

JELLY: He's talking about shit he knows absolutely nothing about, Mike.

MIKE: You was asking if anybody has seen your sister. All he did was answer.

JELLY: I wasn't asking for no speculation as to where she was. I asked you if she had been by here. Hell, I know where she is.

MIKE: Is that right?

JELLY: We're tight, Mike. She don't go nowhere without letting me know.

MIKE: So where is she?

JELLY: She's in Detroit.

MIKE: Detroit?

JELLY: She's visiting relatives, Mike. I know that. I was just trying to figure out when she left.

MIKE: What relatives?

JELLY: What's it to you? You the FBI or something?

MIKE: I thought it was just you and your sister. I never knew you had other relatives.

JELLY: It's just me and my sister here. We've got other relatives. What? You think she would just take off and leave without letting me know where she was at?

MIKE: I don't know, Jelly. I don't know what to think.

JELLY: She's in Detroit, Mike. I know that. Everything's okay.

MIKE: All right.

JELLY: So why don't you go inside and tell Barbara to come out here.

MIKE: Barbara hasn't seen your sister either.

JELLY: Why don't you let me ask Barbara that.

MIKE: I'm not waking her up.

KENNY: She's sleeping, Jelly Belly. You don't want to wake her up if she's sleeping.

JELLY: Mike? Guess who was the first person I saw this morning after I got my walking papers?

MIKE: Who?

JELLY: Bruce.

MIKE: Naw.

JELLY: I'm telling you, man. I walk out of the court house and there he is, standing right outside of the door, right in the middle of the sidewalk, nodded out, dead to the world.

MIKE: I didn't even know you was getting out. How he know?

JELLY: Hell if I know. Junkie radar or something. And that mutherfucker was the last person I wanted to see this morning. So check what I did. I told him, I said, "Bruce, I got to go to the West Side to score some dust. You want to ride along?" And you know Bruce. "Yeah, Brother Jelly, you and me, we're partners." I figured that I'd put his ass on a train, and by the time he discovered that I wasn't on there with him, I'd be gone. We get to the station, the train comes, doors open and I say, "This is it, Bruce." Bruce gets on the train. Now Mike, I'm thinking that this is a local train, and he'll be able to get off at the next stop. But I look up and see that this mutherfucker is an express train. It don't stop until it gets out past West Hell someplace.

MIKE: You bullshitting.

JELLY: I'm telling you, Mike. So I figure, I can't do this, not even to Bruce. I start knocking on the window and shit. And what does Bruce do? Bruce finds him a seat, sits down, gets comfortable, turns and looks at me through the window and starts to wave.

MIKE (*Laughing*): Naw, Jelly.

JELLY: Yeah, man. I'm hollering, jumping up and down, knocking on the window, and this silly mutherfucker is sitting there waving. So I said, what the hell? I waved back. The train pulled out of the station and he was gone.

MIKE: So how he find his way back?

JELLY: Junkie radar.

MIKE: He made it here before you did.

JELLY: They ought to get rid of dope-sniffing dogs and use Bruce. Mutherfucker'll do a better job.

MIKE: And probably won't eat as much.

    MIKE and JELLY laugh.

KENNY: I'm sorry I said that about your sister, Jelly Belly.

JELLY: It ain't nothing, Kenny. Forget about it. You and me, we're still partners.

KENNY: Thanks, Jelly.

JELLY: Now what's this drawing that you got here? What's this all about?

KENNY (*Handing JELLY the drawing*): These are blueprints, Jelly Belly. Blueprints to the house I'm going to build.

JELLY: So Kenny's going to build a house.

KENNY: I already know plumbing. I know about electricity. The electricians let me wire some of the breaker boxes when the foreman's not around. Mike's teaching me carpentry work and bricklaying.

JELLY: You been a busy little son of a bitch, ain't you?

KENNY: Me and Mike, we're going to start our own construction company. Ain't that right, Mike?

MIKE: That's right. We going to build ourselves an empire.

KENNY: And when we do, I'm going to build a house for my mother. New stove, refrigerator. New everything, Jelly Belly.

JELLY: That's a nice thought, Kenny. That's very American of you.

KENNY: You got them upside down.

JELLY: What?

KENNY: The blueprints.

JELLY: I knew that. I just wanted to look at them from a different perspective.

KENNY: From upside down?

JELLY: Look, Kenny, it don't matter how I look at the damn things.

KENNY: Yes it do, Jelly Belly. That's stupid thinking you can look at them from upside down. You see that, Mike? He thinks he can read blueprints from upside down.

JELLY: You can turn them upside down, sideways, or catercorner to the moon, it's all going to end up to equal the same nothing.

KENNY: What you mean nothing?

JELLY: You don't actually believe this shit, do you?

KENNY: Believe what?

JELLY: This shit about you and Mike starting a construction company.

KENNY: Yeah, I believe it.

JELLY: You're dumber than I thought.

MIKE: Then that makes us both dumb, Kenny.

JELLY: You, don't surprise me, Mike. You always was a sucker for hard work and impossible dreams. But why the hell do you have to pull Kenny into this shit? He don't need this sort of heartache.

MIKE: Ain't no heartache, Brother Jelly.

KENNY: Yeah. We going to build ourselves an empire.

JELLY: You going to get your feelings hurt, that's what's going to happen.

MIKE: Why don't you just give him the blueprints back and let's leave it at that.

JELLY: I can't let Kenny start believing in no shit like this.

MIKE: It ain't up to you what the boy believes in.

JELLY: As long as I got breath in this body and strength to take it, I'm going to look out for this boy.

MIKE: So give him a chance, Jelly. It might surprise you. It just might work.

JELLY: You been taking some new type of drug or some shit? If so, you better leave it alone cause it's done fucked up all of your thinking. You know good and goddamn well that the world don't work like that, Mike. For some people, maybe, but for this boy, no.

MIKE: You selling him short, Jelly Belly. You don't know what the boy's capable of.

JELLY: There are three types of people in this world, Mike. Sheep, shepherds, and lamb chops. Now the shepherds are the gods. They tend to the flock. They make sure the sheep stay out of trouble. While the sheep, being the dumb critters that they are, follow the shepherds wherever they go. They take the orders, do as they're told, and tend to stick together. Now this boy right here is a sheep. He was born a sheep, been a sheep all of his life and will remain a sheep until the day when he is transformed into a lamb chop.

MIKE: You ain't changed one bit, have you?

JELLY: And never will. Now you take somebody like Bruce. He ain't a sheep. He ain't even a lamb chop. That mutherfucker is a pork chop. And you got to treat him like a pork chop, smothered in gravy with a little rice on the side.

MIKE: I really don't feel like hearing this shit, Jelly Belly.

JELLY: I speak the truth, Mike, and you know it. Take you and your job for example.

MIKE: Don't you worry about me and my job.

JELLY: They got you, Mike. They know you ain't going nowhere cause they know you're a sheep. Just a sheep who will one day be lead to the slaughterhouse and butchered for meat.

MIKE: Give him his money, Kenny, and let's get this over with. I've got to go in the house and get some sleep.

JELLY: I didn't mean to hurt your feelings, Mike, but you know I speak the truth.

MIKE: I said give him his money, Kenny. I got to go to bed. Got to go to work in the morning.

JELLY: That's right, Kenny. Give me my money. I done hurt Mike's feelings. Now he wants to go in the house and go to bed.

KENNY hands JELLY a large roll of bills.

KENNY: It's all there, Jelly. You can count it if you want, but it's all there.

JELLY (*Counting the money*): I ain't got to count it, Kenny. I trust you. You're my boy.

KENNY: Thanks, Jelly.

JELLY: You have any trouble?

KENNY: No trouble at all. People come to my house, just like you said.

JELLY: You like that dust you just tooted, Mike?

MIKE: It was all right.

JELLY: I got a whole pound of that coming in in a couple of days. It ought to sell like popsicles on a hot summer day. Any of those construction dudes like to toot dust?

KENNY: I don't know.

JELLY: Find out.

KENNY: I'll find out for you, Jelly, but I can't sell none.

JELLY: Why not?

KENNY: Too dangerous.

JELLY: Ain't nothing dangerous about it. Just keep your cool, keep your mouth shut, don't let too many people find out what you're doing, you'll be all right.

KENNY: Naw, Jelly. Too dangerous.

JELLY: All right. You scared to make a little cash, I'll find somebody else.

KENNY: I ain't scared, Jelly. I ain't scared of nothing.

JELLY: Then what's your problem?

MIKE: He doesn't have a problem. He just doesn't want to sell for you no more. That's all.

JELLY: Why don't you let the boy speak for himself, Mike?

MIKE: Cause I don't want you taking advantage of him.

JELLY: Now I realize that your little feelings are hurt, but that ain't no reason to get sassy. In fact, if I didn't know you as I do, I'd take that as an insult. Kenny's my boy. Ain't that right, Kenny?

KENNY: Right, Jelly.

JELLY: If something's bothering him, I want to know what it is. Now tell me, Kenny. Why are you afraid to sell my dope for me?

KENNY: I told you. I ain't afraid of nothing.

JELLY: So what the fuck's your problem!

KENNY: I got robbed! That white boy that hangs out in front of the liquor store with them Puerto Ricans came into my mama's house one night with a gun and robbed me. Took all the money and the dope. I ain't scared. I just don't want to do it no more. Too dangerous.

JELLY: So what the hell is this if you got robbed?

KENNY: That's money, Jelly. Your money. The money I owe you for the dust. I got a job. I'm working.

JELLY: Okay, Kenny. You don't want to peddle no more, I'm not going to ask you to peddle no more.

KENNY: Too dangerous.

JELLY: But what I am concerned about is the welfare of that white boy. What're you going to do about him?

KENNY: What should I do? I can kick his ass if you want.

JELLY: Kick his ass? Ain't you learned nothing, you dim-witted son of a bitch?

MIKE: You got your money, Jelly. Now what's your problem?

JELLY: The problem is, I ain't got my money. This is Kenny's money. Here, Kenny.

> JELLY hands the money back to KENNY.

I don't want this shit. I want my money.

MIKE: I thought it didn't matter to you as long as you were able to spend it.

JELLY: That's where you're wrong, Mike. See, I got pride. A lot more pride than a ditch digger like yourself. You don't hear me crying about how I got fucked over at work and you don't see dirt under my nails or calluses on my hands. My hands are smooth and clean.

MIKE: That's because you've been in jail for the past six months.

JELLY: My hands were clean before I went to jail. I keep myself clean, Mike. My hands, my nose, my mind, all stay clean. I keep it that way by handling only crisp and new money. Money that crackles when you fold it. Not that limp shit, damp money, money that you get after a hard day's work. Clean money, Mike. Money from the bank. New money. Money from the pockets of Buick-driving, blue suit-wearing, fat bald white men with a taste for black women and white dope. That's the money I spend and the only money I spend. Not that bullshit you done sweated over.

KENNY: But this is your money, Jelly Belly. I owe you this.

JELLY: You don't owe me nothing. Forget about it.

KENNY: But what about the dope?

MIKE: He said forget about it, Kenny.

JELLY: What I want to know is, what are you going to do about that white boy?

KENNY: You think I should kick his ass? I can get Pookey Dee and a couple other dudes and kick his ass if you want.

JELLY: So you get a couple of your walking partners and kick his ass. He gets a couple of his walking partners and kick your ass. You get a couple more of your walking partners and kick him and his walking partners' ass and what do you got? A whole bunch of sore-assed walking partners who are tired of walking.

KENNY: So what should I do, Jelly?

JELLY: Kill him.

MIKE: Wait a minute . . .

JELLY: If he don't, you know what's going to happen? Word's going to get out that he's a pork chop. That he let a white boy burn him. Next thing you know, every sorry mutherfucker on the street is going to think that they can burn him too. He's going to have mutherfuckers waiting for him when he gets off of work, waiting in the alley to bust him in the head, knocking on the door of his mama's house in disrespect of the woman who had him. Is that what you want, Kenny? People like Bruce busting your mama in the head while laughing in your face?

KENNY: I'll kill Bruce, he try something like that.

JELLY: You're going to have to kill a whole lot of Bruces if you don't kill that white boy first.

MIKE: But we're the only people who even know that it happened.

JELLY: Where the hell do you think you're at, Mike? This ain't Cincinnati or some shit. There is a wire service out on that street that would make Ma Bell look like two tin cans and a string. You got people passing on information, information moving faster than electricity. I'd bet you half the people in this neighborhood knew he was going to get ripped off before it even happened. You would've known too if you would've kept your ear to the ground instead of fuckin around, building houses and shit. Disgrace has been laid upon this boy's head. He's going to have to take revenge or live with it for the rest of his life.

MIKE: You mean go to jail for the rest of his life.

JELLY: Bullshit.

MIKE: Five to ten with no chance for parole.

JELLY: He ain't going to get no five to ten for killing no dope-pushing, whore-hustling white boy. If anything they'll give him a carton of cigarettes, and a pat on the back. If you doubt my word, try it.

MIKE: Don't listen to this shit, Kenny.

JELLY: Stay out of this, Mike.

MIKE: He wants you to do his dirty work for him.

JELLY: I'm talking to Kenny, so stay out of it!

MIKE: You got to be crazy if you think I'm going to stand here and let you talk him into killing a man just to make you feel better.

JELLY: I've never talked Kenny into doing anything he didn't want to do, now have I, Kenny?

KENNY: No.

JELLY: And never will. All I can do is lay out the facts and let him decide. So. Kenny? What's it going to be? Are you going to be a coward and live in disgrace for the rest of your life or are you going to finally stand up and be a man?

KENNY: I can't kill him, Jelly Belly.

JELLY: So you're telling me that you're not going to do it?

KENNY: You're talking five to ten with no chance for parole.

JELLY: Okay. Great. Fine. See? Wasn't that hard. You made up your own mind and that's what I like about you, Kenny. You don't let other people influence you.

KENNY: Thanks, Jelly.

JELLY: Now, you want a little toot of this dust?

MIKE: Kenny's getting ready to go home and go to bed.

JELLY: I didn't hear Kenny say that.

MIKE: You heard me say it. That's good enough.

JELLY: Kenny's a grown man, Mike. Let him make his own decisions.

KENNY: Yeah, Mike. I got a mind. I can make it up if I want.

MIKE: Is that right?

KENNY: Yeah, Mike. That's what you said.

MIKE: So you want to toot some dust? Is that what you're saying?

KENNY: You tooted some, Mike. How come I can't toot some?

MIKE: We ain't talking about me, Kenny. We're talking about you. You want some dust? There it is.

KENNY: I'm just like you, Mike. I want to toot some dust.

MIKE: Go right ahead. Do what you like.

JELLY (*Offering KENNY a foil*): Here you are, Kenny. Treat your nose to heaven.

KENNY: I don't want any.

JELLY: Come on . . .

KENNY: Mike'll get pissed at me.

JELLY: Forget about Mike. That's just his mother instinct coming through.

MIKE: Fuck you, Jelly Belly.

JELLY: I would let you, Mike, but you wouldn't enjoy it. How about splitting this dust with Kenny instead.

MIKE: I've had enough.

JELLY: Kenny?

KENNY: Mike won't let me.

MIKE: I said do what you want to goddamn it. You want to end up like Bruce, be my guest.

JELLY: Why don't you split it with him, Mike?

MIKE: You got trouble hearing or something? I said I didn't want any more.

JELLY: Well, I never thought I would see the day when Mike turned down a nose full of dust.

MIKE: You've seen it before and you'll see it again.

JELLY: Ole Mike here used to have one of the biggest noses around. In fact, I've seen Mike toot enough dust to kill a horse. Ain't that right, Mike?

MIKE: I don't know what you're talking about.

JELLY: I understand. I know it's a touchy subject, going to jail and all.

MIKE: Why don't you shut your goddamn mouth!

KENNY: You never told me you was in jail, Mike.

JELLY: He don't like talking about it. You see, there was this little mix up . . .

MIKE: I said shut up, Jelly Belly!

JELLY: Cool out, Mike!

> *Beat. JELLY and MIKE stare at each other.*

All I was going to do was tell the boy how you was a victim of mistaken identity.

> *Beat.*

You see, Kenny, one night we was all sitting out here on Mike's front porch getting high on some of the baddest dust that ever came across the tubes. Mike went to the store to get some beer and never came back. Found out the next morning that he was in jail.

KENNY: For what?

JELLY: Murder one. Some dude got beat to death in the alley behind the liquor store. Whoever did it used a brick. Bashed the dude's head in, broke most of the bones in his body. Fucked him up really bad. For some reason, they thought Mike did it.

KENNY: You didn't do it, did you, Mike?

JELLY: Of course Mike didn't do it. I even found a witness that testified that he saw Mike sound asleep in the alley right next to that mutherfucker that got murdered. That's how Mike got blood all over his clothes. Ain't that right, Mike?

MIKE: Yeah, Jelly, whatever you say.

KENNY: Wow, Mike. You slept through a murder? You slept while somebody got beat to death right next to you?

JELLY: He was pretty high, Kenny. He don't remember much of what happened that night.

MIKE: That's enough, Jelly Belly.

JELLY: You got married right after that, didn't you, Mike?

MIKE: I said that's enough!

JELLY: And ain't missed a day of work since.

BARBARA (*From off*): Mike?

MIKE: Shit.

KENNY: So everybody's been to jail except me.

BARBARA (*From off*): Michael!

MIKE: Sorry. We'll keep it down.

JELLY: And I got seniority when it comes to time, don't forget that. Yes sir, we're all like peas in a pod. Here you are, Kenny. Toot that up your nose. Let the angels bring us closer together.

> *JELLY hands KENNY a foil. Pause.*

KENNY: Sure you don't want some, Mike?

MIKE: Why don't you go home and go to bed, Kenny?

KENNY: But this is good dust, Mike. Didn't you say it was good dust?

MIKE: Sure, it's good dust. You see what it's done to Bruce.

JELLY: Will you shut up talking about Bruce! Bruce is a pork chop! Punk-ass, gutless mutherfucker. Ain't good for shit but going to the store for you and he can't do that right half the time. Like that mutherfucker I killed. Pork Chop. Worthless-assed piece of meat with a brain.

You know, they should have given me a carton of cigarettes and a pat on the back for killing that mutherfucker instead of putting me in jail for six months. The dude deserved to die. That's how come I'm sitting here and not still in jail. I did society a favor by killing that dude. Nobody likes a gutless mutherfucker. Not even the man. In fact, you know what the police said to me? They said, "Thank you, Jelly Belly, you did us a favor."

KENNY: No shit?

JELLY: I'm telling you, man. Mutherfucker's body was sitting in the chair next to me, hole in his head, brains spilled out on the floor. I was watching TV. Police came in, let me finish watching my program. Even sat down with me and watched it. Now that's what you call respect. They respect me cause they know that Jelly Belly don't mess with nobody. I even told the dude I was going to kill him before I did it. Showed him the gun I was going to kill him with. Even showed him the bullets. Told him, "Mutherfucker, don't come back to this house." And what did he do the very next day?

KENNY: He came back?

JELLY: Damned right he came back. After I told him not to. That's the reason he's dead.

MIKE: He had to come back, Jelly. He lived there.

JELLY: My mutherfuckin sister lived in that house, Mike. I know who lived in that house. And I gave the dude fair warning. Apparently he didn't take me seriously. I mean, shit man, I didn't want to kill the dude. I used to like him. He was my boy. But he never should've threatened to call the police on me. I told him not to come back but he came back anyway so I blew his mutherfuckin brains out, turned on the television, called the police, and told them to come and get his body. My sister was freaking out and shit. Cussing at me.

KENNY: I don't blame her. You killed the man she was married to.

JELLY: He was a pork chop, Kenny. Much like yourself. Dumb piece of meat with a brain that don't work.

KENNY: Don't call me dumb no more, Jelly.

JELLY: You've lost your pride and you're too dumb to see that when you lose your pride, people start walking on you, pushing you around, telling you what to do. Like Mike here.

KENNY: Me and Mike are friends.

JELLY: Beware, Kenny. First you lose your pride. Next thing you know, you're planted in the ground, just a dead piece of meat, waiting for the maggots to eat out what's left of your brain.

KENNY: I got a job, Jelly. I ain't lost my pride.

JELLY: You let that white boy burn you.

KENNY: He didn't burn me. He just took some money, that's all.

JELLY: Same difference. Toot the dust.

KENNY: I can't kill him, Jelly Belly.

JELLY: Nobody's asking you to. Now toot the dust.

> *Pause. KENNY carefully unwraps the foil.*

MIKE: You know, Kenny, there's a difference between pride and revenge.

JELLY: No difference.

MIKE: Pride comes from building something, then stepping back and admiring what you've built.

JELLY: You talking about using a brick, Mike? Is that what you're talking about?

> *KENNY looks at MIKE for a response, MIKE looks away, pause. KENNY toots the dust. As he does, BRUCE enters. He has a bloody bruise on his face.*

JELLY (*Cont'd*): I knew all we had to do to get this mutherfucker back was to toot a little dust.

> *BARBARA looks out through the door.*

BARBARA: Mike? What's going on out here?

JELLY: Barbara.

BARBARA: Mike?

BRUCE: I got the beer.

JELLY: Come on out and join us. It's party time.

BARBARA: Mike? I asked you a question.

JELLY: Don't be a party poop. Come on out and join us.

BRUCE: I got the beer.

JELLY: So I see, boy. What happened to your face? Somebody kick your ass or something?

BRUCE: I fell.

JELLY: You fell?

BRUCE: I was just walking. And I fell.

KENNY (*Taking the beer from BRUCE*): You didn't shake up the beer, did you?

BRUCE: I fell before I got the beer. Can I have a little bit of that dust?

JELLY: What dust, boy? What you talking about?

BARBARA: You got dust, Jelly Belly?

JELLY: No, ma'am. Ain't nobody got any dust.

BRUCE: Kenny had some dust. He just got through tooting some.

BARBARA: Kenny?

JELLY: Kenny didn't have no dust, did you, Kenny?

KENNY: Nope.

JELLY: That fall must've fucked up the boy's brain.

BRUCE: Come on, Jelly. Why don't you let me get high?

JELLY: You already high.

BRUCE: Naw, Jelly.

JELLY: You get any higher, you going to touch the moon.

BRUCE: My high went away when that concrete hit me in the head.

KENNY: Why don't you sit down and shut up, Bruce.

BRUCE: Fuck you, bitch. You sit down and shut up.

JELLY: Hey, boy, goddamn it! Can't you see that lady standing there! Come here, Bruce! What the hell's the matter with you! Come here!

    BRUCE moves to JELLY.

You want me to rip your mutherfuckin face off?

BRUCE: That would hurt like hell.

MIKE: Cool out, Jelly Belly.

JELLY: You got a mouth like a goddamn garbage can.

BRUCE: I'm sorry, Jelly Belly. Don't rip my face off.

BARBARA: You all got mouths like garbage cans if you ask me. Out here keeping up a racket like you was in a bar somewhere.

JELLY: I'm sorry, Miss Mike, but the boy is a fool. Now apologize to that woman, Bruce. Apologize for your uncouthed behavior.

BRUCE: I'm sorry, Miss Mike. I didn't see you standing there.

BARBARA: And what's your excuse, Jelly Belly?

JELLY: Excuse me, Miss Mike, but like the idiot here, I did not realize you was standing there, or I would've been more careful with my French. I promise to take more caution in the future.

BARBARA: Kenny? You been tooting dust?

KENNY: No, Barbara, I didn't have any.

BARBARA: Mike?

MIKE: Naw, baby, Bruce is just messed up in the head. That's all.

BRUCE: No I ain't. I saw Kenny . . .

JELLY: Shut up, boy!

BARBARA: Kenny, I find out you been tooting dust and you will never, ever come in this house again. You understand that?

KENNY: Yes, ma'am.

BRUCE: Goddamn. How about a beer? Can I at least have a beer?

JELLY: Naw, you can't have no beer. Take your butt over there and sit down. Everybody here can have a beer except Bruce. Mike, get a beer for your wife. And wipe off the top of it. Kenny, get yourself a beer. Bruce, you go near that beer, I'll kill you. You understand that?

BRUCE: Aw, Jelly Belly.

JELLY: Shut up and sit down before I kick your ass because of general principle. Excuse my French.

BRUCE: I'm sorry, Miss Mike.

MIKE: You want a beer?

BARBARA: I want ya'll to keep the noise down, that's what I want.

JELLY: We'll keep it down, Miss Mike. We was having such a good time, I guess we got carried away. Go on and get yourself a beer there. Mike, get your wife a beer.

BARBARA: I don't want a beer, Jelly Belly. I want ya'll to find someplace else to go.

JELLY: We'll keep it quiet. I promise.

BARBARA: I'll tell you what. You wake up my son and there'll be hell to pay. You understand that?

JELLY: I understand, Miss Mike. Your husband here said my sister came by here.

MIKE: I ain't said no such thing.

JELLY: That's not what you said verbatim, but that's what you meant.

BARBARA: I ain't seen your sister, Jelly Belly.

JELLY: Now, Miss Mike, do I look like a fool to you?

BARBARA: It depends on which angle I approach you from.

JELLY: You must be feeling good tonight.

BARBARA: I was feeling good, until I heard all that noise out here.

JELLY: Why don't you cut out the small talk and you tell me when my sister came by.

BARBARA: I told you. I ain't seen your sister.

JELLY: Now, Miss Mike, both you know and I know that in the history of the world, a week has not gone by without my sister coming by here and jacking off at the jaws with you. Now you trying to tell me that you ain't seen her?

BARBARA: That's exactly what I'm telling you.

MIKE: She's telling you the truth, Jelly Belly. Your sister ain't been by here.

JELLY: I refuse to believe that, Mike.

BARBARA: Then sounds like you got a problem, don't it?

JELLY: Come down off the porch, Miss Mike. You're starting to make me nervous.

BARBARA: I live here, Jelly Belly. I will stand wherever I please. If you don't like it, you can leave.

JELLY: I come here on business. And of course to visit my friends. Now come out from behind me, Barbara.

MIKE: This is her porch and her house, Jelly Belly. She can stand wherever she wants.

JELLY: So everybody's feeling good tonight.

BARBARA: You give him his money, Kenny?

KENNY: I gave it to him.

BARBARA: Then your business here is finished, Jelly Belly.

JELLY: Kenny? You tell this woman what you been doing?

KENNY: I didn't tell her nothing, Jelly Belly.

JELLY: Mike?

BARBARA: What difference does it make who told me what and why? You got no secrets around here just like you got no friends.

JELLY: Look, Barbara. I apologize for any distress I might have caused you . . .

BRUCE: I'm sorry too, Miss Mike.

JELLY: So why don't you just sit down, cool out, have a beer and we'll discuss the situation at hand.

BARBARA: You got what you came for, there's nothing to discuss. Your business here is finished, I am going to bed. I would appreciate it if everybody cleared off the porch.

BARBARA exits.

MIKE: You heard the word. Time to clear the porch.

JELLY: Tell me something, Mike. You tell your woman everything or only the things which concern me?

MIKE: I don't think my relationship with my wife is any of your business.

JELLY: I'm disappointed in you, Mike. I'm disappointed in you in a major way.

MIKE: Come on, Kenny. Time to clear the porch.

JELLY: You've bought lock, stock and barrel into an American pipe dream which will never work for you, Brother. The only thing that pipe dream is going to do for you is crack your skull.

MIKE: Time to go, Kenny.

JELLY: Let me tell you something, Mike. When I was in jail, I met this dude named Frosty. Frosty the Snowman. He was in for one hundred and ninety-nine years. Killed his wife, killed his mother-in-law, and killed two of his neighbors when they knocked on the door trying to figure out what was going on. He said that killing his wife was cheaper than getting a divorce.

MIKE: So what's that supposed to mean?

JELLY: Frosty was the coolest white boy I ever met in my life. You'd see Frosty in the chow line and say, "Frosty, what's happening, man?" And Frosty would say, "Just got back from Paris." Or he would say, "Spent the weekend in Vegas and lost all my money." At first, I thought the mutherfucker was crazy. So did everybody else until Frosty killed a guard when the guard pushed him and didn't have five other guards to back him up. They added another ninety-nine years to Frosty's sentence, which didn't bother him none, so they put his ass into solitary confinement. In solitary, there's no light, no people, no voices, there's nothing but darkness. Thirty days past, they didn't let Frosty out. Forty-five days, fifty-five days, sixty days passed and they still got Frosty down in solitary confinement. Everybody knew he was going to be crazier than a jailhouse ho when they finally let him out, if he wasn't crazy already. Ninety-one days after they locked him down, here comes Frosty, walking into the yard. Finally somebody said, "Frosty, what's happening man?" Frosty stopped, looked around and said, "Just spent three of the most beautiful months of my life in the Bahamas and baby it was nice." But that's not the kicker. You know what the kicker is? The mutherfucker had a suntan.

KENNY: Naw.

JELLY: I'm telling you. Mutherfucker was blacker than me. Had a beautiful tan. Tan all over his body except his butt.

KENNY: I don't believe that, Jelly Belly. You believe that, Mike?

MIKE: Of course not.

JELLY: It's the honest to God truth, I swear on my mother's grave. Mutherfucker was smiling, glowing, had sand in his shoes.

KENNY: I don't believe that, Jelly Belly.

JELLY: It don't matter whether you believe it or not. Point is, some people are free even though their bodies might be incarcerated, while some people are slaves to any damned thing that comes along, like that half-assed job you and Mike working.

MIKE: Come on, Kenny. Let's go in.

JELLY: See? Got to go in. Got to go to bed. Can't come and go as you please. Got to do what Mike tells you to do.

MIKE: Come on. We can play some Monopoly.

KENNY: What about all the beer?

JELLY: Yeah, Mike. What am I supposed to do with all this beer?

MIKE: You can take it with you. Come on.

KENNY: Not yet, Mike.

BRUCE: Don't worry about the beer. I'll take care of that.

JELLY: That's right, Bruce. Get yourself a beer. You too, Kenny. Get yourself another beer.

KENNY: But Mike wants me to go in the house.

JELLY: Mike ain't dictating your drinking habits. Go on, get yourself another beer.

MIKE: Leave the beer where it is, Kenny.

JELLY: Give the boy a break, Mike. I ain't seen him in what . . . six months? I know that little job he got don't demand all his time.

MIKE: Let's go, Kenny.

KENNY: Not yet, Mike.

BRUCE: Take your ass to bed, Bitch. Now, Jelly, how about a toot of that dust?

KENNY: Bitch?

JELLY: You want another toot of dust, Mike?

KENNY: Where's the change from the beer, Bruce?

MIKE: Come on, Kenny.

KENNY: Bruce!

BRUCE: Come on, Jelly. Just a little bit and I'll go away.

MIKE: Kenny?

KENNY: BRUCE!

BRUCE: What the fuck do you want now?

KENNY: Where's the change?

       Pause. BRUCE thinks.

BRUCE: What change?

KENNY: Call me a bitch.

JELLY: The change from my mutherfuckin twenty, that's what change.

BRUCE: There wasn't no change, Jelly Belly. Now how about letting me toot a little bit of that dust.

JELLY: You ain't getting shit until I get my change.

BRUCE: I told you. There wasn't none.

JELLY: You cough up my change, mutherfucker, or I'm going to have Kenny kick off in your ass.

BRUCE: Kenny ain't going to do shit.

KENNY: What! What you say, punk! You punk-ass mutherfucker, you! I ain't going to do what!

MIKE: Leave him alone, Kenny!

KENNY: I'll stomp a mud hole in your ass, boy!

BRUCE: Go ahead. I don't give a good goddamn.

JELLY: Don't let him talk to you like that, Kenny.

MIKE: I said, leave him alone, Kenny!

JELLY: Hit him!

> KENNY hits BRUCE, knocks him down. MIKE intercepts KENNY.

KENNY: Punk-ass mutherfucker!

MIKE: Take it easy, Kenny.

KENNY: I'm all right, man.

JELLY: Don't let him push you around, Kenny!

KENNY: Get away from me, Mike.

MIKE: I'm not going to let you fight out here!

JELLY: Hit him, Kenny! Don't let him push you around! Hit him.

KENNY: Leave me alone, Mike!

> KENNY pushes MIKE in the chest. MIKE comes back at KENNY to retaliate, but stops short. MIKE and KENNY square off to fight. JELLY watches with enjoyment.

JELLY: Get him, Kenny. Fuck him up. Hit him.

> MIKE and KENNY prepare for battle. Beat.

BRUCE: Goddamn, Kenny, man. You didn't have to do that. I already fell once.

> MIKE and KENNY relax on each other as BRUCE attempts to pick himself up without success.

JELLY: Where's my change, Bruce?

BRUCE: Wasn't no change, Jelly Belly.

JELLY: Kenny?

> JELLY tosses a set of keys to KENNY.

Go get my gun out of my car.

BRUCE: Aww Jelly Belly, wait a minute . . .

MIKE: Don't bring no guns out here, Jelly Belly!

JELLY: Where's my change, Bruce?

BRUCE: I told you, there wasn't none.

MIKE: No guns, Jelly! I don't want no guns in front of my house!

JELLY: Go get my gun, Kenny.

MIKE: Don't do it, Kenny. I'm warning you. Don't go get that gun.

JELLY: What you going to do, Mike? Make Kenny lose his job?

KENNY: Yeah, Mike. What you going to do?

JELLY: We're just playing around, that's all.

KENNY: Yeah, Mike, just a little fun and games.

MIKE: You go get that gun, Kenny, you can forget about going to work in the morning.

JELLY: Aww, he's just bullshitting, Kenny. Go ahead.

MIKE: I'm not bullshitting.

KENNY: Why you taking everything so serious, Mike? We're just playing around, that's all. You know, like we used to. I mean, hell, give me a break, Mike. I'm a grown man. I do what I want to do.

> *KENNY exits.*

MIKE: You're fuckin up, Jelly Belly. I don't play around like this.

JELLY: You mean not anymore.

MIKE: Why don't you get out of here! Why don't you just leave! Why don't you take your goddamn guns and your drugs and leave!

JELLY: I come to visit my friends.

MIKE: You don't have any friends around here. Leave!

JELLY: I thought you and me was partners.

MIKE: You get your ass off of my porch and out of this neighborhood right this minute or I'm going to call the police on you Jelly Belly. I'll have your ass arrested.

JELLY: You wouldn't do that, would you, Mike?

MIKE: I'll have your ass put under the jail.

JELLY: How old did you say that little boy of yours was?

MIKE: Don't threaten me, Jelly Belly.

JELLY: You threatened me.

MIKE: Get off of my porch.

JELLY: Five, six years old?

MIKE: I don't play that shit.

JELLY: And what's his name? Michael Junior, ain't it?

MIKE: Somebody needs to off you, Jelly. Somebody needs to blow your goddamn brains out.

JELLY: It ain't going to be you, is it, Mike? I'm safe around you. That is, as long as there ain't no bricks around.

MIKE: Maybe I ought to start looking for one.

JELLY: If you do, I hope you find it before Kenny gets back with that gun.

MIKE: Bruce! Hey, Bruce! Bruce!

BRUCE: What?

MIKE: Go on! Get out of here! Run! Leave before Kenny gets back!

BRUCE: I'll pay you back, Jelly Belly. I'll get your money for you.

MIKE: Why don't you just leave, you stupid-ass!

BRUCE: I know I owe you a lot of money, but I'll pay you back. I'll get a job or something.

JELLY: Mutherfucker, you could work from now until doomsday and never pay me back the money you owe me. I've supported your habits since you were in diapers, Bruce. I own you. You understand that? I own everything about you, Bruce.

BRUCE: I know, Jelly.

JELLY: I own your body, I own your soul, I own your dreams, Bruce. You're just like a piece of property to me. Just like my car.

BRUCE: I know, Jelly Belly, and I'll get your change for you.

MIKE: Why don't you just leave!

JELLY: He ain't going nowhere until I tell him to.

BRUCE: I went to the store, just like you told me. I got the case of beer and gave the man a twenty-dollar bill and he didn't give me no change back. So I left. There wasn't no change.

> KENNY enters with a sawed-off shotgun and hands it to JELLY.

JELLY: You forgot, that's what happened.

BRUCE (*Seeing the gun*): I can go back! I can go back and get your change for you, Jelly! I'll make that dude give me your change!

JELLY: Too late, Bruce. I don't want it now. You are in debt beyond repair and like a loan company, I am about to repossess what's rightfully mine.

BRUCE: What?

JELLY: Get on your knees, mutherfucker.

BRUCE: Aww, Jelly man . . .

JELLY: Don't make me have to say it again, Bruce.

BRUCE: Naw, Jelly Belly.

JELLY: Bruce! You hear me talking to you? Bruce! Did you hear what I said?

BRUCE: I heard you.

JELLY: What did I say?

BRUCE: You said get on my knees.

JELLY: So what are you waiting for?

BRUCE (*As he goes to his knees*): Please, Jelly Belly. I thought I was your boy. I thought me and you was partners.

JELLY: Say good-bye to Mike.

BRUCE: Naw, Jelly.

JELLY: I don't want to have to tell you again, Bruce.

BRUCE: I'll get your money for you.

JELLY: Bruce! Say good-bye to Mike!

> *Pause. BRUCE whimpers.*

BRUCE: Good-bye, Mike.

JELLY: Say good-bye to Kenny.

BRUCE: Good-bye, Kenny.

KENNY: Bye Bruce. Been nice knowing you.

JELLY: Now close your eyes.

BRUCE: Naw, Jelly Belly! Please man! Don't kill me!

JELLY: Shut up!

BRUCE: I ain't worth killing, Jelly Belly! I ain't shit! You ought to let me live!

JELLY: I said shut up!

>*JELLY kicks BRUCE. BRUCE tumbles backwards.*

Close your eyes. Die like a man, mutherfucker.

>*BRUCE whimpers, collects himself, crawls back to the foot of the stairs and closes his eyes. JELLY lowers the barrel of the gun to BRUCE's forehead, then quietly says:*

Bang.

>*BRUCE falls over, holding his head, screaming. JELLY and KENNY laugh.*

Get up, mutherfucker!

KENNY: Shut up all of that screaming!

BRUCE: I'm dead!

KENNY: Shut up, Bruce!

BRUCE: My sweet Lord!

JELLY: The gun wasn't loaded, Bruce.

BRUCE: The whole back of my head is gone! I'm dead!

JELLY (*Nudging KENNY*): Hold it, hold it. Check this out.

Well, that takes care of ole Bruce, huh?

KENNY: Yep. Poor ole Bruce.

JELLY: Shame he had to die like that.

KENNY: Yeah, what a shame. I'm going to miss the ole dude.

JELLY: I'm not going to miss him. The mutherfucker owed me a lot of money.

>*JELLY and KENNY laugh. Bruce hears this and starts to listen.*

JELLY: Hey, hold it, hold it. How did you like the funeral?

KENNY: Oh, sad funeral. Real sad.

JELLY: Too bad nobody came.

KENNY: Yeah, too bad.

JELLY: But then again, who would want to see scum put into the ground?

JELLY and KENNY laugh.

BRUCE: Hey, man. I ain't no scum.

JELLY: You're scum, boy. Dead scum.

BRUCE: If I'm dead, then how come I can hear you talking to me?

JELLY: Cause you're a ghost, Bruce. You're dead, your body is burning in hell but your spirit is right here on earth. You are doomed to walk the streets of the city for all eternity looking to get high, but you know what? Ghosts can't get high.

BRUCE: They can't?

JELLY: Nope.

BRUCE: Oh, Lord Jesus.

MIKE: You're not a ghost, Bruce. Get up off the ground!

JELLY: Don't spoil it for him, Mike.

MIKE: The gun wasn't loaded, Bruce.

BRUCE: You mean I'm alive?

JELLY (*Holding up two shotgun shells*): He didn't say you was alive. He said the gun wasn't loaded.

MIKE: He didn't shoot you, Bruce.

JELLY: I should have, though. Walking off from the liquor store and leaving my change like that. I ought to blow your ass away!

BRUCE: Naw, wait, Jelly Belly! I'll go back to the store and get your change.

JELLY: Forget about it.

BRUCE: I'll go back right now.

JELLY: Bruce! Listen to me, Bruce! Forget about the change. You see that white boy that ripped off Kenny?

BRUCE: Yeah, I saw him.

JELLY: See? Even Bruce knows you got ripped off.

BRUCE: He's down at the liquor store, Kenny.

JELLY: So. What you going to do, Kenny?

JELLY offers KENNY the gun.

KENNY: I'm going to kick his ass.

JELLY: You ain't shit, you know that! You, your whoring mama, your drunken daddy, the whole lot of you ain't shit. I don't know how I got hooked up with you in the first place. You ain't my partner, Kenny. You ain't even my friend. You ain't shit. Go home and go to bed. I don't want you around me.

BRUCE: I told you, Jelly Belly. I tried to tell you about Kenny a long time ago. Now if you would've listened to me—

JELLY: Shut up, Bruce!

MIKE: I'm going in the house.

JELLY: Well, go ahead, goddamn it! Don't nobody need you out here anyway.

MIKE: You're sitting on my porch.

JELLY: And will continue to sit on your porch until I get ready to leave. I don't know what's happened to you mutherfuckers. I go away for a couple of months and Mike's done got pussy-whipped and Kenny's done lost all of his nerve.

MIKE: Kenny hasn't lost anything. And me, I don't care what you say about me. Now I'm going in the house and going to bed.

JELLY: And I ain't leaving, Mike. All of that dust you and me snorted on this porch? Every night we sat out here and snorted enough dust to pay my rent, your rent and everybody's rent for months. You ever think about how much that cost, Mike? Did you ever, for one minute, think about where it came from? Who was paying for it? I never asked you for a dime, Mike. Not one thin dime. I always gave you everything you asked for cause you was my friend. And now you want to throw me off your porch. Call the police on me and shit.

KENNY: You calling the police on Jelly Belly? Why you want to do something like that, Mike? Jelly Belly don't mess with nobody.

JELLY: You even tried to turn Kenny against me. Kenny! This boy has been like a son to me.

KENNY: I ain't turned against you, Jelly. I'm still your boy.

JELLY: Then give me one of those beers. Bruce, open this.

JELLY hands BRUCE a foil. BRUCE attempts to open it.

We were friends, Mike. You and your wife needed money, I gave you money, no questions asked. You asked me not to tell her where it came from, I never said a fuckin word. You got yourself in trouble and I went out of my way to help you. If it wasn't for me, you would be in jail right now. I've always gone out of my way to give you everything you asked for, Mike. And now you want to act as if we're strangers? Act as if you don't know me? It ain't that easy, Mike. It just ain't that easy.

JELLY looks at BRUCE who is having trouble opening the foil.

What the hell you doing with that dust, Bruce!

BRUCE: Trying to open it.

JELLY: You spill it, I'm going to kick your ass.

BRUCE: Open this for me, Kenny.

MIKE: You figure out what I owe you, Jelly. I'll pay you back.

JELLY: I don't want your money, Mike. What you owe me can't be repaid in dollars.

MIKE: So you're going to hold this over my head for the rest of my life?

JELLY: I ain't holding nothing over your head. I just don't want you to forget who your friends are.

KENNY: Got it open, Jelly.

BRUCE: Can I have a little bit?

JELLY: You got any money?

BRUCE: No.

JELLY: Then how do you expect to pay for it? That shit don't grow on trees, you know.

BRUCE: I know. But I figured that you'd let me have a little bit. You know, like you always do.

JELLY: See what I mean? You boys are living in a dream world, but let me tell you something. You get nothing for free in this world. Absolutely nothing. I own you, Bruce. You know that?

BRUCE: I know, Jelly.

JELLY: And Mike, you owe me a lot. A hell of a lot.

MIKE: You tell me what you think I owe you and I will pay you back.

JELLY: And you, Kenny, you hurt me most of all. You let Mike turn you against me, let him strip you of all your pride. You've turned into a punk, Kenny. A gutless mutherfucker.

BRUCE: Since you already own me, mind if I have a little toot of that dust?

JELLY: Go ahead, boy. Toot the whole thing. I hope you get sick and die.

BRUCE: Thanks, Jelly.

KENNY: What about me? Can I have a little toot too?

JELLY: Hell no.

KENNY: I can pay for it if you want.

JELLY: There ain't enough money in the world to make me sell to somebody I don't want to sell to.

KENNY: Then can I buy a beer from you?

MIKE: You don't need a beer, Kenny. You need to go home and go to bed.

KENNY: I need a beer, Mike. Why can't I have a beer?

JELLY: Go on and get a beer and shut up. Keep your money. Just get the beer and get away from me. You make me sick.

MIKE: I'm going in the house and going to bed. You ought to do the same, Kenny. If they want to sit out here all night, let them.

KENNY: After this beer, Mike. My throat is dry. You know how that dust is, Mike. I need something to wet my throat.

JELLY: No pride, Kenny. No pride, no dignity. Working a slave's job for slave wages.

MIKE: Honest work, Jelly Belly. Honest work with plenty of pride. The money we spend doesn't come from the pockets of people who were stepped on and kicked aside. The money I spend is mine. Money I worked for.

JELLY: And where does that leave you, Mike? Sitting on the porch of your cracker box house crying about how you got fucked over at work, talking about how you got to go to bed so you can get up the next morning to go back to work so you can get fucked over again. You're building houses that you'll never see the insides of, in neighborhoods with streets that they won't let you drive down. Why don't you build a house for yourself if you got pride, instead of living in this cardboard cut-out? Why don't you build a house for your friends, the people you know, the people down the street and spread your pride around? Cause they won't let you, that's why. You're a slave, Mike. You spend your life breaking your back, building things for people who would rather spit on you than look at you. If that's what you call honest, you can have it. I'd rather have my pride. I'd rather be a man. Men don't bend their backs at the feet of other men, only slaves do that. Men don't take orders from other men, only slaves do that. Men don't sell their pride for two dollars an hour or a bag of dope and men don't allow other men to walk into their houses without just retribution. Only slaves do that.

> *BRUCE, who has tooted the last foil, comes out of his stupor and speaks in general.*

BRUCE: That was some damned good shit, Jelly Belly. Damned good. I'm glad I'm your boy.

JELLY: People are laughing at you, Kenny. They're saying what a dumb mutherfucker you are. They're wondering why you're taking the little pride you got and putting it into things you'll never see. If that's the type of life you want to lead, be my guest. But I thought you were a man. I thought you had potential.

KENNY: I am a man.

JELLY: Yeah, sure, Kenny. I just lay out the facts for you and let you decide. You want another toot of this dust before I go?

KENNY: I can pay for it if you want.

JELLY: You ain't got to pay me, Kenny. I like you. You're my boy. Here, take two. They're small.

> *JELLY hands KENNY two small foils.*

I got to piss. Mind if I use your bathroom, Mike? Or you want to try to keep me out of there too?

MIKE: Barbara's asleep.

JELLY: I didn't ask you if I could spend the night. I asked if I could piss in your bathroom. If not, tell me and I'll piss right here.

MIKE: Use the bathroom. But be quiet.

> *JELLY climbs to the top of the stairs and exits. KENNY begins to open one of the foils.*

You shouldn't do that shit, Kenny. It's not good for you.

KENNY: I can handle it, Mike.

MIKE: You see what it's done to Bruce.

KENNY: Why don't you just leave me alone, okay?

MIKE: Be sure you're ready when I come to get you in the morning.

KENNY: I'll be ready, Mike. Ain't I always ready? Don't I always be sitting there waiting for you when you come? Don't I, Mike? Don't I?

MIKE: Yeah, Kenny.

KENNY: Don't I always do what you say? Don't I always do what everybody says? Foreman says, "Kenny, we need a wheelbarrow of sand out back." I take a wheelbarrow of sand out back. "Kenny, we need a flat of bricks on the second floor." I take a flat of bricks to the second floor. "Kenny, dig a hole." I dig a hole. I always do what everybody tells me to do and I'm tired of it, Mike. For once, just this once, I want to do what I want to do and right now I want to toot this dust!

MIKE: Okay, Kenny. I'm sorry. Toot the dust.

Pause. KENNY opens the foil and is about to toot the dust.

I know how you feel, Kenny. I feel the same way sometimes. But remember the things we talked about? Remember, Kenny? Remember the business? Kenny and Mike's Construction Company. You and me, Kenny. We're going to have our own business. Then we won't have to put up with that shit anymore. We can come and go as we want. There won't be anybody telling us what to do.

KENNY: But when is that going to be, Mike? When?

MIKE: Soon, Kenny. Soon.

KENNY: That's the same thing you said about your promotion, Mike. You said, "Kenny, I'm going to be a supervisor soon." Same thing you said about me working labor. You said, "Kenny, work labor for now, but soon you're going to be an apprentice." Well, you ain't no supervisor, Mike. And I'm still working labor.

MIKE: We need patience, Kenny. Like the brick layers. Remember?

KENNY: Yeah, Mike. Sure. Patience.

KENNY toots the dust. Aroused by the sound, BRUCE comes out of his stupor and stumbles over to KENNY.

BRUCE: Heyyyy, Kenny! Can I have a little bit of that dust?

KENNY: Get the fuck away from me, Bruce, before I kick your ass.

BRUCE: You can kick my ass, but you can't hurt me. You know why? Cause I got a strong mind. You see, you can be at home in your house, you can be cruising down the street, or you can be in jail. It's all the same, you know what I mean?

MIKE: It's not the same!

BRUCE: I mean, shit, man! You got to be somewhere! Right? Am I right? That is one fact that you cannot deny . . . that you got to be somewhere. And the mutherfuckers out there got a lock on your jock no matter where you at. They get you coming and they get you going. The chains are all the same, baby. The only difference is, some of them clink, and some of them clank. But if you got a strong mind like me, it don't matter, clink, clank, coming, going, I could be working your mutherfuckin job. It's all the same. So! Since I made my point, Kenny, you might as well let me have a little bit of that dust.

KENNY: Get the fuck away from me, Bruce!

> *KENNY pushes BRUCE in the face. BRUCE tumbles backwards and lands in the same spot from which he began.*

JELLY (*Entering*): Bruce giving you a little trouble?

KENNY: Bruce ain't shit. Bruce is scum.

JELLY: You toot that dust, Kenny?

KENNY: Yeah, Jelly. And it was some good dust.

JELLY: Don't you got to piss?

KENNY: Yeah, Jelly. I got to piss. Can I use your bathroom, Mike?

MIKE: Go ahead.

KENNY: Thanks a lot, Jelly. That was some good dust. Some real good dust.

> *KENNY exits.*

JELLY: Thank you for the use of your facilities, Mike. Pretty wife you got in there. I almost forgot how pretty she was.

MIKE: You son of a bitch, you.

> *BARBARA enters.*

BARBARA: What the fuck is going on out here? People coming in and out of my house.

JELLY: All I did was look at her.

BARBARA: He stood over my bed, Mike. This mutherfucker came into my room and stood over my bed.

JELLY: You shouldn't let your wife sleep in the nude like that. You never know who might walk in your house.

BARBARA: You're sick, Jelly Belly, you know that? You're the sickest son of a bitch I've ever seen in my life.

JELLY: I was looking for my sister.

BARBARA: You are a walking wall of destruction. People try to build something, try to have a little bit, and you come along and tear it down.

JELLY: It was an honest mistake, Miss Mike. I was looking for my sister.

BARBARA: She ain't here, goddamn it. And with God as my witness, you will never see her again. She came by here shaking and crying . . . she wanted to kill herself, Jelly Belly.

JELLY: So you did see her.

BARBARA: Yeah, I saw her. I gave her the money to leave town. Even found a place for her to go. Took her to the bus station myself. She's doing fine, Jelly Belly. She's doing just fine.

JELLY: So where is she?

BARBARA: That, Brother Jelly, is one thing you will never know.

JELLY: This is a damned shame. I don't like to hit a woman. It makes me feel bad afterwards, you know what I mean, Mike?

MIKE: You're not going to hit that woman. That's one thing I know you're not going to do.

JELLY: But if a woman lies to you, what else can you do?

BARBARA: I'll tell you what you can do. You can take that lie for all it's worth. You hold onto it. You can use that lie and believe it. Let that lie be your salvation, cause one of these days, you're going to hit a woman, and she's going to have a straight razor under her robe. She's going to take that straight razor and run it across that fat belly of yours. Then you're going to feel rather foolish standing there with your mouth open, your belly split wide, and your intestines laying in the dirt.

JELLY: Where's my sister, Miss Mike?

BARBARA: I ain't got the slightest idea, Brother Jelly. Now get the fuck off my porch.

JELLY: She can't live without me. She needs me. It's always been just me and her. What she going to do without me?

BARBARA: Live a very happy life.

JELLY: Listen. I didn't want to kill the dude.

BARBARA: This is the last time I'm going to tell you. Get off my porch.

JELLY: Mike? Talk to your wife for me, okay? For me, Mike. Talk to her.

MIKE: What you want me to tell her?

JELLY: Tell her it's okay, Mike. Tell her, you and me, we're partners. We got to stick together, Mike.

MIKE: Go to hell, Jelly Belly.

JELLY: Yeah, Mike. My partner. My man. You ain't got to be subtle with me. I can pick up on the nuances. Hey, Bruce! You sorry son of a bitch. BRUCE!

BRUCE: Yo, Brother Jelly, Brother man.

JELLY: Come on, Bruce. Let's go.

BRUCE: Go? Go where?

JELLY: We're going to hell, Bruce. You want to go to hell with me?

BRUCE: Yeah, Brother Jelly. You know I want to go with you. You and me, we're partners.

> BRUCE exits.

MIKE: Aren't you forgetting something, Jelly Belly?

JELLY: What's that, Mike?

> MIKE holds up the shotgun.

That ain't mine, Mike. I ain't never seen that before in my life. Jelly Belly don't mess with guns. Got no reason to mess with guns. Jelly Belly don't mess with nobody. And Mike? Keep the beer. Consider it a memento.

> JELLY exits as KENNY enters.

KENNY: Where's Jelly?

MIKE: He left. Why don't you go home too.

KENNY: He left these shotgun shells in your bathroom, Mike.

BARBARA: What the hell has been going on out here?

MIKE: Give them to me.

KENNY: For what?

MIKE: I'm going to get rid of them.

KENNY: Naw, Mike. These are some good shells. You can blow a punk away with these. He left the gun too.

MIKE: Give me the shells, Kenny.

KENNY: He left them for me, Mike, didn't he? He left the gun and the shells for me.

MIKE: He didn't leave them for anybody. Now give me the shells.

KENNY: You afraid I'm going to hurt myself or something?

BARBARA: He didn't say that, Kenny.

KENNY: You think I'm stupid and I'm tired of you thinking I'm stupid. And I'm tired of you telling me what to do.

MIKE: Give me the shells, Kenny.

KENNY: I ain't doing what you say no more, Mike. I'm a man. I got pride. I'm tired of working construction and breaking my back while people laugh at me. I'm tired, Mike.

BARBARA: You're high, Kenny. Go home and sleep it off.

KENNY: Don't tell me what to do!

MIKE: They're going to be people telling you what to do for the rest of your life so you might as well get used to it. It's going to be me or it's going to be Jelly Belly or it's going to be somebody at work. Killing that man who robbed you isn't going to change a thing. There will still be people laughing at you, people thinking you're dumb, people telling you what to do. You can't kill them all, Kenny, so you might as well get used to it.

KENNY: Give me the gun, Mike.

MIKE: Take your ass home and go to bed.

> KENNY knocks MIKE to the ground, grabs the gun, and loads it as MIKE scrambles to his feet.

BARBARA: Oh shit.

MIKE: What you going to do now, Kenny? Shoot me?

KENNY: Just leave me alone, Mike. Okay?

MIKE: You going to shoot me, Kenny?

KENNY: Barbara, tell him to leave me alone.

BARBARA: Leave him alone, Mike.

MIKE: You leave here with that gun, you can forget about the morning, Kenny. You can forget about going to work, you can forget about the business, you can forget about everything. You hear me, Kenny?

BARBARA: Just let him go.

MIKE: And that house you was going to build for your momma. You can forget about that too.

KENNY: But it ain't going to happen. None of it. I'm never going to build no house.

MIKE: You can try, goddamn it. If you was a man, you'd try.

BARBARA: Please, Mike. Let go.

MIKE: Give me the gun, Kenny. Come on. Take the blueprints and give me the gun.

KENNY: It ain't going to happen, is it, Mike? The house, the business, none of it's ever going to happen, is it?

MIKE: We can try, Kenny. That's all we can do, is try.

KENNY: I've tried every way I know how, Mike, and I can't try no more. I stopped trying. I stopped trying when I saw those tears in your eyes. I felt so helpless, Mike. Well, I'm not going to feel helpless no more.

KENNY exits with the gun. MIKE moves to go after him.

BARBARA: You hear that?

MIKE stops.

We done woke up Mikie. Come on, Mike. Let's go in the house.

MIKE doesn't respond.

He's got to go to school in the morning, Mike. Did he tell you? He says he wants to go back again.

MIKE doesn't respond.

Please, Mike. He says he wants to be like his daddy.

MIKE gives one last look in the direction in which KENNY exited, then slowly turns, climbs the stairs, and exits into the house.

BARBARA follows MIKE into the house.

Lights fade.

END OF PLAY

KNOCK ME A KISS

PRODUCTION HISTORY

Knock Me a Kiss was originally produced by Victory Gardens Theater, Chicago, Illinois, Dennis Začek, artistic director, Marcelle McVay, managing director, January 21 through February 27, 2000. The production was directed by Chuck Smith, with set design by Mary Griswold, costume design by Birgit Rattenborg Wise, lighting design by Todd Hensley, and sound design by Benjamin T. Getting and Benjamin Recht. Tina M. Jach was the production stage manager.

Countee Cullen	Jason Delane
Yolande Du Bois	Yvonne Huff
Jimmy Lunceford	Morocco Omari
Lenora	LeShay Tomlinson
Nina Du Bois	Celeste Williams
W. E. B. Du Bois	Dexter Zollicoffer

Knock Me a Kiss was produced in New York by Woodie King Jr.'s New Federal Theatre in association with Legacy Creative Arts Company, Chuck Smith, artistic director, November 11 through December 5, 2010. The production was directed by Chuck Smith, with set design by Anthony Davidson, costume design by Ali Turns, lighting design by Shirley Prendergast, and sound design by Bill Toles. Bayo was the stage manager.

Countee Cullen	Sean Phillips
Yolande Du Bois	Erin Cherry
Jimmy Lunceford	Morocco Omari
Lenora	Gillian Glasco
Nina Du Bois	Marie Thomas
W. E. B. Du Bois	André De Shields

(*above*) Yvonne Huff as Yolande Du Bois and Jason Delane as Countee Cullen in the Victory Gardens Theater production of *Knock Me a Kiss. Photo by Liz Lauren.*

(*left*) Dexter Zollicoffer as W. E. B. Du Bois, Yvonne Huff as Yolande Du Bois, and Jason Delane as Countee Cullen in the Victory Gardens Theater production of *Knock Me a Kiss. Photo by Liz Lauren.*

(*right*) Yvonne Huff as Yolande Du Bois and Morocco Omari as Jimmy Lunceford in the Victory Gardens Theater production of *Knock Me a Kiss*. Photo by Liz Lauren.

(*below*) Morocco Omari as Jimmy Lunceford, Yvonne Huff as Yolande Du Bois, Jason Delane as Countee Cullen, Celeste Williams as Nina Du Bois, Dexter Zollicoffer as W. E. B. Du Bois, and LeShay Tomlinson as Lenora in the Victory Gardens Theater production of *Knock Me a Kiss*. Photo by Liz Lauren.

Characters

Yolande Du Bois The twenty-six-year-old daughter of W. E. B. DU BOIS and NINA DU BOIS. YOLANDE is a romantic who has led a very sheltered life. The greatest love in her life is the love she has for her father.

Jimmy Lunceford Twenty-eight-year-old big band leader. Graduate of Fisk University and former high school teacher, JIMMY decided that the hand-to-mouth existence of touring with his band was more important to him than maintaining a job teaching high school. He is down-to-earth and very practical, up on current trends and fashions, and meticulous when it comes to music. He has a good business sense and loves YOLANDE dearly.

Nina Du Bois Midsixties, she is the wife of W. E. B. DU BOIS. NINA has a very provincial attitude toward sex, which she doesn't enjoy but considers to be necessary. She lives in the shadow of her husband, whom she met when she was a student and he was her professor. She never fully recovered from the death of her eighteen-month-old son Burghardt. His death was fundamental in forming her attitude toward her daughter, YOLANDE, who was born later, and toward her husband, W. E. B., whom she considered responsible for Burghardt's death.

W. E. B. Du Bois (Will) Midsixties, but seems much younger. Active in national and international politics, he has come to recognize that he is a better politician than he is a husband and father. Even so, he considers his personal sacrifices for the promotion of his personal agenda well worth the trade-off. He maintains a very businesslike relationship with his wife and his daughter.

Countee Cullen Twenty-five-year-old young boy-poet genius and protégé of W. E. B. DU BOIS, he is clearly a product of the Ivory Tower, Talented Tenth machine. He is very warm and charming, a man who has used words to get into and out of any situation. Although he's a poet, there is nothing effeminate about him.

Lenora Friend and confidante of YOLANDE, she's the down-to-earth, no-nonsense, tell-it-like-it-is type of friend we all would like to have.

On April 9, 1928, Countee Cullen was married to Yolande Du Bois, the daughter of W. E. B. Du Bois. The Reverend Cullen, Countee's father, officiated at the wedding, which W. E. B. Du Bois called "the symbolic march of young and black America. . . . It was a new race, a new thought, a new thing rejoicing in a ceremony as old as the world."

Two months later, Countee Cullen sailed to Paris with the best man from the wedding, Harold Jackman, leaving Yolande, his young bride, behind. Yolande was granted a divorce from Countee on December 9, 1929.

This play is a fictional account inspired by those factual events.

Time: 1928

Place: Harlem

KNOCK ME A KISS

A play in two acts

ACT ONE

The set should consist of six acting areas. The first four together should constitute the Du Bois apartment on West 150th Street in Harlem. These areas include the foyer outside the front door to the apartment, a common area inside the apartment, the book-laden study of W. E. B. Du Bois, and a private area for Yolande.

The other areas, Jimmy Lunceford's rehearsal hall and Countee Cullen's apartment, should only be suggested.

SCENE ONE

Yolande enters the foyer outside the front door to the apartment. She is followed by Jimmy Lunceford. The hour is late — somewhere between one and two in the morning.

As they enter, Jimmy sings. Yolande tries to quiet him as she fumbles with her keys.

JIMMY:

> *I like cake and no mistake*
> *But baby if you insist . . .*

YOLANDE: Shhh!

JIMMY:

> *I'll cut out cake*
> *Just for your sake . . .*

YOLANDE: Quiet!

> *He stops singing.*

JIMMY: Baby, we was swanging.

YOLANDE: If you're gonna come in here, you're gonna have to be quiet.

JIMMY: Am I right?

YOLANDE: Jimmy . . .

JIMMY: Just tell me. Was we swanging or what?

YOLANDE: All right. You were swinging.

JIMMY: Swinging? No, uh uh, baby, we wasn't swinging. The Duke, he be swinging. Cab Calloway was swinging. But us, baby, we was swanging.

YOLANDE: I didn't know there was a difference.

JIMMY: You know what the difference is. When you swinging, you only going through the motions, you doing it how you think it should be done, you only repeating what you've heard. But when you swanging, baby, the motions are going through you, you making it up as you go along, you following a voice that's coming to you from somewhere deep down inside.

    YOLANDE gets the door open, and they enter the apartment.

YOLANDE: You're gonna have to be quiet, Jimmy.

JIMMY: Ain't nobody home.

YOLANDE: My father isn't home. My mother, she's always here. She never goes anyplace.

JIMMY: Exactly what I expected.

YOLANDE: Is that right?

JIMMY: Yes, sir. This here is one swank stack of bricks.

YOLANDE: Swank?

JIMMY: That's right. I expected your old man to live in a joint like this. Books. Very intellectual. All in the head, you see. Nothing in the heart.

YOLANDE: How you know?

JIMMY: I know your ole man.

YOLANDE: I didn't realize you two were such aces.

JIMMY: Don't have to be his boon coon. Don't even have to meet the man. Listen to you talk bout him all the time. Talk bout how you used to sit here waiting for him to come home.

YOLANDE: You want your drink or not?

JIMMY: I'd rather get a lil taste of somethin else.

YOLANDE: I swear to God you got a one-track mind.

JIMMY: Ain't my fault you put a conjure on me. Every time I close my eyes, all I can see is you. Your eyes, your lips sweet like candy, peaches and bananas, like a couple of Louisiana plums.

YOLANDE: Jimmy . . .

JIMMY: Come here and let me run my tongue across those sweet plums of yours.

YOLANDE: Please.

JIMMY: Come on and knock me a kiss.

YOLANDE: My mother's here.

JIMMY: I'll be quiet. I swear. Quieter than a mouse pissing on cotton.

YOLANDE: How many times I have to tell you?

JIMMY: And I won't go too far. When you want me to stop, I'll stop. Promise.

YOLANDE: I'm not fooling around with you. Especially not here.

JIMMY: Then come back with me to my place, Yolande. Come on.

YOLANDE: I'm not going back to that rattrap you call a room.

JIMMY: Well, I'm sorry, but we all can't afford to stay at the Waldorf.

YOLANDE: Maybe not.

JIMMY: We ain't all connected like you.

YOLANDE: Don't have to be connected to afford to stay someplace better than you staying now.

JIMMY: Okay. Tell you what I'm gonna do. If it's that important to you, snatch up your stuff and let's go down to that swank stack on the Boulevard and get ourselves a real nice room. A suite, order a bottle of bubbles, somethin to eat . . .

YOLANDE: You can't even afford a decent room. How you gonna afford a bottle of bubbles?

JIMMY: I got kick.

YOLANDE: Since when?

JIMMY: Since the hen broke wind. Check it out.

> *JIMMY produces an envelope, which contains a stack of bills. He fans the money out and begins to count it.*

Ten, twenty, thirty . . .

YOLANDE: Where d'you get that?

JIMMY: Forty, sixty, eighty, one hundred.

> *There is more.*

YOLANDE: Jimmy . . .

JIMMY: As you can see, I can obviously afford to purchase a bottle of bubbles.

YOLANDE: That's the band's money, ain't it?

JIMMY: My money.

YOLANDE: You better not be messing with them men's money.

JIMMY: Who's the head nigger in charge? I'm the head nigger in charge.

YOLANDE: Why you always have to use that word?

JIMMY: What word?

YOLANDE: You know what word.

JIMMY: Nigger?

YOLANDE: That word.

JIMMY: Hell, it's true. I am the head nigger in charge. It is my band, I'm the HNIC, and I say, if you want a nice room, you want a lil champagne, we go get ourselves a sweet suite and a bottle of bubbles. Nothin' but the best for my baby.

YOLANDE: Do I look like I just got off the boat?

JIMMY: What boat?

YOLANDE: You think that all you have to do is rent a room and buy a bottle of booze to have your way with me?

JIMMY: I'm trying to give you want you want.

YOLANDE: What I want is to get married, Jimmy.

JIMMY: Okay. Let's get married.

YOLANDE: When?

JIMMY: Name the time and the place.

YOLANDE: How bout here and how bout now?

JIMMY: Unless you got a preacher in your pocket, baby, we gonna least have to wait till the morning. So how bout this? Tonight, we get ourselves a nice room and get real comfortable. Let me curl your toes a lil bit, you curl mine. Then, first thing in the morning, we'll go down to city hall and jump us some broom. What you think bout that?

YOLANDE: Was that supposed to be a marriage proposal?

JIMMY: All right. I can see where this is going. Yolande, will you marry me?

YOLANDE: No one will ever accuse you of being a Valentino.

JIMMY: You said you wanted to get married.

YOLANDE: You make it sound like I asked you to clean out my bathtub drain.

JIMMY: I said I'd do it. Damn.

YOLANDE: I want to get married with a little romance, Jimmy. I don't want to get married by no judge. Judges shouldn't be marrying people. Judges send people to jail.

JIMMY: Don't matter who says the words. Long as we believe them.

YOLANDE: We get married tomorrow, where we gonna go on our honeymoon?

JIMMY: Dayton.

YOLANDE: Dayton?

JIMMY: Dayton, Ohio. Got a gig at a stomp shop there Friday next. We get married, get on the bus, go to Dayton and indulge ourselves in some sweet honeymoon.

YOLANDE: Is that all you ever think bout?

JIMMY: My lips and your plums on our honeymoon.

YOLANDE: Jimmy . . .

JIMMY: I'm a man, baby. Shit, if I wasn't thinking bout it, somethin be wrong.

YOLANDE: All right. I want you to do something for me.

JIMMY: You know I'll do any damn thing for you.

> YOLANDE hands him a silver-tipped walking stick.

YOLANDE: Here.

JIMMY: What's this?

YOLANDE: What's it look like?

JIMMY: Looks like a cane, but I ain't gimpy. Nothing wrong with my legs.

YOLANDE: It's not that type of cane, Jimmy. Here. Take it. Stand over here.

JIMMY: For what?

YOLANDE: I wanna see what you look like.

JIMMY: Don't you already know what I look like?

YOLANDE: Jimmy!

JIMMY: All right.

JIMMY takes the stick and moves to the bookcases.

YOLANDE: Stand up straight. Come on. Hold your chin up, Jimmy. When was the last time you talked to your mother and father?

JIMMY: My mother and father?

YOLANDE: The people who gave birth to you?

JIMMY: This is your daddy's cane, ain't it?

YOLANDE: It's nobody's cane.

JIMMY: You trying to make me look like your daddy.

YOLANDE: I'm trying to imagine what you gonna look like at the wedding.

JIMMY: I can tell you this: Whatever I look like, I'm not gonna be carrying your daddy's silver-tipped walking stick. I can tell you that.

YOLANDE: And I'm not getting on a bus and going to Dayton, Ohio, for a honeymoon with you. When I get married, I wanna get married in a church, Jimmy. With flowers and a ring.

JIMMY: What kinda ring?

YOLANDE: Diamond ring. I want a diamond engagement ring and I want a wedding ring. I want a church wedding with lotsa flowers and ushers and bridesmaids. And on my honeymoon, I wanna sail on a boat, Jimmy, first class. I wanna sail to Paris or Vienna. I'm not getting on nobody's bus going to no damn Dayton, Ohio.

JIMMY: You want a society wedding.

YOLANDE: I want a wedding that corresponds to my stature. According to who I am.

JIMMY: You are sounding more and more like your daddy every day.

YOLANDE: And what's wrong with that?

JIMMY: Nothing, if you don't mind sounding saditty.

YOLANDE: Saditty?

JIMMY: Your daddy is one of the sadittiest Negroes I've ever seen in my life. Saditty and self-righteous, that man's nose so high up in the air if it rained, he'd drown. And now here you come, you starting to act just like him.

YOLANDE: I'm bout tired of you passing judgment on my father.

JIMMY: I don't care nothing bout your daddy. Hell, he don't care nothing bout me. I don't fit into his master plan of producing a batch of upper-crust Negroes. Shit, what I care bout him for? And I'll tell you somethin else: I ain't scared of him either. Everybody walking around this country scared of that nigger. I ain't scared of him and I don't care who knows it. In fact, I can't wait till I meet him. Hell, I'll tell him to his face exactly what I think of him. Shit, the way I see it, he's just like every other nigger walking the face of this earth. He's just as—

YOLANDE: That's enough, Jimmy.

JIMMY: I'm sorry, Yolande, but I got to call it like I see it.

YOLANDE: And now I'm gonna call it like I see it. If you ever wrap your mouth around my father or his reputation again, I swear to God, Jimmy Lunceford, I will break it off with you so hard, fast, and complete I won't even leave a memory behind. You understand me?

JIMMY: All I'm saying is, your daddy—

YOLANDE: I know what you saying and I'm tired of hearing it. My father has worked too long and too hard to have some ignorant son of a Negro like you come along and bad-mouth him.

JIMMY: So why I got to be ignorant?

YOLANDE: Call it like I see it.

JIMMY: Let me say somethin before we start to drift too far from land. I love you, Yolande, and I will marry you any day, any time, all you have to do is say the word. However, I can't afford no diamond rangs and no church weddings and no honeymoons in Vienna. At least not now. I'm struggling right now, baby. If somethin comes outta tonight, if that cat from the Cotton Club dug us or if that cat from the Lafayette liked what he heard, if either one of 'em books us for a gig here in Harlem, baby, we'll be picking in high cotton. Hell, we just as good as the Duke. We just as good if not better than Cab Calloway. I mean, what the hell is hi-de hi-de ho? Don't nobody know. People sing it, but they don't know what the hell they singing. So why did Cab come up with it? Cause it distinguishes him and his band from everybody else and they band. And that's all I got to do. Distinguish me and my band from everybody else. Soon as I figure out a way to do that, I guarantee you, we'll be playing all over this town and maybe then, I'll have enough money for diamonds and church weddings. But until that happens, I got to keep on playing Dayton, and Cincinnati, and Buffalo, and every lil gut-bucket in between. You wanna come along? Baby, you're certainly welcomed.

YOLANDE: I'm not traveling with you as your concubine.

JIMMY: I already told ya I'd marry ya.

YOLANDE: You just don't understand romance, do you?

JIMMY: I guess that's just somethin I'm just gonna have to work on. You wanna go back to my place with me or not?

YOLANDE: What did I tell ya?

JIMMY: Can I at least have a good-night kiss?

> *She acquiesces. He kisses her. She kisses him. After a moment, his hands develop a mind of their own.*

YOLANDE: Jimmy . . .

> *He continues.*

Please don't touch me there.

> *He likes it.*

Jimmy!

JIMMY: All right. Sorry. Sleep tight, Honeymoon.

> *JIMMY exits. NINA, who was eavesdropping on the scene, enters.*

YOLANDE: Jesus. Must you always spy on me?

NINA: Must you always use that type of language?

YOLANDE: You'd think a woman could have a little privacy.

NINA: A woman doesn't need privacy. Not a proper woman. The only type of woman that needs privacy is a woman who's doing something she's not supposed to be doing. But then, you wouldn't call that type of woman a woman, now would you?

YOLANDE: I wasn't doing anything improper.

NINA: I heard a man's voice.

YOLANDE: That was Jimmy.

NINA: He's a man.

YOLANDE: I wasn't doing anything, Mother.

NINA: Two o'clock in the morning.

YOLANDE: He walked me home.

NINA: Man, woman, two o'clock in the morning.

YOLANDE: So what? If I stayed out until five o'clock in the morning, what's it to you?

NINA: Doesn't mean anything to me. Might mean something to your father, though.

YOLANDE: I haven't done anything wrong.

NINA: Didn't say you did. Just saying that your father might be interested in knowing about this behavior.

YOLANDE: Jimmy is a friend of mine, Mother.

NINA: A friend?

YOLANDE: That's all. There is no behavior.

NINA: You've been out with your friend almost every night this week.

YOLANDE: I am twenty-six years old. I should be able to go out with whomever I please.

NINA: We'll see what your father has to say about that.

YOLANDE: Tell him. I don't care. You think I live my life to please Daddy? Is that what you think? I don't care what you tell him. I'm not gonna be here when he gets here anyway.

NINA: And where do you think you're going?

YOLANDE: Daddy's not here, I'm going back to Baltimore.

NINA: Why do you have to keep an apartment in Baltimore, Yolande? What's wrong with living here in New York?

YOLANDE: I plan to begin my work in Baltimore, Mother.

NINA: What work?

YOLANDE: I plan to follow in Daddy's footsteps and dedicate my life to the betterment of the Negro race.

NINA: And somebody told you that Baltimore was the place to go if you wanted to begin this betterment?

YOLANDE: I plan to teach high school in Baltimore, Mother.

NINA: High school?

YOLANDE: I plan to help the downtrodden and the less fortunate.

NINA: That's like the blind leading the blind. You're just as downtrodden and are at least less fortunate as everybody else.

YOLANDE: I'm not gonna allow you to depress me.

NINA: You should forget about helping others and think about helping yourself, Yolande.

YOLANDE: They want me, Mother. They need me. They asked me to come in for an interview at three o'clock tomorrow afternoon.

NINA: Then you will miss seeing your father because he'll be here tomorrow morning.

YOLANDE: Tomorrow morning?

NINA: The 10:45 from Pittsburgh.

YOLANDE: Why didn't you say something?

NINA: You weren't here to say something to.

YOLANDE: Look at me. I have to go to the beauty shop. I have to get my hair done. And look at this dress. Mother, you should have said something. I have to go shopping. There's not enough time.

NINA: Doesn't matter what you look like once your father finds out that you've been carrying on with that musician.

YOLANDE: I haven't been carrying on.

NINA: We'll let your father be the judge of that.

SCENE TWO

The next morning.

COUNTEE CULLEN and W. E. B. DU BOIS in the Du Bois study.

COUNTEE: I turned in the application. They sent me a letter, we set up an appointment, I went in and met with them. Everything is exactly how it should be. They asked about you, how you felt about it. I told them that I'd talk to you.

WILL: What do they want?

COUNTEE: I think what they want is some sort of acknowledgment.

WILL: From me?

COUNTEE: Something simple. A good word, a note perhaps.

WILL: You mean a recommendation.

COUNTEE: I've been after this for the past six years, Dr. Du Bois. If I get this award, I'd be able to study abroad for at least a year if not two. I'll be able to walk in the footsteps of Shelley and Keats.

WILL: And what of your brethren here at home, Countee? Tell me how your walking in the footsteps of dead European poets would benefit the Negro of the United States?

COUNTEE: You mean besides the obvious contribution to my personal growth as a poet?

WILL: It's time for you to look beyond your personal growth. It's time for you to take into consideration the impact of your actions upon the lives of others. You are in the public eye. You are a Negro and you're a poet. Like it or not, everything you do from here on in will have meaning. Every action you take will be dismantled, examined, and interpreted, then reassembled and reinterpreted.

COUNTEE: I am aware of the glare of public scrutiny.

WILL: Are you?

COUNTEE: Well aware.

WILL: Then why haven't you married?

COUNTEE: Is that necessary?

WILL: We've spent a great deal of time and energy extolling the virtues of marriage, the value of family, the importance of Black love within the family. And here you are, in your late twenties, a highly visible vanguard of the struggle and you are, as of yet, unmarried. No matter how you turn it, it does not look good, Countee. It makes it appear as if we do not practice what we preach. Now you know that I support you and your work. But if you want me to give you something more, an acknowledgment, a good word, a note perhaps, you're going to have to help me. Help me help you.

COUNTEE: By taking a wife?

WILL: There must be a host of eligible young women who have caught your eye. Simply choose one.

COUNTEE: How?

WILL: What do you mean, how?

COUNTEE: How do I choose?

WILL: Examine bloodlines. Heredity, physique, health, and brains. Make sure you avoid putting emphasis on beauty or something as fleeting as romantic sexual allure.

COUNTEE: I understand all of this, Dr. Du Bois.

WILL: Then I don't understand your question.

COUNTEE: I'm not sure how to begin.

WILL: Do as I did. Get a piece of paper and make three columns. In the first column, list the names of all of the eligible young women you know. In the next column, list the attributes of each of these women, and in the last column, list their shortcomings. Subtract the shortcomings of each woman from her attributes and the woman with the most attributes, you choose as your wife.

COUNTEE: Sounds a bit impersonal to me.

WILL: Systematic is what it is, my boy. Too often we are ruled by our emotions. We make irrational decisions based on something as silly as love or momentary desire. Love is familiarity. Nothing more, nothing less. For instance, the town I lived in as a child was home to a slaughterhouse. Every week hundreds of hogs were butchered, hung, bled, and dressed for market. The smell of blood and carnage permeated the entire town. Strangers who would come to town would cover their mouth and nose. They'd always ask the same question: "What is that God-awful smell?" And our reply to that question was always the same. "That smell, my friend, is the smell of money." After the slaughterhouse closed, the entire town went into mourning. We mourned not only the loss of the economic river that dried up after the slaughterhouse closed, but we also mourned the loss of the slaughterhouse itself, the activity, the sounds, the sight of it all lit up at night churning out waxed boxes of hams, bacon, pork chops, and steaks. But most of all, we mourned the loss of the smell. It was part of our prosperity, part of who we were. Now, if an entire town can grow to love the smell of spilt blood, carnage, and death, I imagine it wouldn't be difficult for one man to grow to love the woman whom he chose after careful deliberation. That's how I chose my Nina. We've been married now for thirty-two happy years.

COUNTEE: Okay. Make a list.

WILL: And then choose.

COUNTEE: After I choose?

WILL: After you choose, ask your potential wife out on a date. This should be a real date, Countee, don't invite her to a poetry reading or recital. Friends, you invite to hear your poetry. A potential wife, you invite out for an evening of dining. But not dancing. You don't want her to get the wrong idea. Dancing is permitted only after the second or third date. And make sure you buy her some flowers. Women like that sort of thing. Flowers.

COUNTEE: Flowers?

WILL: Didn't your father teach you any of this?

COUNTEE: My father doesn't understand me.

WILL: I'm sure he does.

COUNTEE: Not the way you do.

> *YOLANDE enters.*

YOLANDE: Daddy's home! Daddy! Surprise!

WILL: Ouchie!

> *She hugs him.*

YOLANDE: Surprised?

WILL: Surprised and happy. I thought you were to be in Baltimore.

YOLANDE: I was, but I came in last week to be here to surprise you when you got home but Mother wouldn't tell me when you were coming. First she said you were gonna be here Friday, then she said it was gonna be another week so I decided I was gonna go back to Baltimore for a job interview but last night she told me you were coming home today which didn't leave me with enough time to go shopping or get my hair done cause I couldn't get an appointment on such a short notice and that's the reason my hair looks the way it does. Hey, Countee.

COUNTEE: Hey.

WILL: Your hair looks fine, Ouchie. I like it like this. It's a new look for you.

YOLANDE: The unpressed look?

WILL: It must be your inner splendor that I see shining through. Now what's this about a job interview?

YOLANDE: I'm gonna teach high school, Daddy. In Baltimore. I'm gonna work with the less fortunate.

WILL: Good girl. That's my girl. You hear this, Countee? Yolande is joining the struggle.

NINA enters.

NINA: Will? I must talk to you about your daughter's behavior.

YOLANDE: Here she goes.

NINA: She's been out with a man every night this week.

YOLANDE: I've already told you that he's just a friend of mine.

NINA: He keeps her out until two, three o'clock in the morning.

YOLANDE: Nobody keeps me out, Mother.

NINA: He must be the one keeping you out because I know you do not stay out till the wee hours of the morning on your own.

YOLANDE: I am a grown woman.

COUNTEE: I oughta be going.

WILL: Wait, Countee, please.

YOLANDE: I am fully capable of making responsible choices on my own.

WILL: Ouchie? Is this true?

YOLANDE: Is what true, Daddy?

WILL: Has my little girl met a young man?

NINA: What did I just tell you? I just told you, she's been out with him every night this week.

WILL: Wife, please.

NINA: Am I making words here? Can anyone hear me?

WILL: Yolande?

YOLANDE: He's a friend, Daddy. That's all.

NINA: We know nothing about this man. We know nothing about his background, nothing about his breeding or his upbringing.

YOLANDE: He graduated from Fisk, Mother.

NINA: What about his parents? What do we know about them? And his parents' parents?

YOLANDE: You just eliminated half of all the eligible Negro bachelors in Harlem.

WILL: Ouchie? This friend of yours. What's his name?

YOLANDE: Jimmy Lunceford.

WILL: Is he someone I should meet?

YOLANDE: No, Daddy. There's no need.

NINA: He's a musician.

WILL: Nevertheless, Wife, we could invite him to dinner. Him and his parents. We could get to know his family, discover what type of young man he is.

YOLANDE: I'm telling ya, Daddy, he's just a friend. Somebody I met through Lenora.

WILL: If he's someone you're seeing, I should like to meet him, Yolande.

YOLANDE: The only reason I went out with him in the first place was because I was bored. There's nothing for me to do here in New York or in Baltimore. For example, I would love to go out with a man like Countee . . .

WILL: Countee?

YOLANDE: However, Countee has not asked me out on a date. And if he doesn't ask me out on a date, I can't go out with him, now can I?

WILL: Well I'm sure if Countee knew you were interested . . .

NINA: Excuse me, but I hardly think it appropriate to talk about the young man as if he weren't even here.

COUNTEE: I could leave.

WILL: No, wait, Countee.

YOLANDE: There's a dearth of eligible Negro bachelors in this country. Especially well-traveled, well-bred, sophisticated ones. A man like Countee is exactly the type of man I've been looking for.

NINA: She is shameless.

WILL: Wife, please.

YOLANDE: Thank you, Daddy. At least somebody around here treats me with respect.

NINA: Are you encouraging this type of behavior?

WILL: I think the children need to work this out for themselves.

YOLANDE: We're not children.

WILL: You're right, I'm sorry, you're not.

YOLANDE: We are both mature and responsible adults.

WILL: Capable of making responsible choices on your own, I know. Countee?

COUNTEE: Would you like to have dinner with me, Yolande?

YOLANDE: I would love to have dinner with you, Countee.

NINA: Shameless. She is absolutely shameless.

SCENE THREE

A few days later.

Yolande is getting dressed. Lenora is helping her with her hair.

LENORA: So I go by the rehearsal hall but I don't hear no music. I figure they either taking a break or ain't nobody there. I walk in and find out that everybody's there and they ain't taking no break, they're practicing. But they ain't practicing no music. Get this . . . they're practicing their walk.

YOLANDE: Their walk?

LENORA: Jimmy got everybody on one side of the room, teaching them how to walk to the other side of the room.

YOLANDE: They're grown men. Don't they already know how to walk?

LENORA: Not the way Jimmy teaching them how to walk. Jimmy teaching them how to strut. All together, in step. He's calls it synchronized syncopation.

YOLANDE: He's converting his band to a marching band?

LENORA: I ain't seen them play music when they walk. He got them strutting in step when they walk on stage before they start playing and strutting in step when they walk off stage after they get done playing. He also got them swanging they horns and nodding they heads and waving they hands all together, all while playing.

YOLANDE: Negro's lost his mind.

LENORA: Lost his mind over you is what happened. He told me he asked you to marry him.

YOLANDE: Is that right?

LENORA: That's what he said. 'S'it true?

YOLANDE: If you wanna call it that.

LENORA: He asked you to marry him?

YOLANDE: He only asked me cause he thought I wanted him to ask me.

LENORA: You didn't want him to ask?

YOLANDE: Not the way he did. He didn't mean it. He didn't get down on one knee, he didn't have a ring, he didn't talk to my father and he's gonna have to talk to my father.

LENORA: You need permission to get married?

YOLANDE: I don't need no permission.

LENORA: Then why he gotta talk to your father?

YOLANDE: It's a show of respect, Lenora, to ask the father for a woman's hand in marriage. He wouldn't be asking for my father's permission, he'd be asking for his blessing.

LENORA: I can't see Jimmy asking no man for nothing.

YOLANDE: See what I'm saying? I can't take him seriously cause he really didn't mean it.

LENORA: Wouldn't matter to me. Soon as those words fell from his lips, I'd snatch them up and hold him to it. I'd worry bout whether he meant it later, after the wedding. Shoot. There are plenty of ways of making a man mean it. Long list of ways. The trick is to get him to stay in one place long enough to work some of them ways on him. Get him to sit still, hell, I'll make him mean it.

YOLANDE: Which color?

She holds up a couple of tubes of lipstick.

LENORA: Ain't you going out on a date?

YOLANDE: Right.

LENORA: So why you asking me? Wear the red, baby. Rhythm red. You know what I mean?

YOLANDE: I'm going out with the son of a preacher.

LENORA: You talking bout Countee?

YOLANDE: I ain't talking bout Jimmy.

LENORA: Countee Cullen is not the son of a preacher.

YOLANDE: His daddy is a reverend, Lenora. Got a church on 125th Street.

LENORA: That man is not his daddy. Not the way I heard it.

YOLANDE: No telling what you heard, the people you hang out with.

LENORA: What's that supposed to mean?

YOLANDE: I've known Countee for six years.

LENORA: I don't care how long you've known him. I'm just telling you what I heard. You don't wanna hear it, just say so. You ain't hurt my feelings, cause it don't matter to me.

YOLANDE: All right. Let's hear it.

LENORA: I don't wanna be guilty of foisting upon you any rumor, innuendo, or out your window. I'll keep my little bit of information to myself.

YOLANDE: You want me to beg you?

LENORA: Crawling on your hands and knees.

YOLANDE: I'm not gonna beg you.

LENORA: The way I heard it, Countee Cullen was an orphan. Reverend Cullen and his wife took the boy in when the boy was bout fifteen, sixteen years old.

YOLANDE: This is the first I've ever heard of this lie.

LENORA: Everybody been talking bout it for years. It was real interesting cause the Reverend and his wife couldn't have no kids. Most folks say that it was because of the wife, that she had narrow hips. But other folks say it was because of the Reverend. That he was a bit peculiar, you know what I'm saying? The Reverend was peculiar and then here he shows up with a fifteen-year-old boy that he claimed to be his son.

YOLANDE: I ain't never heard of this before.

LENORA: There's a whole lot out there that you ain't never heard of before.

YOLANDE: My father knows his father, Lenora.

LENORA: You not hearing bout it don't make it not true.

YOLANDE: They've been friends for as long as I can remember. If that was true, I'd know bout it.

LENORA: Why you going out with him for anyway?

YOLANDE: I like him. He's a poet.

LENORA: Jimmy's a poet. And he find out you going out with this man, he really gonna lose his mind.

YOLANDE: Don't nobody care bout Jimmy.

LENORA: When all this change?

YOLANDE: Every time he comes to town he's staying in another nasty room. I don't like those places he stay in. Makes my skin crawl.

LENORA: Not his fault he's a broke negro.

YOLANDE: I'm tired of him putting his hands all over me every time I see him.

LENORA: Let him put them paws on me. I wouldn't complain.

YOLANDE: Every time I see him, he's got only one thing on his mind.

LENORA: Wouldn't complain one bit.

YOLANDE: I want a little romance and all he can think bout is sex.

LENORA: What's the difference?

YOLANDE: Romance is tender kisses and caressing in the moonlight. And sex is . . . sex. It's dark and it's groping and poking and although won't nobody admit it, it's a bit scary.

LENORA: I don't know what kind of sex you having but sound like you doing something wrong.

YOLANDE: I want him to bring me some flowers every now and then. What's wrong with that? What's wrong with me expecting him to dust off a few sweet words to say to me instead of talking bout his music all the time? You know what I would like? I would like to spend an evening with him without him trying to hop on top of me at the end of that evening. Is that asking too much?

LENORA: He won't even buy you flowers?

YOLANDE: I ain't seen none yet.

LENORA: You give a man a lil trim, least he can do is buy you some flowers. You did give him some trim, didn't you?

YOLANDE: Why you always asking me that?

LENORA: Damn, Yolande, I thought you was ready to do this.

YOLANDE: I am ready.

LENORA: Don't sound like it to me.

YOLANDE: I can't think bout nothing else. No matter what I'm doing, walking down the street, I imagine what it's gonna be like to touch him. To touch his chest, his arms, his hands. My God. Have you seen his hands? They're huge.

LENORA: Seen them? I've had dreams bout them.

YOLANDE: I wanna touch those hands. I wanna kiss those hands.

LENORA: Then what's the problem?

YOLANDE: I wanna touch and kiss and all he wants to do is hump and bump.

LENORA: Sounds to me like he wants to do the exact same thing you wanna do.

YOLANDE: I want romance, Lenora. I want flowers.

LENORA: Did you ask him for some flowers?

YOLANDE: Shouldn't have to ask him.

LENORA: Damn, Yolande. You gotta ask the man for what you want. Man won't know what you want unless you tell him.

YOLANDE: What am I supposed to do? Write out directions?

LENORA: That's one way to do it.

YOLANDE: A set of rules bout what he's supposed to do?

LENORA: Step by step, in explicit detail.

YOLANDE: That would ruin it.

LENORA: Ruin what?

YOLANDE: If a man do something for me, I want him to do it cause he wants to do it. Not cause he's following some instructions.

LENORA: Ain't nothing wrong with a lil instruction. Especially detailed instruction. You want the man to bring you flowers, you got to tell him what kind of flowers you like and how often you expect to get them. You want him to whisper some sweet words to you in the middle of the night, first thing you got to do is teach him how to talk, then turn out the lights and ease his lips over to your ear while you softly whisper to him. You got to tell him where to touch and when. Got to tell him how hard, how soft, how fast, how slow. Got to let him know when to stop moving altogether and how to hold it right there. You want a man to do these things for you, you got to tell him, Yolande.

COUNTEE enters with a bouquet of flowers.

COUNTEE: Excuse me. Your mother said you were here and I should come right in. I didn't know you had company.

YOLANDE: It's all right. We were just talking.

COUNTEE: I can wait . . .

YOLANDE: No, I'm ready.

COUNTEE: I brought these for you.

He presents the flowers.

YOLANDE: How sweet. Thank you.

COUNTEE: You're welcome. Ready?

YOLANDE: Oh, yes. I'm ready.

SCENE FOUR

Later that night. Countee and Yolande enter the foyer outside the door to the apartment. A barefoot Yolande carries her shoes.

COUNTEE: You okay?

YOLANDE: I think I danced up a blister on my foot.

COUNTEE: I think I have a blister on both of my feet.

YOLANDE: And you're still perspiring.

COUNTEE: Perspiring? Yolande, I am sweating like a racehorse.

YOLANDE: That's what you get for commandeering the dance floor at the Sugar Cane.

COUNTEE: I was just trying to keep up with you.

YOLANDE: I haven't danced that hard in a very long time.

COUNTEE: I haven't danced that hard since I was in Paris.

YOLANDE: Paris?

COUNTEE: Oh, yeah. There's this dance hall in Paris.

YOLANDE: I know. Dance halls all over Paris.

COUNTEE: But there's this one in particular. On the Left Bank. Near the old Latin Quarter . . .

YOLANDE: Bal Blomet?

COUNTEE: You know Bal Blomet?

YOLANDE: The doorman's name is Michel.

COUNTEE: Yes.

YOLANDE: Negro from Martinique.

COUNTEE: You know Michel.

YOLANDE: And he knows me. Last time I was there, he remembered who I was. Remembered my name.

COUNTEE: This is divine providence.

YOLANDE: It's my favorite place to dance when I go dancing in Paris.

COUNTEE: It's a wonder we haven't run into each other.

YOLANDE: Wouldn't that be something? Run into each other while hopping at the stomp shop at Bal Blomet.

COUNTEE: Yeah, that would be something.

YOLANDE: You been there a lot?

COUNTEE: To Bal Blomet?

YOLANDE: To Paris.

COUNTEE: Twice. Went once with my father and once with a friend of mine.

YOLANDE: Harold Jackman?

COUNTEE: You know Harold?

YOLANDE: Oh yeah. Tall, black, good-looking man?

COUNTEE: You know Harold.

YOLANDE: Extremely good-looking.

COUNTEE: Be careful, because he's also quite the lady's man.

YOLANDE: And you went to Paris with your father?

COUNTEE: My father loves to travel.

YOLANDE: And you travel with him?

COUNTEE: The first trip my father and I took together was home from the hospital right after I was born and we've been traveling together ever since.

YOLANDE: I want to go there on my honeymoon.

COUNTEE: To Paris?

YOLANDE: I want to sail first class. During the day I wanna sit on the deck with my husband and sip champagne. And at night . . .

COUNTEE: Oh, yeah.

YOLANDE: You know that you can never, under any circumstances, tell my father that you and I went dancing on the first date.

COUNTEE: Believe me. I know.

YOLANDE: He finds out that we went dancing and he'll have you locked up and me put away.

COUNTEE: You don't have to worry. It'll be our little secret.

YOLANDE: You want to come in for a drink?

COUNTEE: I would like to, but your mother . . .

YOLANDE: My mother's gonna have to get used to the idea that I have men calling on me.

COUNTEE: You consider me to be a caller?

YOLANDE: I'm sorry. I didn't mean to assume . . .

COUNTEE: No, it's all right. We've known each other for so long, I didn't know how you considered me.

YOLANDE: How do you want me to consider you?

COUNTEE: If I was one of your callers, I'd probably be last in a long line of men.

YOLANDE: That's not true.

COUNTEE: That I would be the last or that the line is long?

YOLANDE: Neither.

COUNTEE: That's not what I heard.

YOLANDE: What've you heard?

COUNTEE: I heard you were notorious.

YOLANDE: Notorious?

COUNTEE: A regular heartbreaking Aphrodite. Leaving a long, littered trail of brokenhearted men.

YOLANDE: I don't know where you heard that but you heard wrong.

COUNTEE: Then why does your mother get so upset?

YOLANDE: My mother has a nervous disposition, Countee. She worries bout things that are not real. She sees things that are not there. I think she needs a brain doctor, but Daddy won't get her a brain doctor. He seems to think that her behavior is normal.

COUNTEE: Sorry.

YOLANDE: You wanna come in or not?

COUNTEE: I really should get going.

YOLANDE: And you call me a heartbreaker. You're the one, Mister son of a preacher man.

COUNTEE: What?

YOLANDE: I know bout you. I peeped your cards.

COUNTEE: And what did you see when you peeped my cards?

YOLANDE:

> Copper Sun. "Timid Lover."
> I who employ a poet's tongue,
> Would tell you how
> You are a golden damson hung
> Upon a silver bough.

COUNTEE: You've read my work.

YOLANDE: Every woman in Harlem has read your work. They lay awake at night dreaming of being your wife. And you're such a cucumber, you act as if they don't even exist. What is it with you?

COUNTEE: Maybe I've been saving myself.

YOLANDE: For who?

COUNTEE: Somebody special.

YOLANDE: She better get here quick.

COUNTEE: Maybe she's already here. Maybe she just arrived.

YOLANDE: You trying to sweet-talk me, Countee Cullen?

COUNTEE: I'm afraid I'm not doing a very good job of it.

YOLANDE: You're doing just fine. But you know my father wants to meet the parents of any man that I'm seeing.

COUNTEE: I know.

YOLANDE: And somebody told me you were adopted.

COUNTEE: Where d'you hear that?

YOLANDE: I just heard it.

COUNTEE: Negroes won't let you rest for one minute, I swear. Just cause you operate in the public eye, Negroes think that your entire life should be laid open and placed on a buffet table for them to pick over.

YOLANDE: I'm sorry.

COUNTEE: I get so tired of the rumors.

YOLANDE: I apologize, Countee. I shouldn't have said anything. It was stupid.

COUNTEE: It's not your fault. You heard a rumor. Am I right?

YOLANDE: I heard a rumor.

COUNTEE: And what other rumors did you hear?

YOLANDE: Just that you were adopted.

COUNTEE: Just wait. You'll hear others.

YOLANDE: I shouldn't have repeated it.

COUNTEE: I'm gonna tell you this because I feel as if I can trust you, Yolande. I mean, I can trust you, can't I?

YOLANDE: Of course you can trust me.

COUNTEE: It's true. I was adopted. The Cullens are not my real parents.

YOLANDE: Then the story bout your father bringing you home from the hospital?

COUNTEE: Is true. I was adopted as an infant. My mother died in childbirth. I never talk about it because I don't think I should have to talk about it. People think that because I'm a poet, I'm like Langston. That I should plunder the details of my life for fodder for my poetry. But I'm not like Langston. I don't care to share every embarrassing little detail of my life with the entire world. Everyone has something in their life that they would like to keep private, whether it be a very personal thought or desire, or perhaps it's a memory or single moment from the past. Well, this is my private memory, the single moment from my past that I have never cared to share with anyone other than the very few people who are close to me. I hope I can now include you in that circle.

YOLANDE: Of course you can.

COUNTEE: I had hoped I could.

YOLANDE: I guess this means that now, we both have secrets.

COUNTEE: I should go.

YOLANDE: I've had a wonderful evening.

COUNTEE: So did I.

YOLANDE: And I do consider you to be a serious caller. Is that all right?

COUNTEE: That suits me just fine, Miss Du Bois.

YOLANDE: I suppose you want to kiss me good night now.

COUNTEE: I would very much like to kiss you good night. However, there are pleasures in this world that are far greater than those of carnal pleasure. Like the memory of your smile. The cocoa smooth curve of your cheekbone, or the way the corner of your mouth curls when you laugh. These are the ethereal pleasures I would like to take with me and keep until we see each other again.

> COUNTEE *puts his index finger to his lips, then to hers. He exits. She swoons, regains her composure, and moves into the apartment to find NINA waiting.*

YOLANDE: I should have known.

NINA: You were with that boy, weren't you?

YOLANDE: Actually . . .

NINA: The poet.

YOLANDE: It's none of your business who I was with.

NINA: That boy is just like your father.

YOLANDE: And what's wrong with that?

NINA: Your father groomed him.

YOLANDE: You make it sound dirty.

NINA: You don't understand your father.

YOLANDE: I understand him far better than you ever will.

NINA: You think.

YOLANDE: I see nothing wrong with going out with a man like my father because I happen to love my father.

NINA: You are placing your head right into the jaws of the beast.

YOLANDE: Mother, please . . .

NINA: You don't understand the nature of the beast, Yolande. The beast is blind and the beast is greedy . . .

YOLANDE: I had a wonderful evening . . .

NINA: This beast is insatiable.

YOLANDE: I am not in the mood to hear this tonight.

NINA: And you're placing your head right into its hungry gaping mouth.

YOLANDE: There is no beast, Mother. It doesn't exist. There's nothing under the bed. There's nothing hiding in the closet. There is nothing there, Mother. Nothing's gonna gobble me up. Nothing's gonna eat me.

NINA: Just like Burghardt.

YOLANDE: Nothing like Burghardt. I'm not like Burghardt, Mother. I am not gonna die.

NINA: Is that what you think? That Burghardt died?

YOLANDE: Jesus . . .

NINA: That's what your father told you, isn't it?

YOLANDE: Nobody told me, Mother, this is what everybody knows. Burghardt died when he was seventeen months old.

NINA: Your brother didn't die, Yolande.

YOLANDE: He died of diphtheria, Mother.

NINA: That's what they want you to believe. But I know better. I was there. Remember?

YOLANDE: God . . .

NINA: Burghardt did not die of diphtheria.

YOLANDE: Please help me.

NINA: Burghardt was sacrificed. By your father. Your father sacrificed his only son.

YOLANDE: Daddy loved Burghardt, Mother.

NINA: Of course he loved him. I never said your father didn't love him. Your father loved that boy fiercely. Just like Abraham loved his son, Isaac. But when God asked Abraham to sacrifice Isaac, Abraham didn't think twice, did he? He didn't think twice.

YOLANDE: Mother, please . . .

NINA: Abraham built himself an altar, then placed his son upon that altar and with his hand picked up a knife to slay his son that he loved so fiercely. Both Burghardt and Isaac were placed upon the altar. Only difference, Burghardt received no last-minute reprieve. There was no intervening angel to appear on Burghardt's behalf. No. The voice of God was conspicuously silent when Burghardt was sacrificed. There were no angels singing. No booming voice of God coming down from on high to save my Burghardt with the golden-spun hair. There was nothing but me and Burghardt laying there waiting for your father to come home. Me and Burghardt with the golden-spun hair whose body had grown cold.

YOLANDE: Would you like your medicine, Mother?

NINA: Your father sacrificed my only son.

YOLANDE: Would you like a headache powder?

NINA: And now he's about to sacrifice you.

SCENE FIVE

Jimmy and Lenora in the rehearsal hall.

JIMMY: Where is she?

LENORA: I don't know.

JIMMY: Six thirty.

LENORA: I know what time it is.

JIMMY: She ain't here.

LENORA: I can see that.

JIMMY: What she say?

LENORA: She said she was gonna meet us.

JIMMY: What time?

LENORA: I already told you.

JIMMY: Tell me again.

LENORA: She said she was gonna meet us at six o'clock.

JIMMY: And now it's six thirty.

LENORA: I know, Jimmy.

JIMMY: So where the hell is she?

LENORA: Damn, Jimmy. What did I just tell you? I don't know where she is.

JIMMY: Then maybe you can tell me this. What's the nigger's name?

LENORA: What nigger?

JIMMY: The nigger she been messing with.

LENORA: She . . . she ain't messing with nobody.

JIMMY: Don't try to give me that tissue-paper lie.

LENORA: Not that I . . . that I know of.

JIMMY: You can't lie, Lenora, not to me. I can read you like a piece of sheet music.

LENORA: I . . . I'm not lying.

JIMMY: See? There you go. You get that yammer in your voice. Every time you tell a lie.

LENORA: I . . . I . . .

JIMMY: You gettin ready to tell a big one.

LENORA: Shit!

JIMMY: What's the nigger's name?

LENORA: Honest to God, Jimmy. I . . . I do not know if she's seeing somebody else or not.

JIMMY: I tell you what. I find out who he is, I'm gonna scramble his ass like a pair a fresh country eggs.

LENORA: You ain't got to do all of that.

JIMMY: You know who it is, don't you?

LENORA: All you got to do is talk to her every now and then. Treat her nice.

JIMMY: I talk to her. Hell, I treat her nice.

LENORA: When was the last time you bought her some flowers?

JIMMY: Flowers?

LENORA: They look like collard greens with little decorations on top.

JIMMY: Don't get smart with me.

LENORA: When was the last time you bought her some flowers, Jimmy?

JIMMY: She ain't said nothing to me bout buying her some flowers.

LENORA: Some things, a woman shouldn't have to ask for.

JIMMY: She ain't got no problem asking for everything else she want. She wanted me to find a new stack. I found a new stack. Got a nice kitchenette, real nice, two rooms on 110th Street. You think she been around to see it? Hell naw. I ain't seen her. She's out running around with some other nigger. She wants to get on a boat and sail first-class to Paris. Well, I can't afford no goddamn first-class honeymoon in Paris.

LENORA: When d'you get a new place to live?

JIMMY: Few days ago.

LENORA: I thought you were broke.

JIMMY: I was broke.

LENORA: Then where d'you get the money?

JIMMY: Who you supposed to be? Policeman, wanna know where I got my money?

> YOLANDE enters.

JIMMY: Well if it ain't the Queen of Sheba, coming here to grace us with her presence.

YOLANDE: Excuse me?

JIMMY: What did we do, almighty queen, to deserve to be in your company?

YOLANDE: I came here thinking we were gonna go have some dinner after you were done with rehearsal but apparently I was mistaken.

LENORA: How you doing, Yolande?

YOLANDE: I'm fine. How bout you?

JIMMY: Thought you was going back to Baltimore for a job interview.

YOLANDE: I went back to Baltimore for a job interview. Went back last week.

JIMMY: Told me you was going three weeks ago.

YOLANDE: And right after I told you that, I found out at that my father was coming home and I decided to stay here and see him.

JIMMY: Why didn't you tell me?

YOLANDE: I'm telling you now, Jimmy.

JIMMY: Why couldn't you tell me before?

YOLANDE: Before what?

JIMMY: Before you decided to go out to The Sugar Cane and stay till 2 AM tearing up the dance floor with some nigger. That's before what. Now after you pick your mouth up off the floor, I want you to tell me one thang. What's the nigger's name?

YOLANDE: That ain't nothing for you to worry bout.

JIMMY: Tell me the nigger's name and let me decide whether or not to worry.

YOLANDE: He's a friend.

JIMMY: Apparently.

YOLANDE: A friend of my fathers.

JIMMY: I don't care whose friend he is. I wanna know the nigger's name.

YOLANDE: Nothing happened between us, Jimmy. He's like a cousin to me.

JIMMY: Is he a man?

YOLANDE: Is he a what?

JIMMY: A man. Either he's a man or he's not. If he's a man, friend of the family, cousin, uncle, third nephew removed, I don't care what, you got no business being out dancing with him till two o'clock in the morning.

YOLANDE: Every time a man and a woman get together, they don't have to be thinking bout all that mess that you always thinking bout.

JIMMY: Did he tell you that? That bullshit? Let me tell you sumthin. Every time a man and a woman get together, they only thinking bout one thing. Getting nasty. Am I right? Lenora? Am I right?

LENORA: Well, I . . . I . . . uh . . .

JIMMY: Course I'm right. You take a man, you take a woman, put them together and unless they brother and sister, they thinking bout getting nasty with each other. And in some parts of this world, I hear it don't even matter if they brother and sister. They get nasty with each other anyway.

YOLANDE: We're not in some parts of the world. We're in Harlem and in Harlem, not all men are thinking bout that.

JIMMY: That what the nigger tell you? That he wasn't like that? That he was different?

YOLANDE: Not every man in this world is like you, Jimmy.

JIMMY: If he tried to tell you he was different, he was lying to you, Yolande. I been on this earth for a very long time and I'm here to tell you that man's hunger is eternal. A man will always be attracted to the sway of a woman's hip and to the curve of a woman's breast. It ain't a choice that the man makes, the man can't help it, it's the way the man is made. I don't care who he is, where he come from, or where he think he's going, every time a man looks at a woman, he's thinking bout only one thang and that's getting himself some juice. The only time he ain't thinking bout getting himself some juice is right after he done got himself some juice. And there ain't nothing you or anybody else can do to change that. Everything that a man does in his life, whether he's playing some music, building a house, sporting some clean vines, working a job, or taking a bath, he's doing it for only one reason. To get himself some juice. Getting juice is a man's number one priority in life.

YOLANDE: You are so vulgar.

JIMMY: His number two priority in life is making sure some other nigger don't come along and take his juice away.

YOLANDE: So now you trying to tell me that even jealously is natural?

JIMMY: As natural as a warm summer rain. I'm talking bout survival of the fittest. See? Your old man ain't the only educated nigger around here.

YOLANDE: Jealously is not natural, Jimmy.

JIMMY: It's part of human nature, Yolande. You don't like it, your argument ain't with me. It's with the man upstairs.

YOLANDE: I got a telegram for you. Human civilization has advanced beyond the Stone Age. We are no longer hunters and gatherers. There are pleasures in this world that are far greater than those of carnal pleasure.

JIMMY: What kind of shit is that?

YOLANDE: What?

JIMMY: Pleasures greater than carnal—what's this nigger's name?

YOLANDE: I'm not telling you.

JIMMY: Ain't I done right by you? Ain't I tried to give you everything that you ask for? You ask me to find a new place to live. I found a new place to live. You didn't even know that, did you? No, you didn't even know. I got a two-room kitchenette, separated by a door that you can close if you want.

YOLANDE: I didn't ask you to do that for me.

JIMMY: You told me you didn't like the place I was staying.

YOLANDE: I didn't tell you to go out and find another place.

JIMMY: What you expect me to do? Stay in a place that you don't like? And look at this. Look what else I got for you.

> *He produces a small ring box.*

JIMMY: Here.

YOLANDE: What is this supposed to be?

JIMMY: Supposed to be a ring.

LENORA: Let me see.

JIMMY: I was gonna give it to you tonight but you might as well have it now.

YOLANDE: Where d'you get the money for this?

JIMMY: Don't you worry bout it. Point is, I done right by you. I give you everything you ask for. Still can't afford no goddamn honeymoon in Paris, but I'm working on it.

YOLANDE: Where d'you get the money for the ring, Jimmy?

LENORA: I'll tell you where. The band ain't been paid for the past three weeks. That's where he got the money.

YOLANDE: You spend that money you were supposed to use to pay the band?

JIMMY: Everybody's gonna get paid.

YOLANDE: When?

JIMMY: Everybody's gonna get every dime that's coming to them.

YOLANDE: When, Jimmy?

LENORA: You have to admit, this is a gorgeous ring.

JIMMY: Soon as we get that gig at the Cotton Club.

LENORA: A diamond and two sapphires.

JIMMY: We get that gig at the Cotton Club, everybody gonna be rolling in dough.

YOLANDE: You talk to the man at the Cotton Club?

LENORA: My size and everything.

JIMMY: Not yet.

YOLANDE: Then how you know you gonna get the job?

JIMMY: I can feel it.

YOLANDE: You can feel it?

JIMMY: In my bones.

LENORA: You better hope that's not just a touch of bursitis.

JIMMY: Ain't no goddamn bursitis. I've figured it all out. I've discovered the thing that distinguishes us from the other bands. Lenora knows. Tell her, Lenora.

YOLANDE: I can't accept that ring, Jimmy.

JIMMY: What you mean you can't accept it?

YOLANDE: You spending money that ain't yours to spend. Take this back to where you got it and get your money back. Then take that money and do what you was supposed to do with it and pay the men in your band, Jimmy.

JIMMY: Yolande . . .

YOLANDE: No. Pay the men in your band.

SCENE SIX

The Du Bois apartment.

WILL and COUNTEE enter.

WILL: Fine meal. Yes indeed, very fine meal. Wife is a very good cook. Don't you think?

COUNTEE: Yes, sir.

WILL: She received excellent household training from her mother and in turn, has done everything in her power to pass on those skills to Yolande. And while I cannot personally vouch for Yolande's culinary dexterity I would be negligent if I failed to point out that she is her mother's daughter and if you enjoyed the meal you just had, remember that the apple never falls far from the tree. Would you like a glass of wine?

COUNTEE: Wine?

WILL: A Rhine I purchased while I was in Berlin. Ordinarily I do not partake of alcoholic beverages which dull the senses, especially American whiskeys which I find to have the taste and texture of formaldehyde. However, this wine is singular in its purpose and character. It's German, made from a special hybrid grape which the Germans developed after years of careful crossbreeding. You see, that's the secret of superior quality. Careful crossbreeding. Care to join me?

COUNTEE: I'd be honored.

WILL: You and Yolande seem to have hit it off quite well.

COUNTEE: Yes, sir.

WILL: Dinner, the theater. I even understand that you two went out dancing together on your first date.

COUNTEE: How did you . . .

WILL: Very little escapes me, Countee. I know everything worth knowing.

COUNTEE: With your permission, sir, I would like to ask Yolande to marry me.

WILL: Why? Because you love her? Or because you think it's the right thing to do?

COUNTEE: I think that Yolande has all the attributes that I'm looking for in a wife. I also believe that she and I have many things in common and that we're very well matched, Dr. Du Bois.

WILL: In that case, you don't need to ask me for my permission. You want the girl to marry you? Ask the girl to marry you.

COUNTEE: But what do you think? If I asked her?

WILL: I think if we announced to the world that Countee Cullen was to marry the daughter of W. E. B. Du Bois, it would create such a sensation that your marriage would be the marriage of the decade. It would represent the prefect union of Negro talent, brains, and beauty. It would shatter old stereotypes of the Negro in this country. The walls of prejudice would come crashing down. It would be a star in the pinnacle of the Harlem Renaissance. However, you mustn't allow any of this to influence your decision, Countee. First and foremost in my mind is your work and my daughter's happiness. Moreover, you may also be interested to know that I've spoken with the foundation regarding your fellowship. They asked me for a written recommendation, which I've already completed.

He offers COUNTEE an envelope.

I believe this fulfils my part of the agreement.

YOLANDE enters with plates.

YOLANDE: Everybody ready for dessert?

WILL: What're we having?

YOLANDE: Peach cobbler and pecan pie.

WILL: I'll have the cobbler. Countee?

COUNTEE: No peaches for me. I'll have the pecan.

YOLANDE: Pecan pie it is.

WILL: I'll get it. You have a guest. Entertain him.

WILL exits.

YOLANDE: How d'you like the dinner?

COUNTEE: It was very good.

YOLANDE: My mother may be a bit daft but she knows how to cook. Me? I can't even boil water.

COUNTEE: Guess what? I have some good news.

YOLANDE: So do I.

COUNTEE: You first.

YOLANDE: Okay. I got the job in Baltimore. I'm gonna be teaching high school. This is the beginning of my career.

COUNTEE: Congratulations.

YOLANDE: Thank you. Now you, what's your news?

COUNTEE: I'm going back to Paris, but this time, I'll probably be gone for at least a year.

YOLANDE: Lucky you.

COUNTEE: And I want you to go with me, Yolande.

YOLANDE: To Paris?

COUNTEE: During the day we can sit on the deck sipping champagne and at night . . .

YOLANDE: Yeah, right. You and me. Sailing to Paris. Together. Unchaperoned. Wouldn't that be a scandal?

COUNTEE: Wouldn't be if we were married.

YOLANDE: To each other?

COUNTEE: I like being with you, Yolande. We know each other and I feel as if I can trust you. We trust each other and we have fun when we're together. You wanna go back to Paris. We can go back together.

YOLANDE: Are you proposing marriage to me?

COUNTEE: If you can promise me one thing. If you can promise me that, if we got married, things between us would not change. If you can stand in the center of your heart and swear to me that you would do everything in your power to freeze this moment in time, to preserve as we are now, for the rest of our lives . . .

YOLANDE: I wouldn't want anything between us to change.

COUNTEE: Then, yes, I am proposing to you. Yolande, will you marry me?

YOLANDE: Countee . . .

COUNTEE: You don't have to answer now. Think about it. Think about all the things you want to do. Think about Paris.

YOLANDE: I've been seeing someone else.

COUNTEE: My faith in human goodness would be shattered if there were not at least one other man competing for your affections.

YOLANDE: This other man I've been seeing. We've been together for a very long time.

COUNTEE: You had a life before you met me, just as I had a life before I met you. I'm not asking you to change that.

YOLANDE: He and I are very close, Countee.

COUNTEE: Is he your lover?

YOLANDE: No. Lover? Heavens no. He's a friend, Countee. He's a very good friend.

COUNTEE: If he's a friend, then you must promise me that you will keep him as a friend. Even if you and I are married.

YOLANDE: That would be impossible.

COUNTEE: Good friends are like precious jewels. They're very rare and very hard to find. Once you find one that's authentic, you should keep it, hold onto it, and cherish it because you never know when or if, indeed, you'll ever find another. For example, Harold Jackman's a good friend of mine and I would never sever my relationship with him. Likewise, I would not expect you to sever your relationship with your friend even if we were married.

YOLANDE: You wouldn't be jealous?

COUNTEE: Why would I be jealous?

YOLANDE: All men are jealous. It's human nature.

COUNTEE: Most men I know are very sophisticated. They understand that a fully rounded and complete life consists of many different elements and many different people. That spectrum includes trust, but it also includes very good friends.

YOLANDE: What bout my job in Baltimore?

COUNTEE: If you want to teach high school in Baltimore, Yolande, I suggest that you teach high school in Baltimore. Our marriage should not interfere with the development of your vocation. Remember, our goal here is to keep things as they are.

> WILL *enters.*

WILL: Pecan pie for Countee. And what're you having, Yolande?

YOLANDE: I would like some peaches.

WILL: The pecan pie is better. How about some pecans?

COUNTEE: I'll get it.

WILL: No, I'll get it.

COUNTEE: Please. Allow me.

> COUNTEE *exits.*

WILL: What did you do? Ouchie? What happened?

YOLANDE: Nothing happened, Daddy.

WILL: What did you say to him?

YOLANDE: I didn't say anything. He asked me to marry him.

WILL: Congratulations. My girl's getting married. (*He calls out*) Wife! Get in here! Congratulations, Ouchie. Wife!

YOLANDE: He asked me to marry him, Daddy. I didn't say I would.

WILL: But you will, right? Ouchie? Did you tell him no?

YOLANDE: I wanted to talk to you first.

WILL: Good. Good choice. Very good. Now listen to me, Ouchie. It is impossible for me to love you any more than I already do. And it is through my love for you that I tell you that you and Countee are two of a kind. You're of the same breeding, the same stock. Marrying Countee Cullen is one of the best things you could ever do.

YOLANDE: Then why do I feel so uncertain?

WILL: You're moving into an unchartered area, Ouchie, into a land which you've never before explored. It's natural for you to feel a bit apprehensive. The question is: do you love him?

YOLANDE: Shouldn't I feel something?

WILL: You should.

YOLANDE: I don't.

WILL: That's not surprising. You're probably a bit confused.

YOLANDE: I care for him, Daddy.

WILL: That's good.

YOLANDE: But I do not love him.

WILL: Love is not a lightning bolt that strikes in the middle of a storm. It's not a panacea that will wash away all of your pain and worries. If anything, love is like a very slow-burning fire that may smolder for years before finally catching ablaze. I want you to be happy, Yolande. Please don't wait for lightning to strike.

> *NINA enters with desserts, followed by LENORA and COUNTEE.*

NINA: Yolande, I thought you wanted peach cobbler?

YOLANDE: That is what I wanted.

NINA: Then why is Countee bringing you pecan pie?

> *JIMMY has entered the foyer and now rings the bell. NINA moves to the door and looks through the peephole.*

LENORA: You ought to get yourself a piece of that cobbler. I'm here to testify, those peaches are good. This here is my third piece. But then again, the pecan ain't so bad either.

NINA: It's that man.

WILL: What man?

NINA: Yolande's friend. The musician.

LENORA: Oh oh.

NINA: Looking for Yolande.

WILL: We're in the middle of a family dinner.

NINA: What should I do?

WILL: Yolande, are you expecting him?

YOLANDE: No.

WILL: Then why is he here?

YOLANDE: I don't know, Daddy.

NINA: What do you want me to do, Will?

WILL: I'll take care of it.

YOLANDE: No, I'll do it.

WILL: You sure?

NINA: Yolande, let your father take care of it.

WILL: Wife, Yolande can handle herself. She's a grown, mature woman. It's time for her to start making decisions on her own.

LENORA (*To COUNTEE*): Can you box?

COUNTEE: Can I what?

LENORA: Throw down. Stick and jab, bob and weave, cause if not, if I was you, I'd find me someplace to hide.

YOLANDE opens the door.

JIMMY: Hey, baby. Hope I'm not disturbing . . .

YOLANDE: What do you want, Jimmy?

JIMMY: I know this is not . . .

YOLANDE: What d'you want?

JIMMY: Ain't you gonna invite me in?

YOLANDE: Now's not a good time.

JIMMY: I just wanted to stop by to give you . . .

YOLANDE: You're interrupting a family dinner.

JIMMY: I'm sorry. I hadn't seen you, I wanted to give you this.

> *He hands her a small box.*

YOLANDE: What is it?

JIMMY: You know what it is. Open it. I talked to the man from the Lafayette. He's gonna book us for the next six weeks. You know what that means? That means we ain't got to go to Cleveland or Dayton ever again. We can stay right here in Harlem. Well? Open it.

WILL: Yolande?

JIMMY: I bought it with my own money. That was after I paid every dime I owed to every swinging dick in the band.

YOLANDE: Jimmy . . .

JIMMY: I know, I know. Lenora already told me. I gotta talk to your daddy first. And I plan to do right by you, Yolande, so that's the reason I'm here, to talk to your daddy. I still ain't walking around carrying no damned silver-tipped walking stick, but I'll talk to the man. Where is he?

> *JIMMY pushes inside.*

JIMMY: Sorry. Looks like I'm interrupting a party or somethin.

WILL: You're interrupting a very personal family gathering, young man.

JIMMY: Sorry. (*To YOLANDE*) All right, baby, I'll see you tomorrow and we'll—(*He sees COUNTEE*) Who's that? That's him, ain't it? That's the other nigger you been seeing.

WILL: See here, young man . . .

YOLANDE: Jimmy, you're outta line.

JIMMY: I'm outta line? You sitting up here with some other nigger and you calling me outta line?

YOLANDE: We'll talk bout this tomorrow.

JIMMY: What you mean tomorrow? Ain't no tomorrow. We gonna straighten this shit out today. Right here and now.

YOLANDE: Jimmy, please.

JIMMY: That's him, ain't it?

YOLANDE: If you'd wait till later, I can explain everything.

JIMMY: Ain't no later.

LENORA (*To COUNTEE*): Don't try to hide behind me.

JIMMY: Who the hell is he, Yolande?

WILL: See here, young man. My daughter is not beholden to you or any other man.

JIMMY: I'm gonna ask you one more time, Yolande.

YOLANDE: Why you got to do this, Jimmy? Why you got to come in here and ruin everything?

JIMMY: Why you got to keep playing me for a fool?

YOLANDE: Ain't nobody playing you for a fool. If you just wait till later . . .

JIMMY: I'm not waiting for later. I'm sick of this. I'm sick of sniffing up behind you like a lil dog while you flash your precious lil tail all over town. I'm sick of begging you, I'm sick of waiting for you while you try to figure out what you gonna do. Ain't no later, Yolande. You're gonna have to make up your mind right here and now. You're gonna have to choose between me and that nigger over there.

YOLANDE: In that case, I already made up my mind.

JIMMY: Good.

YOLANDE: I appreciate your gift but I can't accept it. I'm getting married, Jimmy. I'm getting married to Countee Cullen.

JIMMY: To who?

YOLANDE: Now if you don't mind, we're in the middle of a family dinner.

JIMMY: You gonna marry this nigger?

YOLANDE: And I'd appreciate it if you would leave.

JIMMY: This ain't right.

WILL: You've been asked to leave, young man.

JIMMY: Come on, Yolande. Go with me. Let's take a walk.

YOLANDE: No.

JIMMY: We can talk bout this . . .

YOLANDE: There's nothing to talk bout.

WILL: You've been asked to leave.

JIMMY: Tomorrow. We'll talk tomorrow.

YOLANDE: No, Jimmy.

JIMMY: Come with me. Come and look at the apartment . . .

YOLANDE: Listen to me.

JIMMY: We'll stop and get some coffee . . .

YOLANDE: It's over, Jimmy. I'm getting married.

JIMMY: Lenora, do somethin.

YOLANDE: I want you outta my house.

JIMMY: Talk to her.

YOLANDE: You understand what I'm saying to you?

JIMMY: Help me. Lenora, please.

YOLANDE: Get out.

JIMMY: Lenora . . .

YOLANDE: Go away, Jimmy. I don't wanna ever see you again.
Understand? I hate you. Get out.

JIMMY: All right, Yolande.

YOLANDE: Get out.

JIMMY: All right. Okay. I'm leaving. I'm gone.

   JIMMY exits.

WILL: Good girl.

NINA: Yolande's getting married?

WILL: You did good.

NINA: My little girl's getting married.

   End of Act One

ACT TWO

The Du Bois apartment.

NINA and YOLANDE. NINA arranges flowers in a vase.

NINA: Miss Otis was by the other day. Ten weeks later and she is still
talking about your wedding. But I'm not surprised. Everybody in
Harlem is still talking about your wedding. Ten ushers in black tie
and tails. Sixteen bridesmaids in dresses that were gorgeous, Yolande,

just gorgeous up to heaven. Miss Otis still can't get over how many flowers were at the church. Roses and orchids and tulips and lilies. She said she had never seen so many flowers in one place before. She said it looked like the Garden of Eden. How she would know what the Garden of Eden looks like, I don't know, I'm just telling you what she said. You know what Mrs. Pingree said? Mrs. Pingree said that she thought there were too many flowers. Said it looked like somebody's funeral instead of a wedding, looked like somebody had died. But she's just jealous cause she didn't receive an invitation. I tried to explain to her that there wasn't enough room to invite everybody to the wedding. As it was, there were over one thousand people at the church that day. We sent out invitations to only five hundred because the church only seats five hundred. Your father was not happy with the prospect of providing food and drink for five hundred people, but when I saw your father standing at that altar with you on his left and Countee on the right, and I saw the pride bursting from your father's face as he looked out over the church full of Negro artists, politicians, businessmen, and dignitaries from all across the country, I realized that your father would have gladly spent twice as much for that moment. That moment, for him, will always be frozen in time.

She finishes the arrangement.

There. That's very nice, don't you think? Yolande? You okay? Would you like me to make you some tea?

YOLANDE: When did you say Daddy was gonna be home?

NINA: Not for another week. He's in Philadelphia, I think. Yes, Philadelphia. Either that or Washington, I'm not quite sure. I get a little confused every now and then. And where did you say Countee was?

YOLANDE: He's in Boston, Mother.

NINA: Boston? Did I already ask you that?

YOLANDE: Yes, you did.

NINA: I'm sorry. Would you like me to make you a cup of tea?

YOLANDE: No, Mother. Thank you.

NINA: Miss Otis said that green tea will help ease your morning sickness.

YOLANDE: I don't have morning sickness.

NINA: Who do you think you're kidding, Yolande. I heard you having difficulties this morning.

YOLANDE: Difficulties?

NINA: In the bathroom. Of course, not that I was listening.

YOLANDE: It was the flowers, Mother.

NINA: These are the same flowers you had at your wedding.

YOLANDE: The smell makes me sick.

NINA: Sounds like morning sickness to me.

YOLANDE: I'm sick of smelling them, I'm sick of looking at them, I'm sick of thinking bout them . . .

NINA: Let me make you a cup of tea.

YOLANDE: Didn't I tell you I didn't want any of your damn tea?

NINA: I hope this attitude of yours is not indicative of the next nine months, cause if so, we're gonna be in for a very long and bumpy ride.

YOLANDE: What is it with you? Why do you always see things that are not there?

NINA: I don't know, Yolande. Why do you have such a problem seeing things that are standing right in front of you?

YOLANDE: This is useless.

NINA: You know what I think?

YOLANDE: No, but I'm sure you're gonna tell me.

NINA: I think it's high time you and I had a talk.

YOLANDE: A talk?

NINA: A heart to heart.

YOLANDE: With you?

NINA: I am your mother.

YOLANDE: Please, don't remind me.

NINA: Have I done something to you, Yolande?

YOLANDE: I'm sorry.

NINA: Something to hurt you?

YOLANDE: I'm sorry, Mother. It's just . . .

NINA: You wanna talk about it?

YOLANDE: What makes you think I have something I wanna talk bout?

NINA: You went on your honeymoon ...

YOLANDE: Yes.

NINA: To Niagara Falls. And the Falls are very romantic, Yolande.

YOLANDE: Yes, very romantic.

NINA: But you left. You came home almost a week early.

YOLANDE: Because of my job, Mother. I had to come home to prepare for my job.

NINA: I hope you're not still considering accepting that job.

YOLANDE: I've already accepted it.

NINA: You don't need a job. You already have a job. You're married, for God's sake.

YOLANDE: I don't plan to give up my professional vocation just because I got married.

NINA: What vocation? You don't have a vocation.

YOLANDE: Not yet, but I plan to have one. I plan to have a life, Mother.

NINA: You have a life.

YOLANDE: Being married is a life?

NINA: And what's wrong with that?

YOLANDE: It's not enough for me.

NINA: It was enough for me.

YOLANDE: Well, I don't plan on ending up like you.

NINA: I see. Yes, that would be the worst thing that could ever happen to you, wouldn't it?

YOLANDE: I didn't mean it like that.

NINA: I know how you meant it. I know exactly how you meant it. You don't want to end up like me for good reason. But I was not always like this. I used to be like you, you know. I used to be a soldier. I marched right into battle. Right after Burghardt was born, your father moved us to Atlanta, and Atlanta was not a pretty place for Negroes to live. Everything was segregated. The parks, the theaters, public transportation, the restaurants, train stations, even the public library was segregated. And the schools and hospitals, Negroes weren't even allowed in the schools and hospitals. Even back then I refused to patronize any system of segregation, which meant I had to walk every place I went, and since Negroes were lawfully prohibited from using any park, water fountain, or even stopping to rest on a public bench, whenever I left the house I could not stop walking, not to rest, not to get a drink of water, not for one moment, not until I had reached my destination. I pictured myself as that woman who I heard speak the other day. Gertrude Ederle. She swam from France to Great Britain, across the entire English Channel, without stopping once. That's how I felt every time I left that house in Atlanta. Like Gertrude Ederle, I had to continue to press on, I could not stop, I could not rest, not for one moment lest I drown in a sea of hate.

YOLANDE: You okay, Mother?

NINA: I find it very difficult to believe that Countee has agreed to forsake New York in favor of Baltimore.

YOLANDE: He hasn't.

NINA: Then how do you plan to teach in Baltimore?

YOLANDE: I plan to live in Baltimore, Mother.

NINA: And what is Countee supposed to do?

YOLANDE: Countee plans to stay in New York.

NINA: That doesn't make any sense.

YOLANDE: We plan to keep both apartments, Mother.

NINA: Two apartments?

YOLANDE: His is in New York and mine'll be in Baltimore.

NINA: No sense at all.

YOLANDE: We don't plan to surrender to convention. We liked the way our relationship was before we were married and we plan to keep things the way they were.

NINA: Yolande, baby. Listen to me. It's not such a bad thing, being a wife. Not once you get used to it. That's the hardest part, Yolande, getting used to it. That's the part that takes a while. After your father and I were married, I cried practically every time he touched me for almost a year. But I got used to it. Every woman has a tough time at first. But the trick is, what I've found, is to lie real still. You lie as still as you can, go ahead and let the man do his business, and it'll be over before you know it.

YOLANDE: What're you talking bout?

NINA: I'm talking about tolerating your duties, Yolande. Your marital duties.

YOLANDE: You talking bout sex?

NINA: There's no need for that type of language.

YOLANDE: My mother's talking to me bout sex.

NINA: I'm talking about the difficulties of being a wife.

YOLANDE: Ain't this bout a clock-stopper.

NINA: I know, we should have had this conversation a long time ago. If we had this conversation, maybe you and your husband wouldn't be in the midst of these difficulties.

YOLANDE: What difficulties? There are no difficulties.

NINA: You ended your honeymoon early.

YOLANDE: I've already explained that to you.

NINA: I know what you said, but you have to understand how it looks.

YOLANDE: Countee and I do not have to be together every single moment of every day. You and Daddy are not together every single moment of every day and nobody talks bout how that looks.

NINA: Your father is doing very important work.

YOLANDE: In case you haven't heard, my husband is doing very important work as well. Now, is there anything else you would like to know?

NINA: You're gonna have a baby, Yolande. You cannot live in Baltimore with a child while your husband lives in New York. It makes no sense. Your duty, as a wife, is to be with your husband and to, occasionally at night, tolerate your marital obligations.

YOLANDE: I'm not talking to you bout this.

NINA: You're not ready yet. But you will be. And when you are ready to talk about tolerating your obligations, promise me that you'll come to me, your mother, to talk. Okay? Yolande? You promise?

SCENE TWO

COUNTEE and WILL in Will's study.

WILL: I'm sorry I couldn't get back any sooner. I was detained in Pittsburgh at a meeting of the National Association for the Advancement of Colored People. Now I want you to tell me. What happened?

COUNTEE: Yolande decided to come home early.

WILL: From your honeymoon?

COUNTEE: She wanted to get back early in order to prepare for her job.

WILL: You ended your honeymoon early for a teaching job in Baltimore?

COUNTEE: She wanted to take time to prepare her lesson plans and to meet with some of the other teachers. You know Yolande. Once she makes up her mind to do something, there's nothing I can do.

WILL: And have the newspapers been notified of this fact?

COUNTEE: I don't know.

WILL: No matter what you do, no matter how you move or what you say, you must be aware of how it will appear to the public.

COUNTEE: I understand that, Dr. Du Bois.

WILL: Apparently your understanding was only marginal, since you ended your honeymoon early and failed to notify the newspapers as to the reason why. Do you know what happens when you fail to supply the newspapers with facts? They make up their own facts, and we cannot allow that to happen.

COUNTEE: I'm sorry. It was an oversight.

WILL: Is there anything else I should know?

COUNTEE: Like what?

WILL: Are you two having any problems?

COUNTEE: No, no problems.

WILL: I want you to feel free to confide in me.

COUNTEE: We're not having any problems, Dr. Du Bois.

WILL: What about your trip to Paris?

COUNTEE: There has been a slight change of plans, but it's not a problem.

WILL: What kind of change of plans?

COUNTEE: Yolande has always wanted to travel first class and I simply cannot afford for her to travel first class.

WILL: How much do you need?

COUNTEE: I cannot, in good conscience, accept any more money from you, Dr. Du Bois.

WILL: It's not a problem, Countee. How much?

COUNTEE: No.

WILL: Countee, I consider you to be like a son to me, like my Burghardt who was taken away from me at a very young age. Many times I close my eyes and, in my mind, paint a picture of what my Burghardt would have looked like had he lived. I try to imagine the glow of his face, the texture of his voice, I try to imagine happiness dancing in his eyes. I must have painted a hundred different pictures of Burghardt using a hundred different faces, and in the end, the person I see is you. And as my son, in law and in spirit, I will gladly give you any type of assistance you will ever need, Countee, without exception, as if you were the issue of my own flesh.

COUNTEE: But it's time for Yolande and me to take responsibility for our own lives.

WILL: This marriage involves more than just you and Yolande. The future of practically every Negro in this country is enmeshed in your marriage. Do you know what this is?

> He holds up an envelope.

This is a letter from Dr. Walter Beekman, provost at Harvard University.

> He holds up another envelope.

Dr. Roger Crogman, president of Atlanta University. And this is from Judge Julian Mack, United States Circuit Court of the City of New York. All of them expressing their heartfelt congratulations and best wishes for the bride and groom. And if you listen carefully, you will hear, somewhere off in the distance, a sound. A rumble, barely perceptible, but it's there, nevertheless. That sound you hear is the crumbling of the walls of segregation, the walls of prejudice which are about to come tumbling down. I feel a monumental change about to happen in this country, and your marriage is the avant-garde of that change. You cannot march into the fray alone, Countee. There's too much at stake.

COUNTEE: If I needed your help, I would gladly accept it, Dr. Du Bois. But I've already made other arrangements. My friend, Harold Jackman, has pledged to make a financial contribution to the trip to Paris. Yolande has decided not to join me in Paris until December. This way, she can spend a semester teaching and we both can save money so that when she does join me for the holidays, she can travel in the style to which she is accustomed. You see, Dr. Du Bois, it's all been taken care of.

WILL: And what about the newspapers?

COUNTEE: Again, an oversight.

WILL: It's an oversight we cannot afford. I'll take care of the newspapers and make sure they have all the facts.

COUNTEE: Thank you.

WILL: No need to thank me, son. I do what I do not only for you but for us all.

SCENE THREE

LENORA and YOLANDE.

LENORA: It was a slaughter. They never knew what hit them, never knew which way to look, never knew which way it was coming from. The first wave moved in from the left. They were marching in step, lockstep, axes under their arms, moving with military precision. The second wave moved in from the right, marching in step, lockstep, keeping the beat, boom pop, boom pop, boom pop pow. Suddenly, dead center, Jimmy rises up from what appears to be nowhere, and make no mistake about this: Jimmy is cleaner than a broke-dick dog. White tie and tails. Ofay sitting at a table in the front fell out into the aisle. Jimmy got his ass and hadn't even played one note yet. Jimmy looks around, raises his baton, the brass raise up with him. Old wrinkled wench at a table in the back throws up her arms and falls out. Jimmy got her, still ain't played note one. Baton comes down, the band blows out the first notes of "For Dancers Only," and the place goes up for grabs. People moving thisaway and thataway. Arms, legs, and sweat flying all over the dance floor. But Jimmy is not perturbed, he ain't broke a sweat. Even the razor-sharp crease in his tuxedo pants is undisturbed. He's out front of that band and he's leading, and he's listening, and he's watching them ofays on the dance floor and he's killing them with a cool, calculated, syncopated precision that would make a diamond cutter pack up his tools and walk away in shame.

YOLANDE: Good for him.

LENORA: That's what I thought. But later, after the last set, after all the white folks had gone, Jimmy's looking around the room like he's searching, like he's looking for somebody. Then I realize who he's looking for. He's looking for you. But you ain't there. That's when I realized that he's still waiting for you, Yolande.

YOLANDE: Waiting for me for what?

LENORA: To make an appearance. To hear him play.

YOLANDE: I've already heard him play, more times than I care to remember.

LENORA: Then maybe he's waiting for you to tell him what happened.

YOLANDE: I got married. That's what happened. I thought he was aware of that fact.

LENORA: Why you being so hard on Jimmy?

YOLANDE: Why you got to keep bothering me bout this man? Don't nobody care bout him.

LENORA: You cared about him. Or at least you did at one point in time.

YOLANDE: That point in time has passed, Lenora. You are revisiting ancient history.

LENORA: Least you could do is sit down and talk to him.

YOLANDE: I am married, Lenora.

LENORA: Help ease his pain a bit. That ain't gonna kill you.

YOLANDE: Why is this so hard for you to understand? I cannot be hanging out with Jimmy Lunceford anymore.

LENORA: All right, I got it.

YOLANDE: You wanna help ease his pain? You talk to him. You help him understand.

LENORA: What's the matter with you?

YOLANDE: I thought it was gonna be different.

LENORA: You thought what was gonna be different?

YOLANDE: Everything. Being married. Being a wife. But it's not different. At least I don't feel any different.

LENORA: Is that all?

YOLANDE: I don't feel any different than I felt before.

LENORA: You are so typical.

YOLANDE: Typical?

LENORA: You think you the only woman that's going through what you going through right now? Well, you're not. Women been going through what you going through since the beginning of time. In fact, what you got is a well-known documented medical condition. They call it the "I just got married and it ain't what I thought it was gonna be" blues.

YOLANDE: That ain't no medical condition.

LENORA: Saw it in a medical book.

YOLANDE: Don't nobody believe you.

LENORA: Medical book said that women, they expect to wake up the morning after they get married and hear harp music and see butterflies flying around the room and shit like that.

YOLANDE: I never heard of none of this you talking bout.

LENORA: I know you, and I know you expected to wake up and see blue skies, butterflies, and hear string music.

YOLANDE: Ain't nobody said nothing bout hearing no string music.

LENORA: But you did expect to see blue skies and butterflies, didn't ya?

YOLANDE: I expected to feel like a wife.

LENORA: But how do you feel?

YOLANDE: I feel exactly the way I felt before I got married.

LENORA: "I just got married and it ain't what I thought it was gonna be" blues.

YOLANDE: I feel like I made a mistake.

LENORA: What happened? Did that nigger beat you?

YOLANDE: Oh, heavens no.

LENORA: Did he hit you?

YOLANDE: No.

LENORA: Did he threaten to hit you?

YOLANDE: No, Lenora.

LENORA: Did he embarrass you?

YOLANDE: No.

LENORA: Did he try to get you to commit some sort of unnatural sex act on him?

YOLANDE: What?

LENORA: Uh huh. I knew it.

YOLANDE: What're you talking bout?

LENORA: You shouldn't be such a prude, girl. I know what men like and I know that men like it when women do things like that. They like the attention. If fact, I don't see anything unnatural about it. Especially when the man responds in kind.

YOLANDE: What do you mean, respond in kind?

LENORA: When they do it back to you, honey. I like the feel of a man's lips down there. His tongue. I like the warmth of his breath.

YOLANDE: What on earth are you talking bout?

LENORA: I'm talking about using your mouth, girl. And I'm not talking about talking.

YOLANDE: Oh, no.

LENORA: You ought to try it. You might like it. And who knows? He responds in kind, and maybe you could find them blue skies and butterflies you been looking for.

YOLANDE: That was not the problem, Lenora.

LENORA: Then what was the problem? How did it go on your wedding night?

YOLANDE: What do you mean, how did it go?

LENORA: You know what I mean. Was he happy? Did you satisfy him?

YOLANDE: That's none of your business.

LENORA: It's never been anything other than none of my business. Now tell me. How many times did you do it?

YOLANDE: I don't know.

LENORA: You lost count?

YOLANDE: It was a very long night.

LENORA: What about the very first time that you did it? Did it take him a real long time to get done or did he get done real quick and keep coming back for more?

YOLANDE: Why are you asking me so many questions?

LENORA: Why you being so defensive?

YOLANDE: My life is not on public display.

LENORA: Since when did I become the public?

YOLANDE: You are asking very personal questions.

LENORA: This is a very personal matter, Yolande. Somebody told me that he was going to Paris without you. Is that true?

YOLANDE: We decided to meet there around Christmas.

LENORA: Then who is he going to Paris with?

YOLANDE: He's not going with anybody.

LENORA: Then he's going alone.

YOLANDE: Not exactly.

LENORA: Either he's going alone or he's going with somebody, Yolande. It's got to be one or the other. Who is he going with?

YOLANDE: Harold Jackman.

LENORA: The best man from your wedding?

YOLANDE: I don't understand what any of this has got to do with the price of butter.

LENORA: All right, then forget it.

YOLANDE: What you mean by that?

LENORA: By what?

YOLANDE: "All right, then forget it."

LENORA: It means "All right, then forget it."

YOLANDE: You not fooling nobody. I know what you thinking.

LENORA: Is that right?

YOLANDE: That's right.

LENORA: You now a mind reader on top of everything else?

YOLANDE: That little mind of yours is not that difficult to read.

LENORA: Is that right?

YOLANDE: That's right.

LENORA: What you might be reading are your own thoughts. You ever think of that? Some people see only what they wanna see, no matter what's standing right in front of them. Now I'm gonna ask you something. You can answer if you feel like it, but you know what? It really don't matter to me. But I'm only gonna ask you once. That night, after your wedding, did Countee make you his wife?

YOLANDE: He had some problems.

LENORA: What kind of problems?

YOLANDE: Man problems.

LENORA: What about the night after that?

YOLANDE: He needed time to rest.

LENORA: Rest? According to you, he wasn't doing nothing.

YOLANDE: He's been doing a lot of work.

LENORA: What kind of work?

YOLANDE: He's a poet, Lenora.

LENORA: I understand that. But you still ain't told me what kind of work he's doing that requires him to need time to rest.

YOLANDE: If we do it too much, it'll fatigue his brain and interfere with his work and the work he's doing is very important.

LENORA: Has this man even laid a hand on you yet?

YOLANDE: He's been under a lot of pressure.

LENORA: Ain't that much pressure in the world.

YOLANDE: What do you know bout it?

LENORA: The man hasn't touched you yet. That's the reason you don't feel any different. And now he's ready to sail to Paris with the best man from your wedding.

YOLANDE: You think that maybe ...

LENORA: You're not dumb, Yolande. If you're happy with this, it's not my place to tell you anything different. You the only person who can say what you see when you look at that man and can't nobody get inside of you and look out through your eyes. Just make sure that what you're looking at is something that's outside of you, Yolande. Just make sure that what you're looking at is not a reflection of the world that you've created inside of your own head.

YOLANDE and COUNTEE. COUNTEE is packing.

COUNTEE: Every time I think I'm done packing I find something else I think I ought to bring. So I open the trunk thinking I'm gonna add just one item. Next thing I know, the trunk is empty and everything that took me ten days to put into the trunk is spread out all over the room and I'm right back where I was when I started packing ten days ago. Think I ought to bring this seersucker?

YOLANDE: I think it's gonna be a lil too cool for seersucker.

COUNTEE: You're right.

YOLANDE: Course I am.

COUNTEE: Don't know what I'd do without you.

YOLANDE: Funny. I was just asking myself the same question.

COUNTEE: Everything all right?

YOLANDE: I wanna go with you.

COUNTEE: I know you do. And I want you to go with me.

YOLANDE: That's not what I mean.

COUNTEE: But we're gonna have to wait till December.

YOLANDE: I've changed my mind, Countee. I want to go with you now.

COUNTEE: That's not possible right now.

YOLANDE: Why isn't it possible?

COUNTEE: We don't have the money.

YOLANDE: We have enough.

COUNTEE: Not for you to travel first class.

YOLANDE: I don't care bout traveling first class anymore. I'll travel second class or tourist class if I have to.

COUNTEE: You're willing to travel tourist class to Paris?

YOLANDE: I'll ride in steerage if that's what it takes. But when you sail, I wanna sail with you, Countee. I don't wanna stay here alone.

COUNTEE: What about your job?

YOLANDE: My job can wait.

COUNTEE: You told them you were going to start in September.

YOLANDE: I know what I told them, and I'll tell them something different. If they don't like it, they can hire somebody else, but I don't wanna stay here alone.

COUNTEE: Yolande, even if we agreed that we should travel together, and even if we both agreed to travel tourist class, and if we kept track of every single nickel that passed through our hands, we still would not have enough money.

YOLANDE: But there's enough for you to travel with Harold Jackman?

COUNTEE: Harold Jackman is making a considerable contribution towards the expenses.

YOLANDE: I will make a considerable contribution towards expenses.

COUNTEE: You don't have the money.

YOLANDE: I will get the money.

COUNTEE: From where?

YOLANDE: All you have to do is tell me how much we need.

COUNTEE: Your father?

YOLANDE: Don't worry bout where the money comes from.

COUNTEE: Your father's already paid for our wedding and for our honeymoon.

YOLANDE: That's not your concern, Countee.

COUNTEE: I can't accept any more money from your father.

YOLANDE: That money is my money. The money is in my name, money my father set aside for me. All you have to do is tell me how much we're gonna need. I will get it.

COUNTEE: And what about Harold? What am I supposed to tell him?

YOLANDE: You tell him that there's been a change of plans. That you've decided to travel to Paris with your wife. That's what you tell him.

COUNTEE: What's the matter with you?

YOLANDE: I wanna be on that boat with you when you leave for Paris.

COUNTEE: Yolande, I need to spend some time with Harold.

YOLANDE: Then have lunch with him before we sail.

COUNTEE: It has to be more than just an hour or two.

YOLANDE: Then invite him along. Is that what you want? Invite him along. The three of us. We can travel together.

COUNTEE: Yolande, I need to spend this time with Harold alone.

YOLANDE: What're you talking bout?

COUNTEE: These past few months have been very difficult for me.

YOLANDE: It's been very difficult for the both of us.

COUNTEE: Yolande, it's important for you to understand that the time will always come when I will need to spend time with Harold alone.

YOLANDE: Explain this to me.

COUNTEE: He is a close and dear friend and as a close and dear friend, there are things that he and I need to talk about.

YOLANDE: What things?

COUNTEE: Private things.

YOLANDE: Things you can't discuss with me?

COUNTEE: Things that I may be able to discuss with you one day but not this day.

YOLANDE: How bout tomorrow?

COUNTEE: Why are you doing this?

YOLANDE: I thought I was your wife.

COUNTEE: You are my wife.

YOLANDE: Then why haven't you made me your wife?

COUNTEE: This again.

YOLANDE: Why haven't you touched me?

COUNTEE: We've been over this, Yolande.

YOLANDE: Have we?

COUNTEE: Yes, we have.

YOLANDE: I'm having a bit of trouble remembering that particular conversation. Refresh me.

COUNTEE: I thought we had found pleasures in this world that were greater than those of carnal pleasure.

YOLANDE: You talking bout a peck on the cheek? Is that what you're talking bout? Holding hands and reciting poetry? Is this your pleasure greater than carnal pleasure?

COUNTEE: Now you're mocking me.

YOLANDE: What kind of pleasure do you have with Harold? Is it also a pleasure greater than carnal pleasure?

COUNTEE: Harold is my confidant.

YOLANDE: Lenora is my confidant but I don't have the need to spend private time alone with her.

COUNTEE: Maybe you should try it. Who knows? You might find that you like it.

YOLANDE: What are you saying to me?

COUNTEE: I made it clear to you before we were married that I had no intentions of giving up my relationship with my friend Harold. I even encouraged you to keep your relationship with your friend Jimmy. Nobody told you to go out and cut him off at the knees.

YOLANDE: Jimmy and I were a lot more than just friends.

COUNTEE: Oh, really. Guess what. Harold and I are a lot more than just friends.

YOLANDE: Jimmy wanted to have relations with me.

COUNTEE: Are you sure you want to continue to draw parallels?

YOLANDE: You had relations with Harold Jackman?

COUNTEE: You and I have been chosen, Yolande.

YOLANDE: Answer my question.

COUNTEE: We have a job to do. We have to figure out a way to do that job without laying out our entrails for the vultures to eat. That means we have to be smart, we have to be vigilant, and we have to keep certain things in our lives private.

YOLANDE: You lied to me.

COUNTEE: I never lied.

YOLANDE: What else don't I know bout you?

COUNTEE: You know everything.

YOLANDE: What bout your mother?

COUNTEE: My mother?

YOLANDE: Where is she? You told me she died in childbirth.

COUNTEE: She did.

YOLANDE: Where is she, Countee?

COUNTEE: She lives on a farm in Eastern Kentucky.

YOLANDE: Jesus, no. I'm not staying married to you.

COUNTEE: Because I lied about my mother?

YOLANDE: Because I don't know who you are.

COUNTEE: You know everything about me, Yolande.

YOLANDE: No.

COUNTEE: Look at me. I haven't changed. I swore to you that I would not change. I am the same man who made you laugh at dinner, the man with whom you danced until two AM almost every night. I am the man who stood with you at the altar. The man who put his trust in you after you swore to keep that trust.

YOLANDE: And now you're the man who's about to sail to Paris with his best friend instead of me. No, Countee. I'm not staying married to you.

COUNTEE: Is that what this is about? You want to go to Paris with me?

YOLANDE: Not anymore.

COUNTEE: Fine. It's done. I'll see Harold later today. I'll explain the situation to him.

YOLANDE: Nothing to explain.

COUNTEE: Yolande, listen. I didn't understand how important this was to you. Now that I understand, I can make adjustments.

YOLANDE: Don't bother. I don't want to fatigue your brain and interfere with your work.

COUNTEE: Please don't mock me.

YOLANDE: You mock me.

COUNTEE: But I can make amends. I will speak with Harold.

YOLANDE: I don't want you to speak with him. In fact, I don't even want my name falling from your lips.

COUNTEE: He can stay here in New York and you and I will sail to Paris together.

YOLANDE: I don't wanna go to Paris. Not with you. Not now.

COUNTEE: Why are you doing this to me? We talked about this, Yolande. We swore we would try to keep things as they were.

YOLANDE: What do you want? You want to freeze me in time? You want my yesterday to be like my today and my today to be like my tomorrow? No, I'm not gonna live like that. Not when it began with a lie.

SCENE FIVE

Rehearsal Hall.

JIMMY does a soft shoe as he softly sings. LENORA and YOLANDE watch him. LENORA takes notes with a pad and pencil.

JIMMY:

> *I like cake and no mistake*
> *But baby if you insist*
> *I'll cut out cake*
> *Just for your sake*
> *Baby, come on and knock me a kiss*
> *I like pie I hope to die*
> *Just get a load of this*
> *When you get high*
> *Doggone the pie*
> *Baby, come on and knock me a kiss*
> *When you press your lips to mine*
> *Twas then I understood*
> *They taste like candy*
> *Brandy and wine*
> *Peaches bananas and everything good.*
> *I love jam and no flim flam*
> *Scratch that off my list*
> *This ain't no jam*
> *The jam can scram*
> *Baby, come on and knock me a kiss*

YOLANDE: Working on a new routine?

JIMMY: You could say that. (*To LENORA*) You get all that down?

LENORA: Got it.

JIMMY: Then I'm done. Would you get my stuff for me?

LENORA exits.

YOLANDE: You finished arranging the song.

JIMMY: Finished it a long time ago.

YOLANDE: Sounds good. I heard you play it for the first time last night. Heard the whole thing. That was something, seeing your name up in lights on the marquee at the Cotton Club. I was standing outside. Wish I could have come in, but you know, no colored allowed. Stood outside during the whole show. Baby, you were swanging. I got a chance to peek in every now and then and saw what you did with the orchestra. That was something, the way you got them all moving together. Looked good, too. People loved it. And the place was packed. I did get a chance to come inside after you were done playing. I caught a glimpse of you right before you went backstage but I doubt if you saw me.

JIMMY: I saw you.

YOLANDE: I waited around for you.

JIMMY: I was busy.

YOLANDE: I figured that out after they told me you had left.

JIMMY: Band business.

YOLANDE: Look, Jimmy, I'm sorry bout the way things happened.

JIMMY: Nothing to be sorry bout. You made a choice. People do that in life. They make choices. I just wish I would've known that a choice was being made, that's all. I got this feeling that if I would've known, maybe I could've said somethin or done somethin. Who knows? Maybe I would've carried that damn silver-tipped walking stick. But then again, maybe not. But, we'll never know now, will we?

YOLANDE: Funny how things work out, huh?

JIMMY: Yeah, funny.

YOLANDE: I'm still the same person I was before.

JIMMY: No, Yolande. You are many years older than the young girl you were a few months ago. You have aged. You have turned into a woman. I can see it in the way you walk, in the way you try to smile. No, you're nothing like the way you were a few months ago.

YOLANDE: You don't understand what I'm saying. You see, Countee, that's my husband . . .

JIMMY: I know the nigger's name.

YOLANDE: Countee and I have what I consider to be a modern marriage. We have decided not to adhere to convention.

JIMMY: You mean that you're keeping your apartment in Baltimore and that he's keeping his place in New York? Is that what you're talking bout? That you're gonna see each other once or twice a week or maybe once or twice a month? Is this your idea of a modern marriage?

YOLANDE: I admit it, Jimmy. I made a mistake. But I'm the same person, Jimmy, I'm the exact same person I was before. Nothing's changed. I made a very stupid mistake but I can make it up to you, Jimmy. I can give you what you want.

JIMMY: I doubt that.

YOLANDE: But I can. You'll see. When you touch me, you'll see that I am the exact same person I was before. Only difference, I'm ready for you now, Jimmy. I'm ready to do all of those things that we talked bout. And I want to do them with you again and again and again. I'm gonna keep my apartment in Baltimore. You can come and see me whenever you get ready. And I can come see you when I come to New York.

JIMMY: Sounds wonderful. Only problem is, you happen to be married.

YOLANDE: Doesn't matter.

JIMMY: Doesn't matter to who? To him? Why am I not surprised?

YOLANDE: I will go with you right now, Jimmy. Anywhere, I don't care. Back to your place. I don't care where it is or what it looks like. I will go with you and give you everything that I have to give, if you will take me and make me yours.

JIMMY: That's very nice, Yolande.

YOLANDE: I am offering to give you everything that you wanted.

JIMMY: Is that what you think I wanted? To lay up with you like a dog? To turn out the lights, take off my clothes, and conduct some sort of business with you?

YOLANDE: Doesn't have to be like that, Jimmy.

JIMMY: I wanted all of you, Yolande. Not just the part that I can see and touch. I also wanted the part of you that used to get inside of me and stay with me long after you were gone. But you went and gave that part to somebody else. And now here you come offering me, what? The leftovers? Your carcass? I don't need you for that. There's a whole boatload of women out there who would give me that. If that's all I wanted, I would have gone to one of them a long time ago, cause they know how to do it, probably a lot better than you do, and they only charge a dollar.

LENORA enters with a topcoat, scarf, white gloves, and cane.

JIMMY: I hope you find what you're looking for. I hope you find what you need. I wish you all the happiness in the world and I mean that, sincerely. (*To LENORA*) You ready?

LENORA: How about I catch up with you?

JIMMY: No need to hurry. I'll see you when you get home.

JIMMY kisses LENORA and exits.

YOLANDE: I see.

LENORA: He didn't tell you?

YOLANDE: I should have guessed. The way you would talk bout him all the time. Talk bout his hands, his arms, his chest . . .

LENORA: I know you're not upset about this.

YOLANDE: I guess you know what the men like.

LENORA: What's that supposed to mean?

YOLANDE: Did you use your mouth on him?

LENORA: He wanted somebody to.

YOLANDE: I'm sorry. I shouldn't have said that.

LENORA: Did you think that when you left that the entire world would just stop turning? That everything would just freeze in time? Is that what you thought?

YOLANDE: I don't know what I thought.

LENORA: The world moves on, Yolande, with you or without you.

YOLANDE: You were right bout Countee.

LENORA: I'm sorry.

YOLANDE: I don't know what to do. I don't want to stay married to him.

LENORA: You don't have to stay married to him.

YOLANDE: What am I supposed to do?

LENORA: Get a divorce.

YOLANDE: My father would die.

LENORA: Then don't get a divorce. Divorces are for people whose marriages have failed, and your marriage didn't fail. According to you, you never had a marriage to begin with, so you don't have to be divorced. Tell your father about Countee, then have your marriage annulled.

YOLANDE: Do you know what that would look like? What people would think?

LENORA: It would probably look like he never made you his wife. What people would think would resemble the truth.

YOLANDE: The scandal that would cause.

LENORA: You have to stop thinking about others and start thinking about Yolande.

YOLANDE: I can't even imagine . . .

LENORA: Try to imagine. Imagine Yolande as being first and foremost. Not the poor, not the downtrodden, and certainly not your father. Yolande.

YOLANDE: That's a nice ring you have there. A diamond and two sapphires.

LENORA: This? Yeah, I uh . . . I . . . I . . .

YOLANDE: It's all right, Lenora. Does this mean you're getting married?

LENORA: No. He just gave it to me to wear. I only wear it cause I know it was yours.

YOLANDE: Can I ask you something?

LENORA: Sure.

YOLANDE: You ever . . . you know . . . with another woman?

LENORA: No. You?

YOLANDE: No. You ever think bout trying? I mean, we are friends after all.

LENORA: We ain't never been that good of friends. What's the matter with you? That man's got you thinking all backwards and sideways. You better tell your daddy about him and get this over with so you can get on with your life and stop bothering me with all of this strange-ass behavior. You understand me, Yolande? Go and tell your daddy.

SCENE SIX

The Du Bois home. Early morning.

NINA: Yolande? Wake up, hon. You didn't sleep out here all night, did you?

YOLANDE: I must have.

NINA: You can catch the curvature of the spine by sleeping in chairs like that. You should sleep in the bed, honey. Nice, firm, sturdy bed.

YOLANDE: I know.

NINA: Countee's here looking for you. Says he hasn't seen you for a few days. Didn't you tell him you were gonna be here?

YOLANDE: I haven't told him anything.

NINA: Problems?

YOLANDE: I guess you could say that.

NINA: Countee really looks worried.

YOLANDE: He ought to be worried.

NINA: That's no way to be, Yolande. I'll let him know you're here.

YOLANDE: No, wait. Please. Don't tell him I'm here. Daddy home yet?

NINA: Came in late last night.

YOLANDE: Where is he?

NINA: He's in his room. What's going on, Yolande?

YOLANDE: Nothing.

NINA: You've been crying.

YOLANDE: Everything's fine, Mother.

NINA: What you want me to tell Countee?

YOLANDE: Countee can wait.

NINA: I have something that might cheer you up. A surprise. Actually, it's more like an early present.

> *NINA presents a small package to YOLANDE. YOLANDE opens the package.*

I went to see Helen Keller speak the other day. You know who she is? She's that blind and deaf woman who learned how to talk by touching the lips and the throat of a speaker while the words the speaker spoke were being spelled out on the palm of her hand. Isn't that amazing? Anyway, I was on my way home from hearing her speak and I saw it in the window at Zimmerman's. It was so adorable, I'm sorry, I couldn't resist.

In the package is a baby's jumper.

It's for you. Well, actually not for you, it's for your baby, Yolande. I wanted to be the first one to give you something. I hope that wasn't selfish of me. I know I should've waited a bit. Waited at least until you were showing, but if you don't tell anybody, I won't.

YOLANDE: Mother, there is no baby.

NINA: Of course not. Not yet. But you just wait. In about seven months, you're gonna have the biggest surprise.

YOLANDE: No, Mother.

NINA: You may think you're ready, but believe me when I tell you, when that time comes, you'll find out that it's nothing like you thought it was gonna be.

YOLANDE: Seven, eight, nine, ten months, a year. It doesn't matter. There will be no baby.

NINA: Why not?

YOLANDE: I lost it. I lost the baby.

NINA: Oh, my sweetness. It's happening. All over again. Just like before. Just like Burghardt.

YOLANDE: No, Mother.

NINA: I told your father I didn't want to move to Atlanta. I made it clear to him, Yolande. There were no hospitals for Negroes. And everything might have been fine if Burghardt hadn't gotten sick. The nurse at the desk, she wouldn't admit Burghardt. They wouldn't even look at him. All he needed was a little medicine, and they had the medicine in ample supply behind those huge stone walls. It took us the rest of the night and most of the morning to find one of the three Negro doctors on the other side of town who would treat Burghardt, but by then it was too late. Your father said that it was not his fault, but he moved us to that Godforsaken place, for his work, he said. And that's the reason Burghardt is dead. He never even had a chance to live. Your father, who loved his son dearly, placed his son on the altar and sacrificed him without giving it a second thought.

And now you tell me that you've lost your child, and I can't help but to wonder, what did your father do this time.

YOLANDE: He didn't do anything, Mother.

NINA: How did you lose the baby?

YOLANDE: I just lost it. Daddy didn't have anything to do with me losing it, Mother.

NINA: Okay, Yolande. I'm gonna believe you. I just hope what I'm gonna believe is the truth.

COUNTEE *enters.*

COUNTEE: Excuse me.

NINA: I thought she might have been in here. I guess I was right. I'll get rid of all of this paper.

She gathers up the wrapping paper and exits.

COUNTEE: I have been looking for you.

YOLANDE: I know.

COUNTEE: I spoke with Harold . . .

YOLANDE: I don't wanna hear bout Harold.

COUNTEE: Look, Yolande . . .

YOLANDE: It's over. I'm gonna tell my father.

COUNTEE: Tell him what?

YOLANDE: Everything. I'm sorry, but I have to. I'm gonna have our marriage annulled.

COUNTEE: Yolande, please explain to me what happened between us to make you feel as if you had to consider resorting to this.

YOLANDE: It all began with a lie, Countee.

COUNTEE: But I love you, Yolande. I will do anything. All you have to do is tell me what you want. Just tell me what you want me to do and I will do it.

YOLANDE: I want you to make me your wife.

COUNTEE: Okay. Done.

YOLANDE: Now. I want you to do it now.

COUNTEE: You mean . . .

YOLANDE: Right here and now. We can go on the floor. On the desk. In the chair. Doesn't matter. The choice is yours.

COUNTEE: Are you serious?

YOLANDE: You said you would do anything.

COUNTEE: But . . . your mother . . .

YOLANDE: Did you mean it? Or was that just another lie?

> *She starts to unbutton his shirt. He tries to touch her. She tries to touch him. They pick up a little momentum. Suddenly, COUNTEE stops.*

COUNTEE: I can't do this.

YOLANDE: What do you want? You want me to use my mouth? I could use my mouth.

> *She goes to her knees and starts to unbutton his pants as COUNTEE breaks away.*

COUNTEE: What do you think I am?

> *He fumbles to restore his buttons as WILL enters.*

WILL: Good. You both are here. I have something for you. You've received letters of congratulations from various people, and I've taken the liberty to answer the important letters with notes of thanks, especially to Judge Julian Mack.

> *He hands a letter to COUNTEE.*

All you have to do is sign the letter and I'll have my secretary post it.

> *He offers COUNTEE a pen, which COUNTEE takes to sign the letter.*

I will have the other letters ready for you to sign later today.

> *COUNTEE offers the letter to YOLANDE. YOLANDE takes it and reads it. COUNTEE offers her the pen.*

No need to read it. It's simple enough. "Thank you for your note of congratulations. With your blessing, our marriage will be one of happiness and of bliss."

YOLANDE: And you want me to sign it?

WILL: It's a thank-you note, Yolande.

YOLANDE: I'm not signing this.

WILL: Why not?

YOLANDE: My marriage is not one of happiness, Daddy. It is not one of bliss.

WILL: I understand you're having problems. Problems are to be expected, Ouchie. Usually the problem stems from the fact that we, as a nation, are not forthright when it comes to the subject of relations. As a result, the man quite innocently assumes that his wife will enjoy relations as much as he does, which is usually not the case. Girls are usually extremely sensitive in their organs. Therefore, that which gives the husband pleasure may, for the girl, be exquisite physical torture.

YOLANDE: What are you talking about?

WILL: I'm talking about those problems that come with marriage, Yolande. It was your mother's responsibility to explain these things to you, but she has clearly, once again, failed her responsibility.

YOLANDE: That's not the problem, Daddy.

WILL: Countee, please. I'm going to ask you for your patience in this matter.

YOLANDE: Why are you asking him for his patience? What about me? What about my patience?

WILL: Daughter, please.

YOLANDE: Daughter?

WILL: Countee? Would you excuse us for a moment?

YOLANDE: What're you talking about? Why are you asking him for his patience?

    COUNTEE exits.

WILL: Yolande, you are no longer a little girl. You are a woman and you have been entrusted with a great and exciting responsibility. Stop feeling sorry for yourself and concentrate on your main duty, and that is to be of assistance to Countee so that he may complete a year's work to which the world will listen.

YOLANDE: He's never touched me, Daddy. He's never touched me, he doesn't kiss me.

WILL: What do you think marriage is? Do you expect to continue to carry on like a couple of schoolchildren?

YOLANDE: We never carried on in the first place. Countee doesn't carry on. Not with me, he doesn't. With Harold Jackman, maybe, but not with me.

WILL: What are you saying?

YOLANDE: He is abnormal, Daddy.

WILL: He is carrying a great burden upon his shoulders.

YOLANDE: Sexually. He is sexually abnormal.

WILL: Most women believe that most men are sexually abnormal. But he's a man, Yolande. He has an appetite. This is perfectly normal.

YOLANDE: If he has an appetite, it's not for me, or for any other woman. Countee has an appetite for other men.

WILL: Where did you hear such a vicious and malicious lie?

YOLANDE: From Countee. He told me himself.

WILL: I refuse to believe it.

YOLANDE: Ask him yourself. He'll probably tell you.

WILL: Yolande, if this is true . . . if Countee actually confessed this to you . . . then you have no right to repeat it to me or to anyone else. Your husband spoke to you in confidence, Yolande. It is imperative that you keep that confidence.

YOLANDE: Didn't you even hear anything I just said?

WILL: Countee is doing work that will usher in a new way of thinking in this country. He is writing about love, about music, about the souls of black folks. His work will change the way America views the problem of race in this country and all you can think about is yourself? You've been spoiled, Yolande. And I admit, it's partially my fault for giving you everything you've ever wanted. As a result, you have developed no sense of responsibility.

YOLANDE: Is that what I am? One of your failed projects?

WILL: You are my daughter.

YOLANDE: Or maybe I'm another sacrificial lamb.

WILL: I love you deeply.

YOLANDE: Just like you loved Burghardt?

WILL: I love you both the same.

YOLANDE: Please don't tell me that, Daddy.

WILL: I don't love him any more.

YOLANDE: No.

WILL: I don't love you any less.

YOLANDE: Mother was wrong about you. She said you were a beast, but she was wrong. You're not the beast. You're feeding the beast. You're keeping it alive.

WILL: I am fighting it with every ounce of my existence.

YOLANDE: You are feeding it the flesh and the bones of your own children.

WILL: I have dedicated my life to the end of racism. But I'm only one man, Yolande. I cannot slay the beast alone. I need your help.

YOLANDE: I'm not a soldier. I'm not gonna give my life for your cause.

WILL: It's your cause as well.

YOLANDE: No.

WILL: You want to teach high school? You want to help the downtrodden and the less fortunate? If you were truly committed to joining the struggle you would forget about "i before e except after c," and embrace your real responsibility, and that is of helping a great poet become even greater. Be of assistance to him. Reach up and remove a stone from the wall of segregation and help me push it over onto this rampaging beast so that one day we all may live in peace. Sign the note, Yolande. I'll post it the first thing in the morning.

    YOLANDE takes the note.

YOLANDE: You want the note signed?

    She crumples the note and drops it.

You sign it. I've already been complicit in too many lies.

    YOLANDE moves to COUNTEE as WEB exits.

COUNTEE: You tell him?

YOLANDE: I told him.

COUNTEE: Everything? And what did he say?

YOLANDE: I don't think he understood. Or maybe he didn't care to understand.

COUNTEE: Yolande, please, I know that between the two of us, we can find happiness.

YOLANDE: The happiness you're offering me is not enough. I need more, Countee.

COUNTEE: What more?

YOLANDE: I need you to knock me a kiss.

COUNTEE: What?

YOLANDE: I told you that you could trust me and I plan to keep that trust, but I will not stay married to you. I'm not gonna get an annulment, but I am gonna sue you for a divorce. And you will give me that divorce. And if you make any trouble for me or if you say anything unkind about me, I will take that trust and I will split it open and lay it out on the table for the entire world to feast upon. You understand me?

COUNTEE: I understand.

YOLANDE: Have a good time in Paris. Give Harold Jackman my best.

> *COUNTEE puts his index finger to his lips, then moves to put it to hers. She stops him. He exits as NINA enters.*

NINA: Countee's gone?

YOLANDE: He's gone.

> *NINA picks up the baby jumper.*

NINA: You mind if I keep this? I would like to put it with Burghardt's things as a reminder. Did I tell you about Helen Keller? She was stricken with an illness that left her blind and deaf when she was nineteen months old. I thought what had happened to her must have been the absolute worst calamity that could ever befall a person. I thought that not being able to hear another human voice, not being able to see another human face, must be a fate worse than death. I now realize that there are worse fates in this world. You see, I have eyes that appear to function as eyes, but they see nothing but darkness. And I have ears and I can hear sounds, but the only sounds I hear are grunts, moans, whimpers, and howls. And while a woman who was born deaf and blind was able to learn to speak by touching the lips and the throat of a speaker, I am unable to touch or to be touched and therefore, I will never learn to speak. I open my mouth to speak, but nothing comes out. I flail my arms in darkness and come in contact with nothing. Do you know what that's like? To have all of your senses removed? Not being able to see? To hear? To smell? To touch? To taste? I am old, Yolande. My desire dull. My feelings have been crusted over with memories of what could have been. But here I am talking about me again and you would think that I would know by now that you don't want to hear about me. I think I'll have a bit of tea, that's what I think I'll do. Miss Otis says that the green tea helps and you know what? I think she's right.

NINA moves to exit.

YOLANDE: May I have a bit as well?

NINA: Of tea? You want to have a bit of tea with me?

YOLANDE: Yes. I would like to have a bit of tea with you, Mother.

NINA: Okay. But you must be patient with me, Yolande. It may take a while for me to find another cup.

Lights fade.

END OF PLAY

PUDD'NHEAD WILSON

PRODUCTION HISTORY

Pudd'nhead Wilson was commissioned and produced by The Acting Company, Margot Harley, producing director. The production was directed by Walter Dallas, with set design by Juliana von Haubrich, costume design by Andre Harrington, lighting design by Dennis Parichy, and original music and sound design by Obadiah Eaves. Douglas Langworthy was the dramaturg, and Cole P. Bonenberger was the production stage manager.

This production opened in 2001 at the College of Staten Island Center for the Arts in Staten Island, New York, before embarking on a twenty-two-city national tour. The tour ended when the production opened Off Broadway at the Lucille Lortel Theatre in 2002.

Chambers	Michael Abbott Jr.
Bailiff/Man 3	Spencer Aste
Howard	Bryan Cogman
Tom	Jimonn Cole
Cecil/Man 2	Christian Conn
Judge Driscoll	Michael Lluberes
Reporter	Katherine Puma
Angelo/Lou/Man 1	Thom Rivera
Joe/Luigi	John Livingstone Rolle
Roxy	Roslyn Ruff
Rowena	Jordan Simmons
Nancy	Christen Simon
Pudd'nhead Wilson	Coleman Zeigen

(*above*) Roslyn Ruff as Roxy and Michael Abbott Jr. as Chambers in The Acting Company's production of *Pudd'nhead Wilson*. *Photo by Ken Howard.*

(*left*) Jimonn Cole as Tom and Michael Abbott Jr. as Chambers in The Acting Company's production of *Pudd'nhead Wilson*. *Photo by Ken Howard.*

(*right*) Roslyn Ruff as Roxy and Jimonn Cole as Tom in The Acting Company's production of *Pudd'nhead Wilson*. Photo by Ken Howard.

(*below*) Coleman Zeigen as Pudd'nhead Wilson and Roslyn Ruff as Roxy in The Acting Company's production of *Pudd'nhead Wilson*. Photo by Ken Howard.

Characters

Pudd'nhead Wilson	Forty-year-old white male.
Judge Percy Driscoll	Fifty-year-old white male.
Judge Howard	Fifty-year-old white male.
Chambers	White male in his twenties. The same actor also plays MAN THREE.
Angelo	White male. The same actor plays MAN ONE and LOU.
Cecil	White male. The same actor plays MAN TWO.
Tom	African American male in his twenties. The same actor also plays JIM.
Luigi	African American male. The same actor also plays JOE.
Roxy	African American female in her forties.
Nancy	African American female.
Rowena	White female in her twenties.

Time: 1830 *through* 1855.

Place: *In and about the town of Dawson's Landing, Missouri.*

Production Note: *The actors who play Tom and Luigi should be obviously African American. The blacker, the better. Likewise, the actor who plays Chambers should be obviously Caucasian. The whiter, the blonder, the better. No attempt should be made to make the race of these characters adhere to the awareness of the other characters in the play.*

PUDD'NHEAD WILSON

A Stage Adaptation and Reinterpretation of the Mark Twain Novel

A play in two acts

ACT ONE

PUDD'NHEAD WILSON is alone on stage. He addresses the audience.

WILSON: Wilson is my name. David Wilson. I was named David by my father, Earl Mark Wilson of Buffalo, New York. Although my father was not a religious man, he was familiar with the story of David. You know David. Old Testament. Armed with only a slingshot and a few stones, David single-handedly slew the giant Goliath who was the champion of the Philistines. That's me. David. Slayer of the champion of the Philistines. Remember that. David Wilson.

NANCY, a slave woman, enters.

NANCY: Hey, Pudd'nhead.

WILSON: Not Pudd'nhead Wilson.

NANCY: You's a Pudd'nhead, alright. No mistake 'bout dat.

WILSON: What did you say?

NANCY: Ah said, 'cuse me, Marster Wilson. Ya feelin' alright?

WILSON: What d'you want?

NANCY: Judge Howard sent me out heah to fetch ya inside, sir.

WILSON: Tell Judge Howard that I'm happy right where I am, thank you.

NANCY: But it's warm inside, Marster Wilson.

WILSON: But the company is better out here.

NANCY: What company?

She looks around.

Ya sho ya feeling alright, Marster Wilson?

WILSON: I'm feeling fine, Nancy.

NANCY: Den ya mind if Ah ax ya sumthin'?

WILSON: Ask me anything you'd like.

NANCY: Who ya out heah conversating wid?

WILSON: Nobody.

NANCY: You's holding a mighty heavy discourse to be conversating wid nobody.

WILSON: It's too complicated to try to explain.

NANCY: Maybe ya 'splain it inside whar it's warm.

WILSON: I'm fine.

NANCY: Is it de fire dat ya afeard o'?

WILSON: The fire?

NANCY: No need to be afeard o' de fire, Marster Wilson. Jim built dat fire fer Judge Howard, t'keep him warm. En iffen ya en me was inside, dat fire would keep us warm too. Dat's de reason fer a fire, Marster Wilson. T'keep ya warm en to cook on. Dat fire ain't gwine take up legs en walk. It ain't gwine git ya. Dat fire gwine stay right whar it belong, en as long as we stay whar we belong, everythin' gwine be roses.

WILSON: But that's the problem, Nancy. Don't ya see?

NANCY: What's de problem?

WILSON: None of us know where we belong.

NANCY: Ah knows whar Ah belong. Inside next t'dat fire.

> HOWARD enters.

HOWARD: You coming in, Wilson?

WILSON: Not just yet.

HOWARD: Still bothered by the spectacle? You can't let something like that get to you. You did a good thing, Wilson. You're a hero.

WILSON: Then why don't I feel like a hero?

HOWARD: You will. Once all of the excitement dies down and you've had a chance to reflect. You coming in? I could extinguish the fire if you like.

WILSON: Thank you, but I'm comfortable out here.

HOWARD: Suit yourself. You did the right thing, Wilson. Justice was served.

> HOWARD and NANCY exit.

WILSON (To audience): Pudd'nhead. That name was richly undeserved. I made a remark. An unfortunate remark a few days after I arrived here in Dawson's Landing some twenty-odd years ago. And for that one unfortunate remark, I was christened Pudd'nhead. It happened on February 1st, 1830. I remember the exact date because on the very same day I arrived, two baby boys were born in one house. One was born to the wife of Judge Percy Northumberland Driscoll who died in childbirth. The other was born to one of Driscoll's slave girls, Roxana. I was twenty-five years old at the time, had just finished law school and had come to Dawson's Landing, Missouri, to seek my fortune. I had brought with me a trifle of money which I used to purchase a small house on the western edge of town. Right after I purchased the house, I had a tin sign made up which read David Wilson, that's me, Attorney and Counselor-at-Law. Well, that's what I had planned to do. Practice law.

Three men enter.

The day I was to pick up my new tin banner announcing my chosen profession, I stopped to chat with a couple of the locals. I was new in town and eager to make as many new acquaintances as possible.

WILSON joins the men as a dog barks off in the distance.

MAN ONE: Think it's gonna rain anytime this week?

Dog barks.

MAN TWO: Might rain.

Dog barks.

Then again, might not.

Dog barks.

MAN THREE: You see the new wallpaper Aunt Patsy got?

Dog barks.

MAN TWO: I saw it. It's stripe-ed.

MAN ONE: Stripe-ed?

Dog barks

MAN TWO: Makes me dizzy.

Dog barks.

MAN THREE: I wish somebody would do something about that damned dog.

Dog barks.

MAN ONE: The barking of that dog has upset the entire town.

> *Dog barks.*

WILSON: You know, I wish I owned half of that dog.

> *The dog stops barking as if to listen. The men all look at WILSON as if seeing him for the first time.*

MAN TWO: Why is that Mister . . . Wilson is it?

WILSON: That's right. Wilson. David Wilson.

MAN TWO: Well, Mister David Wilson, why is it that you wish you owned half a dog?

WILSON: If I owned half of that dog, I think I would kill my half.

> *WILSON laughs. The dog yelps. The men look at each other.*

MAN TWO: You hear what he just said?

MAN ONE: I 'spect I heard but I'm not for sure. Thought he said he wish he owned half a dog.

MAN THREE: And iffen he did, he'd kill his half.

MAN ONE: That's what I thought I heard, too.

MAN TWO: You heard right cause that's exactly what he said.

MAN ONE: What do you suppose he reckons would become of the other half of the dog if he killed his half of the dog?

MAN TWO: Don't know. You reckon he thinks it would live?

WILSON: No, gentlemen. You see, that's the point. The dog is clearly an annoyance and if I owned half the dog—

MAN TWO: He must've thought the dog would live cause if he hadn't thought the dog would live, he would have wanted to own the whole dog, knowing that if he killed his half of the dog and the other half of the dog died, he would be responsible for the dead half just the same as if he had killed that half instead of his own. Don't it look that way to you?

MAN ONE: Looks that way to me.

WILSON: No, gentlemen, you don't understand . . .

MAN THREE: Just a minute, fellas. I think we're misapprehending the man.

WILSON: Thank you.

MAN THREE: It makes no sense if he owned one half of the dog, however, if he owned one end of the dog and another person owned the other end, it would be different cause if you kill one half of a dog, there ain't any man that can tell whose half it was; but if he owned one end of the dog, maybe he could kill his end of it and—

MAN TWO: No, no he couldn't either.

MAN ONE: He couldn't kill his end of the dog and not be responsible if the other end died, which it would.

MAN THREE: I see your point.

WILSON: And that's exactly my point. It was an attempt at humor.

MAN TWO: In my opinion the man ain't in his right mind.

MAN ONE: Ain't in no mind if you ask me.

MAN THREE: 'Pears to be a fool.

MAN ONE: 'Pears? Is, I reckon you better say.

MAN TWO: That's right. Is a fool.

MAN THREE: Not only is a fool, but a damn fool. Anybody can think different if they want to, but those are my sentiments.

MAN TWO: I'm with ya on that one. Perfect jackass if you ask me.

MAN ONE: I don't think we'd be going too far to say he's a pudd'nhead. How 'bout you?

MAN THREE: I agree with ya.

MAN ONE: And if he ain't a pudd'nhead, I ain't no judge.

MAN TWO: And you one of the best judges I know.

MAN THREE: That's right. Man's a pudd'nhead.

MAN TWO: Pudd'nhead.

MAN ONE: Pudd'nhead Wilson.

WILSON (*To audience*): Within a week every soul in town knew my name to be Pudd'nhead. But after people got to know me, they realized I wasn't such a bad fella. In fact, I became very well liked around town. Whenever anybody had a problem, they'd come to me, ole Pudd'nhead Wilson. The name stuck and after a while it ceased to carry any harsh or unfriendly feelings with it. However, I have more than made up for my faux pas about the dog. I made up for it seven times over with a bolt of lightning and clap of thunder that shook this entire town. You see, I discovered the answer to the riddle that no one else could understand. I, David, slew Goliath. I, Wilson. David Wilson. Not Pudd'nhead Wilson.

ROXY enters pushing a baby carriage. The men watch.

WILSON: Good morning, Roxy.

He peers into the carriage.

WILSON: What a lovely pair of baby boys. How old are they?

ROXY: Bofe de zat same age, sir—five months. Bawn de fust o' Feb'uary.

WILSON: They're handsome little chaps. One's just as handsome as the other, too. Look at them. They must be twins.

ROXY: Twins?

WILSON: Can't tell them apart.

ROXY: Ah kin tell dem 'part.

WILSON: Then you're the only one. Are they twins, Roxy?

ROXY: Nawsir.

WILSON: Brothers, then.

ROXY: Nawsir.

WILSON: They have to be brothers. Look at the similarities. The shape of the brow, the nose. They are the spitting image of each other. Who do they belong to?

ROXY: Dat one dere is Thomas à Becket Driscoll. He belong to Marster Driscoll. De udder one, his name's Valet de Chambers, but Ah calls him Chambers fer short. He's a nigger. Mighty prime lil nigger, Ah al'ays says, but dat's cause he belongs to me.

WILSON: Belongs to you?

ROXY: Yassir. Mah son.

WILSON: And who's the father?

ROXY shifts uncomfortably, glancing at the men.

It's alright, Roxy. You can tell me.

ROXY: He ain't got no daddy.

WILSON: You mean you don't know who the father is?

ROXY: Ah mean he's a nigger en a daddy is sumthin' dat a nigger don' got.

WILSON: That's biologically impossible, Roxy. You see ...

> WILSON notices that ROXY's discomfort stems from the attention being paid by the men.

MAN ONE: Told ya he was a pudd'nhead.

MAN TWO: Who's the nigger's daddy?

> The men laugh, then exit.

WILSON: What a lovely pair of boys.

ROXY: T'ank you, sir.

WILSON: How can you tell them apart?

ROXY: Don' know but Ah kin. En Ah's de on'y one. Not even Judge Driscoll kin tell dem 'part en he's de daddy. Ah mean he's de daddy o' dat one.

WILSON: I understand. Mind if I add them to my records?

ROXY: Yo' records?

WILSON: You know my law practice isn't going very well.

ROXY: Nawsir, Ah didn't know dat.

WILSON: Seems as if no one wants to be represented in the halls of justice by a man named Pudd'nhead, which has left me with an abundance of free time to devote to my various hobbies, one of which is palmistry.

> He removes a small glass slide from his pocket.

WILSON: If you would allow me to—

ROXY: Nawsir, Ah'm sorry, but ya shouldn't be tetchin' dem chilluns.

WILSON: It's alright, Roxy. I won't hurt them. You see, I believe that the events of a person's life are embedded in the palm of their hand. I believe that their past and their future are printed there, like words in a book. So what I do is record people's palm prints and their finger marks on small strips of glass. Then as these folks grow older, as their lives change, as they change jobs and change temperaments, I try to discern patterns in their palm prints and finger marks which hopefully will correspond with the changes in their lives. And recording a palm print is all very painless.

> He reaches into the carriage.

You see, I put a lil fat right here. Press the palm and fingers to the glass and presto, it's done.

ROXY: Ya mean to tell me dat ya kin tell a pusson's past en dey future by looking at dat lil piece o' glass?

WILSON: I said I believe you can tell their past and their future. Unfortunately, I haven't quite figured out a way to do it yet. You see, that's the tough part, unlocking the secret. I believe it's all there. I just don't know how to read it yet.

DRISCOLL enters, followed by NANCY.

DRISCOLL: Roxy, get ovah heah and tell me where you been.

ROXY: Ah be'n right heah, Marster Driscoll, doing what Ah'm 'posed to be doing en dat's tending to Marster Tom.

DRISCOLL: If you would excuse me, Pudd'nhead, but I seem to have a problem heah.

WILSON: Pay me no mind, Your Honor.

DRISCOLL: Joe, Jim, get over here.

JOE and JIM enter.

ROXY: Marster?

DRISCOLL: Now you all know that I am a fair man. I am fair and I am humane. Humane to all my animals and my slaves. Have I not been fair to you?

ROXY: Oh, yassir, Marster.

JOE: You's be'n fair.

NANCY: Oh, yassir.

JIM: Most fair.

DRISCOLL: And humane?

JIM: Oh, yassir, Marster.

JOE: Yassir.

DRISCOLL: And I allow you all great liberty. As much liberty as any slave is allowed here in these parts. Once your work is done, I let you come and go as you please. Do I not?

JOE: Oh, yassir.

JIM: As we please.

DRISCOLL: I tolerate many things around here, but there is one thing I will not tolerate and that's thievery.

JOE: Thievery?

NANCY: Sumbody stole sumthin'?

DRISCOLL: I am missing a dollar which I laid on the credenza. That means that one of you's a thief and I wanna know who it is.

JIM: Thief? Uh uh.

NANCY: Nawsir.

ROXY: No.

JOE: No thief heah.

DRISCOLL: This is the third time that something like this has happened, and you have all been warned before, but apparently my warnings have done no good, so this time, I plan to teach you a lesson you won't forget. You will tell me who the thief is and then the thief will be sold.

JIM: Sole!

ROXY: Oh mah Lawd!

JOE: Warrn't me, Marster.

NANCY: Warrn't me.

JIM: Warrn't me.

ROXY: Sho warrn't me!

DRISCOLL: My patience is exhausted. I wanna know who the thief is and I wanna know now.

> JIM, JOE, NANCY, and ROXY stand silent.

Come on. Which of you is the guilty one?

> The four stand silent.

I will give you one minute. If, at the end of that minute, the thief has not confessed, I will sell all four of you.

JIM: Please, Marster, Ah beg ya . . .

DRISCOLL: And not only will I sell the four of you, but I will sell you down the river.

ROXY: Down de river!

JOE: It was me, Marster, Ah done it. Ah stole de dollah.

DRISCOLL: Joe?

JOE: But Ah didn't mean to. Ah swear t'God. It was an accident.

DRISCOLL: Accident?

JOE: Dat's right. Accident. Didn't mean to do it. Must've be'n de devil hisself who sneaked up behind me en whispered in mah ear "Joe, take dat dere dollah." But Ah said no, devil, git 'way frum me. Ya cain't make me take a dollah frum Marster Driscoll en even if Ah did take it cause ya made me take it, Marster Driscoll would know dat it was ya who made me do it, cause Marster Driscoll is a kind Marster en a smart Marster en he know Ah love 'em mo' den Ah love life itself en Ah would cut off mah own han' befo' Ah hurt Marster Driscoll.

DRISCOLL: You have hurt me deeply, Joe.

JOE: Ah know, Marster, en Ah's so sorry. Please have mercy on dis heah po' nigger.

DRISCOLL: Very well. I must sell you, you know that.

JOE: Please, Marster.

DRISCOLL: I said I would sell the thief and that's what I plan to do.

JOE: Please.

DRISCOLL: However, I will have mercy and sell you locally, even though you don't deserve it.

JOE: T'ank you, Marster.

DRISCOLL: Go collect your things. Start to say your good-byes.

JOE: God bless you, Marster Driscoll. You's a kind marster. May ya be in heaven a half hour befo' de devil know ya dead.

JOE exits.

DRISCOLL: The rest of you, go on about your business and leave me be.

JIM exits. ROXY stares at DRISCOLL in disbelief.

DRISCOLL: That means you too, Roxy. Take my boy on out away from heah.

ROXY exits.

DRISCOLL: You see what I'm up against, Pudd'nhead? Every day I am faced with these type of decisions. It would have been easy for me to sell them all down the river, to banish them into the far reaches of hell, but no. Humanity dictates that I strive to be godlike, so like God, I stretch forth my mighty hand and close the gates of hell against them.

WILSON: What a great and noble act.

DRISCOLL: I did it, not for their sake, but for the sake of my son, Tom, who, many years from now, may learn what I did here today and be thereby moved to deeds of gentleness and humanity himself.

> *WILSON and DRISCOLL exit as ROXY enters with the baby carriage. She sings. As she sings, she starts to sharpen a small machete against a stone.*

ROXY:

> *Ah'm gonna be ready,*
> *Ah'm gonna be ready,*
> *Ah'm gonna be ready,*
> *Ready to put on my great white robe.*

> *JOE enters and watches ROXY, who continues to sing.*

> *Ah'm gonna be ready,*

JOE: Roxy?

ROXY:

> *Ah'm gonna be ready,*

JOE: What ya doing?

ROXY:

> *Ah'm gonna be ready,*

JOE: Roxy?

ROXY:

> *Ready to put on—*

JOE: Roxy!

> *ROXY stops.*

What ya got in yo' head?

ROXY: Ah'm gwine kill him.

JOE: Ya gwine kill who?

ROXY: Marster Driscoll. Ah'm gwine chop him up.

JOE: Ya out yo' mind?

ROXY: Finally in mah right mind.

JOE: Roxy, listen a me. Ah shouldn't a done what Ah done.

ROXY: Everybody take thangs, Joe.

JOE: But not money.

ROXY: A lil sugar, piece o' cake.

JOE: Never money. Ah shouldn't a done it. White man's money's dearer to him dan life itself. Ah should've known better.

Ah shouldn't have stole it.

ROXY: But what ya done warrn't really stealing, Joe.

JOE: How ya figure dat?

ROXY: Marster Driscoll own dat dollah, sho. Dat dollah his. But Marster Driscoll also own you. Ya belong to him jes like dat dollah belong to him. So if ya pick up dat dollah en put it in yo' pocket, what he done lost?

JOE: He lost a dollah.

ROXY: No he ain't neither. Marster Driscoll owns ya en he owns everythin' ya own. Dat means iffen ya pick up dat dollah en put it in yo' pocket, dat dollah still belong to him cause ya belong to him. Ya ain't gained nothin' en he ain't lost nothin'. Dat dollah still part o' his property. Even iffen ya trade dat dollah fer somethin' to eat, he still gwine git his money werth cause after ya eat, ya gwine be a lil quicker wid de foot when werkin' fer him.

JOE: Dat's some roundabout thinkin'.

ROXY: Ah'll tell ya roundabout thinkin'. Roundabout thinkin' is me, runnin' 'round heah thinkin' dat Marster Driscoll wouldn't sell me.

JOE: He won't sell you.

ROXY: He threatened to sell me.

JOE: Jes a threat, Roxy.

ROXY: Threatened to sell me down de river.

JOE: You his favorite.

ROXY: Favorite what? Ya thank he takes a fancy to me cause he use me in dat way? Dat don' make me no different den all o' de udder niggers running 'round heah. Dere was a time Ah tought it made me different, but it don'. De way Ah sees it, he sell me jes as quick as he sell you, likely quicker.

JOE: Ya wrong, Roxy.

ROXY: Likely sell me en mah baby chile.

JOE: He wouldn't sell Chambers. Dat's one thang Ah kin tell ya fer sho. Chambers semblances him 'bout de eyes, de nose, de mouf.

ROXY: Don' make no difference.

JOE: He sell Chambers, he be sellin' a lil piece o' hisself.

ROXY: Ya think dat matters to dese folks? Chambers semblances Marster, sho. But de way Ah sees it, dats mo' de reason Marster gwine sell him. Chambers git older, e'ry time Marster look at him, he gwine be reminded o' his own wickedness. Not on'y is he gwine sell Chambers, prob'ly sell him down de river en ya know what's awaitin' a nigger if he git hisself sole down de river.

JOE: Ah know.

ROXY: Dey put iron 'round yo' neck, iron en chain 'round yo' ankle, 'round yo' wrist.

JOE: Ah know, Roxy.

ROXY: En Ah cain't let him do dat. Not to mah baby. Not to Chambers.

JOE: Ya killing Marster ain't gwine stop him frum selling ya or Chambers.

ROXY: Ah like to see him do it if he dead. Iffen he chopped up in a hunnred pieces, Ah like to see him try en sell anybody.

JOE: Ya chop him up, sumbody else gwine come 'long en take his place. Fer e'ry lil piece o' him ya scatter out en 'bout, 'nother one o' him gwine sprout up, en instead o' one Marster Driscoll to cope wid ya gwine have a hunnred.

ROXY: Den Ah'll poison him. Put ground glass in his food.

JOE: De on'y thang ya gwine do by tryin' t'kill Marster Driscoll is turn Dawson's Landing into hell fer e'ry nigger here. Ya kill him, dey gwine kill ya en den, dey gwine t'kill everybody who look like ya. En fer peaches en cream, dey gwine sell Chambers deep down de river anyway. Dat what ya want to happen?

ROXY: Ya know it ain't.

JOE: Gimme dat chop-axe.

He takes the machete.

What ya oughts to do is fall t' yo' knees en t'ank God dat ya ain't already down de river. Dat what ya oughts t' do.

ROXY spits.

En ya ought not to blaspheme dat a way.

ROXY: De on'y thang Ah t'ank God fer is Adam.

JOE: Adam?

ROXY: Adam bit de apple. When he done dat, he brought death into dis world en fer dat, we owe him some deep gratitude. But dat's de on'y thang.

JOE: Den be t'ankful fer death en leave Marster Driscoll alone. Ya hear me, Roxy? He's a kind Marster.

ROXY: Nigger, what kinda mushrooms ya be'n eatin' ta come up wid sumthin' like dat? Kind Marster. Ain't no such thang as a kind Marster. It don' exist. Any man what owns 'nother man is by his very nature, unkind.

JOE: He don' mistreat us.

ROXY: Guess dat 'pends on what ya call mistreat.

JOE: Ya know what Ah mean, Roxy. He don' beat us.

ROXY: En ya think dat's enuf? He bought hisself some niggers en put dem niggers to werk fer him en jes cause he don' beat dem niggers, dat make him kind? Ya must've got dat frum de white man's bible cause according to mah book, dat don' make him kind. Dat jes make him a different kind o' cruel. If he was kind, he be like 'most everybody else in dis worl' en bypass buying niggers altogether. But he chose not to do dat. He chose to go out en buy hisself some o' de bes' niggers money kin buy.

JOE: Ya gots to stop thinking like dat, Roxy. Ya heah me? Ah want ya to put dem toughts outta yo' head en swear to me dat ya ain't gwine try en kill Marster Driscoll. Roxy! Do it!

ROXY: Alright.

JOE: Alright what?

ROXY: Ah swear.

JOE: Swear what?

ROXY: Swear Ah ain't gwine try en kill Marster Driscoll.

JOE: Nigger swear?

ROXY: Nigger swear.

JOE: Good. Ah'm glad ya did dat. Now, Ah ain't gotta tell Marster what ya was planning on doing.

ROXY: Oh Marster Joe, you is so kind to me.

JOE: Don' talk to me dat away, Roxy.

ROXY: En Ah's so happy. Look at me. Ah's a happy nigger. Ah's happy to be heah en Ah's happy to be a slave.

JOE: Ya don' know it yet but Ah jes he'ped ya.

> *JOE exits.*

ROXY: Ah swore Ah ain't gwine try en kill 'em en Ah'm gwine keep mah swear. But Ah ain't gwine let him sell mah Chambers down de river either. Since Ah cain't kill Marster, dat means Ah gots to kill ya, Chambers.

> *The baby starts to cry. She picks him up and starts to undress him.*

Don' worry. Ah ain't gwine let ya go alone. Ah'm gwine go wid ya. We gwine wade in de water, together. We gwine jump in de river, wade on over to de udder side, den troubles o' dis worl' is all over— dey don' sell po' niggers down de river over yonder. Ah'm gwine dress ya up real nice. Ah'm gwine put ya in Marster Tom's shirt so dat when de angels in heaven see you, dey gwine admire ya jes as much as all de udder angels in heaven. Marster Tom won't miss dis one lil shirt. Lawd knows he's got enuf o' 'em. Why de Lawd makes thangs de way dey is? Why he give one baby nothin' en de udder baby everythin'? An ought's an ought, a figure's a figure, all fer de white man, none fer de nigger. Dat's what Ah al'ays say. Look at ya heah, in Marster Tom's shirt, pretty as you is, nobody be able to tell ya 'part. Dey'd think ya was Marster—

> *She stops and looks at the two babies.*

Now who would b'lieve clo'es could do de like o' dat? Dog mah cats if it ain't all Ah kin do to tell t'udder frum which, let alone his pappy. Good Lawd, dare Ah do it? T'ain't no sin—white folks has done it. Dey's done it—yes, en dey was de biggest quality o' white folks in de whole buildin', too. Dey was kings en queens. Dat's what de preacher said de Bible said. Queen switched her baby wid 'nother baby, so it ain't no sin. White folks done it. Glory to goodness it ain't no sin.

Frum dis day out, Chambers, you is Marster Tom en Tom, you's Chambers. De white folks done it. Now Ah's gwine do it. Now, Ah's gotta practice to git used to who's who 'round here.

She picks up her baby, CHAMBERS.

Come here, Chambers.

She realizes her mistake and corrects herself.

Marster Tom. You's so pretty in yo' nightgown. Such a pretty baby.

The other baby, baby TOM, cries.

Shut up, Chambers!

She smacks the baby a good one.

Dat felt good.

Baby TOM cries again. She smacks him again.

Shut up, Ah tell ya. Does ya want me to take sumthin' to you? (*To CHAMBERS, now TOM*) Such a pretty baby. Yes you is. Ah could git used to dis.

She alternately smacks one and coos to the other as PUDD'NHEAD enters and addresses the audience.

WILSON: Nobody knew. Nobody suspected. Not even I suspected. You see, Roxy was right. Not even the father, Judge Driscoll, was able to tell the boys apart. But Roxy was wrong about another matter. Judge Driscoll never sold her down the river. He gave her away as a wedding present to his young niece from Philadelphia. But this was many years later, long after the boys were well into their teens. The day Roxy left, she was happy and contented because she knew that her son Chambers, now Master Tom, would never have to face the same hardships that she had to face, and when Roxy left, she took her secret with her. But because of Roxy, I was able to atone for my remarks about the dog. You see, this is where my story begins. This was the beginning of my redemption.

TOM, now in his twenties, enters carrying a pistol. He is followed by CECIL, ROWENA, and CHAMBERS. CHAMBERS, obviously a slave, carries what appears to be a small travel case.

TOM: Stand back, everyone. Please, stand back. I wouldn't want anyone to get hurt by a stray projectile. Now, tell me. Where is the scoundrel?

CECIL: He ain't here, Tom.

TOM: Probably somewhere cowering.

ROWENA: But you're not afraid, are you, Tom?

TOM: Yea, though I walk through the valley of the shadow of death, I will fear no evil if I know that thou are with me.

ROWENA: And I am with thee.

TOM: Prove it.

ROWENA: How?

TOM: Comfort me with thy arms and thy lips.

ROWENA: You rascal.

> *She kisses him.*

WILSON: What you up to, Tom?

TOM: Stand back, Pudd'nhead. I don't want you to get hurt.

WILSON: Hurt by what?

TOM: This heah is something I doubt you would understand.

WILSON: Zat right?

TOM: That's right.

WILSON: And exactly what wouldn't I understand?

TOM: Pride, Pudd'nhead. A gentleman's honor, that's what.

WILSON: You planning to fight a duel?

TOM: I am planning to avenge an injustice, Pudd'nhead.

ROWENA: That's right. An injustice.

TOM: I plan to defend the good name of Driscoll.

ROWENA: Grave injustice.

WILSON: Does your father know about this foolishness?

TOM: Number one, it's not foolishness. But I doubt if that's something you would understand being of northern extraction. Number two, if my father was aware of this match, he would most certainly approve because I am not only defending my good name but his good name as well. Chambers?

CHAMBERS: Yassir.

TOM: Libation.

CHAMBERS: Yassir.

CECIL: Libation?

TOM: I didn't stutter nor did I slur the word.

> *CHAMBERS opens the travel case, extends the legs, and sets up what appears to be a portable bar equipped with bottles and glasses.*

CECIL: I thought you might wanna keep a clear head, you know, with ya upcoming duel and all.

ROWENA: That's right, Tom. You don't want to get yourself hurt or otherwise injured.

TOM: Set your mind to ease. You see, Apple Jack doesn't affect me the way it affects most men. With me, it has a tendency to sharpen the eye, steady the hand, and clear the mind. Others, who are unable to refresh themselves in moderation, overindulge and as a result, their minds become dull and their humor belligerent.

CECIL: Sorry.

TOM: No need to apologize when you're doing the best you can.

CHAMBERS: Yo' libation's ready, Marster Tom.

TOM: Thank you, Chambers.

> *CHAMBERS hands TOM a glass containing a shot of whiskey. TOM knocks it back, then hands the glass back to CHAMBERS.*

TOM: I would offer you a taste, Pudd'nhead, but I wouldn't want to be responsible for sending you any further off your trolley than you already are.

WILSON: Thank you for the consideration.

TOM: Don't mention it.

WILSON: But I happen to be a bit of a teetotaler.

TOM: Wise move on your part.

CECIL: I ain't no teetotaler.

TOM: Help yourself, Cecil. Just make sure you don't hurt yourself. Chambers? Set him up.

> *CHAMBERS makes CECIL a drink.*

And how 'bout you, my lovely Rowena? Would you like a little fortification?

ROWENA: Oh Tom. You know I don't drink.

TOM: Who said anything about drinking?

ROWENA: You rascal.

> *She kisses him.*

WILSON: Just with whom are you planning to joust, Tom?

TOM: Sam Childress, the scoundrel.

WILSON: Sam?

ROWENA: He accused Tom of cheating at cards.

WILSON: Still gambling, are ya Tom?

TOM: I don't gamble, Pudd'nhead.

WILSON: But you were playing cards.

TOM: Card playing is not gambling. Gambling is an occupation for fools, Pudd'nhead. It involves uncertainty. It involves guesswork. It involves unfounded suspicion and conjecture.

WILSON: And card playing does not involve conjecture or uncertainty?

TOM: Not when I play. You see, if you understand Pascal's Laws of Probability and the theory behind binomial coefficients, you would know the exact odds of pulling an inside straight after running a royal flush. I don't gamble, Pudd'nhead. I only bet on sure things. I only bet on what I can see, on what's before me. I never try to guess what's in another man's hand, I only bet on what's in my hand. By following these rules, I have effectively removed the element of chance from the game of poker and reduced it to an exercise in mathematical possibilities. That was how I beat Sam. I beat him fair, I beat him square. I beat him so bad he didn't know left from right, up from down, he looked at a six and thought he was looking at a nine.

ROWENA: And that's when he accused Tom of cheating.

TOM: And that's the reason I'm here: to set the record straight. However, I believe the man to be lily-livered.

CECIL: I wouldn't call him that, Tom.

TOM: Then where is he, Cecil? He ain't here, I can tell you that. Chambers, I want you to go by Sam Childress's house and see if he's there. You think you can do that?

CHAMBERS: Yassir.

TOM: You know where he lives?

CHAMBERS: Yassir.

TOM: You think you can get there and back without getting lost?

CHAMBERS: Yassir.

TOM: Then what you standing there looking at me for? Go, goddamn it. Go and see if he's at home and if so, tell him I sent you to fetch him here for his prearranged rendezvous.

CHAMBERS: Yassir.

TOM: Now get!

CHAMBERS exits.

CECIL: I don't know what you're worried about. Sam's gonna show.

TOM: Think so?

CECIL: I know so. Sam's a good shot, Tom, and I ain't never know him to pass up a challenge from no man.

TOM: You willing to place a wager on your knowledge? Say, five dollars?

CECIL: Five dollars?

TOM: You think Sam's gonna show, and you seem to be confident in your ignorance.

CECIL: I am confident.

TOM: Then let's see exactly how confident you are. I got five dollars that says he won't show.

CECIL: That's a lot of money, Tom.

TOM: I'm sorry, Cecil. I plum forgot. I thought for a moment I was talking to a man of means.

CECIL: I got the money. I got that plus a whole lot more.

TOM: Then place a wager. I got ten dollars that says that Sam Childress will not show up.

CECIL: You know what? I would do it if I had my Judy Boot with me.

TOM: Your what?

CECIL: Judy Boot. My good luck charm. Rhinestone my pappy gave me before he got hit by that train in Kansas.

TOM: You think a piece of pebble's gonna decide whether Sam Childress shows up or not?

CECIL: I don't do no gambling without my Judy Boot.

TOM: Either you believe what you said or you don't. If you believe, put up, and if you don't, shut up. But don't talk to me about good luck, bad luck, or nigger superstition cause I don't want to hear it.

CECIL: Nigger superstition?

TOM: That's what's you're holding onto. Nigger superstition.

CECIL: Alright. I'll bet ya.

TOM: Twenty dollars?

CECIL: Twenty dollars.

TOM: Put up.

> CECIL hands TOM a twenty. TOM adds a twenty to CECIL's bill, then hands them both to ROWENA.

TOM: Why don't you tuck this safely away between those two honeysuckles of yours.

CECIL: Pudd'nhead should hold the money.

TOM: You don't trust me?

CECIL: I didn't say that.

TOM: Then why you want Pudd'nhead to hold the money? You think I would try to cheat you, Cecil? Is that what you're trying to say? Are you accusing me of cheating you?

CECIL: Naw, Tom.

TOM: Et tu, Brute?

CECIL: I ain't trying to say none of that. All I'm trying to say is that on a wager such as this, a disinterested party should be the one holding the money and the only disinterested party here is Pudd'nhead Wilson. Ain't that right, Pudd'nhead?

WILSON: He has a point, Tom.

TOM: Alright. Pudd'nhead, would you do us the honor?

WILSON: This time.

> TOM and CECIL hand money to PUDD'NHEAD.

Although I have to confess that I will never understand this southern sense of pride and honor.

TOM: It's a very complex subject.

WILSON: Aren't you afraid you may be killed during one of these forays?

TOM: I may be killed but I'm not afraid. One should never fear the inevitable, Pudd'nhead. Fear is food for cowards and I am not a hungry man. I am a Driscoll, descendant of a long line of Driscolls. The blood running in these veins is centuries old. My blood has witnessed famine and prosperity, periods of disease and health, the worst of war and the best of social harmony. My blood has witnessed everything there is to witness in this world, which means that nothing on this earth made by man nor God can make me afraid.

WILSON: And you think it's your blood that enables you to stare into the face of death without flinching?

TOM: You ever been to school, Pudd'nhead?

WILSON: Course I have.

TOM: What school did you go to?

WILSON: You know.

TOM: I forgot. Remind me. What school?

WILSON: It was a small university in the east.

TOM: And what did you study at this small unnamed university in the east?

WILSON: You know what I studied, Tom.

TOM: Was it law?

WILSON: Why are you doing this?

TOM: I believe it was. I believe you studied law. And lemme ask you something. In the twenty-some-odd years since you graduated, have you had the opportunity to practice law?

WILSON: No, I haven't.

TOM: The man goes to school and studies law, but he's unable to practice law. What you make outta that, Cecil?

CECIL: He goes to school. He studies law. He's unable to—

TOM: Never mind. You know where I went to school, Pudd'nhead?

WILSON: Everybody knows.

TOM: I went to Yale University. Ever hear of it? I studied many subjects while matriculating at Yale. One of the many subjects I studied was animal husbandry. I studied breeding, propagation, systems of selection, and mating. Did you know that if you took a sheep that produced a fine quality of wool and mated that sheep with a ram which also produced a fine quality of wool that the resulting offspring would produce the exact same fine quality of wool?

ROWENA: He is so smart.

TOM: You see, Pudd'nhead, an offspring will always exhibit the traits of its progenitor.

WILSON: Yes, Tom. I knew that.

TOM: That's the way it is with all of God's creatures. Take the nigger for example. Most niggers are bred for working. The men have wide, strong backs. The women have wide hips for breeding and big bottoms for carrying babies on their backs while working in the fields. Take a look at a nigger's hand and you'll see a hand that was built to hold a shovel, for holding a spade, for swinging an axe, or chopping cotton and tobacco. If you gave a nigger a pistol and tried to teach that nigger how to shoot that pistol, the nigger couldn't do it, no matter how much training you gave him, because a nigger's hand was not made to hold a pistol. His meaty fingers couldn't fit into the trigger guard. Not to mention the nigger's predisposition towards cowardice.

WILSON: I'm sorry, Tom, but I have to disagree with you on that.

TOM: This is not like the hoodoo voodoo you practice with finger marks on pieces of glass, Pudd'nhead. I'm discussing a body of science that is as precise as mathematics. As exact as Pascal's Laws of Probability.

WILSON: All the same, I think you're underestimating the power of good training.

TOM: You think you can train a nigger how to shoot a pistol?

WILSON: I think training is everything. After all, the peach was once a bitter almond; a cauliflower is nothing more than a cabbage with a college education.

CECIL: All of this talk about eating is making me hungry.

ROWENA: You coming to the party tonight, Pudd'nhead?

WILSON: What party?

CECIL: The party at Tom's house.

WILSON: I didn't know Tom was having a party.

TOM: Tom's not having a party. My daddy's having the party. I'm an innocent bystander.

ROWENA: The party's in honor of the new visitors coming to town.

WILSON: What visitors?

CECIL: Them Italian Twins.

WILSON: I haven't heard anything about it.

TOM: I don't know how that's possible, judging by the way the entire town's been abuzz about them.

ROWENA: A pair of royal Italian twins are coming to stay here in Dawson's Landing for a spell and Judge Driscoll's having a reception in their honor.

TOM: I don't know why everybody's making such a big fuss.

CECIL: Cause of the way they look. You seen 'em yet?

TOM: I've seen twins before.

CECIL: Not like these you ain't. It's like one man standing there looking in a mirror. Everything about them is the same. The eyes, the nose, every single hair on their head is the same. Freaky.

ROWENA: That's not what makes them so special, Cecil. We're talking about Italian royalty here.

> *A hooded figure enters, unnoticed by the men. The figure remains on the perimeter of the space.*

TOM: That's nothing special. I knew a couple of Italian fellas when I was at Yale.

> *The group exits as CHAMBERS enters near the hooded figure. The hooded figure calls out.*

ROXY: Chambers.

> *CHAMBERS stops, notices the figure.*

Come here.

> *CHAMBERS hesitates.*

Come on!

She motions him over. CHAMBERS moves closer.

CHAMBERS: Mammy? Zat you?

ROXY: Course it's me, boy.

She smacks him.

Git ovah here.

CHAMBERS: What ya doing heah, Mammy? Ya ain't 'scaped, is ya?

ROXY: Naw, Ah ain't 'scaped.

CHAMBERS: Whacha doin heah den?

ROXY: Ah's free.

CHAMBERS: You's free?

ROXY: Ah's free.

CHAMBERS: How ya git free?

ROXY: De white lady Marster gimme to, his niece? She up en died. But befo' she died, laying dere on her death bed, she sets me free. Now Ah need sumthin' ta eat.

CHAMBERS: Ya free?

ROXY: What Ah jes tell ya? Now Ah need sumthin' ta eat, Chambers. Piece o' bread, lil fat back.

CHAMBERS: You's free! Oh happy day, Mammy. Happy day.

He dances. She smacks him.

ROXY: What's de matter wid ya, boy?

CHAMBERS: You's free, Mammy.

ROXY: En Ah'm hungry.

CHAMBERS: But you's free.

ROXY: Lots o' good it's gwine do me. Ah ain't got no money. Ah ain't got no food. Ah ain't got no place to rest mah head. Ah be'n runnin', dodgin', duckin' en hidin' fer dern near two months now.

CHAMBERS: Why ya duckin' en hidin'?

ROXY: Slave-ketchers on mah trail.

CHAMBERS: But Ah tought ya said ya was free.

ROXY: Ah is free. Got certified papers to prove it. But dat don' stop de slave-ketchers frum snatchin' ya up en sellin' ya to sumbody else. Ah be'n duckin' en hidin', pickin' thru garbage, lookin' fer food.

CHAMBERS: Why don' ya jes buy yoself some food, mammy?

ROXY: Ain't got no money to buy no food, ya fool.

CHAMBERS: But you's free.

ROXY: Dat don' mean Ah got money. Ya got t'werk t'git money en Ah's too ole t'werk. Marster stole all mah good werkin' years. Mah arms is tired en Ah cain't stan' fer long, mah legs give out. En even iffen Ah warrn't too ole t'werk, ain't nobody gwine pay me t'werk when dey kin buy demselves 'nother nigger dat dey don' got t'pay at all. En ya sittin' heah singin' like a fool, oh happy day. Ain't no happy day. Not fer me it ain't. Now Ah needs ya to git me sumthin' to eat.

CHAMBERS: Ah kin git ya a lil ponecake.

ROXY: Good boy. Dat's mah boy. But wait. Tell me 'bout Marster Tom.

CHAMBERS: What ya wants to know 'bout him?

ROXY: How is he?

CHAMBERS: He doing alright, Ah reckon.

ROXY: What he like?

CHAMBERS: What ya mean, what he like? Ya know what he like.

ROXY: He turn out tall en handsome?

CHAMBERS: Ah reckon. Tall en handsome.

ROXY: Turn out to be a good man?

CHAMBERS: 'Pends on what ya call a good man.

ROXY: He kind?

CHAMBERS: Kind?

ROXY: He take pity on po' niggers?

CHAMBERS: Marster Tom?

ROXY: Do he got it in his heart to know when a nigger is hurtin'?

CHAMBERS: He de same Marster Tom he was when ya lef' heah.

ROXY: But everythin' subject t'change.

CHAMBERS: Everythin' 'cept Marster Tom.

ROXY: Please don' tell me dat.

CHAMBERS: What ya so inner-rested in Marster Tom fer?

ROXY: Ah suckled dat boy. Ah raised him like he was mah own.

CHAMBERS: Dere's a whole string o' dem dat ya raised like yo' own. Most o' dem, ya raised better den ya raised yo' own.

ROXY: Ya say dat like it was mah aim to do so.

CHAMBERS: Ah'm sorry, Mammy. Ah didn't mean to say it dat away.

ROXY: Marster Tom's different den de rest o' dem. Ah gave dat boy a lil somethin' extra hoping he'd turn out right. Dat's de reason Ah got to know. Maybe if he turned out right, maybe now he gimme a lil somethin' back fer mah trouble.

CHAMBERS: What lil somethin' ya lookin' for?

ROXY: Tought maybe he might toss a dollah mah way ever now en den.

CHAMBERS: Marster Tom?

ROXY: He's de on'y thang Ah got lef'.

CHAMBERS: Den ya ain't got much o' nothin', cause Marster Tom ain't got no dollahs to be tossing nobody's way even iffen he wanted to.

ROXY: Ain't he rich?

CHAMBERS: His daddy's rich.

ROXY: Dat means Tom's rich.

CHAMBERS: Dat's what it's 'posed to mean but not when it comes to Marster Tom. Marster Driscoll give him fifty dollahs a month but Tom spends dat right up.

ROXY: Marster Driscoll got a lot mo' money den fifty dollahs a month.

CHAMBERS: Sho he do, but Tom cain't tetch it cause Marster Driscoll tuck 'n' dissenhurrit him.

ROXY: Disenwhiched him?

CHAMBERS: Dissenhurrit him.

ROXY: What's dat?

CHAMBERS: Means he bu'sted de will.

ROXY: Bu'sted de will! Tell me dat ya lying.

CHAMBERS: Ah's lying.

ROXY: Ah knowed it, ya good-fer-nothin' nigger.

She smacks him.

CHAMBERS: What ya do dat fer?

ROXY: Fer lying to me.

CHAMBERS: Ah didn't lie to ya, Mammy.

ROXY: Ya jes said ya did.

CHAMBERS: On'y cause ya axed me to.

ROXY: Looka here, Chambers. Ah want de truth outta you. Marster Driscoll dissenhurrit Tom or not?

CHAMBERS: Course he did. Ah tole ya dat.

ROXY: Lawd Jesus.

CHAMBERS: But ole Marster say he forgive Tom en fix up de will ag'in iffen Tom straighten up.

ROXY: Dat's what he said?

CHAMBERS: Dat's what he said.

ROXY: Listen ta me, Chambers. Ah want ya ta go ta Tom en tell him dat his po' ole nigger Mammy jes wanna have one sight o' him ag'in befo' she die.

CHAMBERS: Ah tought ya wanted me t'git ya sumthin' ta eat.

ROXY: Forgit 'bout de food fer now. Go to Tom en tell him dat his po' ole nigger Mammy wants ta see him.

CHAMBERS: It ain't gwine do no good. He ain't gwine see ya.

ROXY: How ya know?

CHAMBERS: Ah know Tom en Ah know how he feel 'bout niggers. He ain't gwine see ya, en he certainly ain't gwine give ya no money even if he had it ta give. De on'y thang he gwine do is liable to gimme a cuff upside de head fer axing.

She smacks him.

ROXY: What Tom will do ta ya be nothin' compared ta de beatin' Ah'm gwine give ya iffen ya don' do as Ah tell ya. Ya unnerstand me?

CHAMBERS: Ah got ya, Mammy. Ah'ma goin'. Good to see ya ag'in, Mammy.

ROXY: Good to see ya too, Chambers.

> *She smacks him.*

ROXY: Now do as Ah tell ya.

> *CHAMBERS moves to PUDD'NHEAD, TOM, and CECIL.*

TOM: One thing you have to understand about the Italians. Back East, folks look at them just like they look at the Irish. They're nothing more than a cut above the niggers.

CHAMBERS: Marster Tom?

TOM: What is it?

CHAMBERS: Got a message fer ya, Marster.

> *CHAMBERS has a note.*

TOM: What does it say?

CHAMBERS: Don' know, Marster.

TOM: Didn't ya read it?

CHAMBERS: Nawsir.

TOM: Why not?

CHAMBERS: Cain't read, Marster.

TOM: Course you can't. Well don't just stand there. Bring it to me.

> *CHAMBERS hands the note to TOM.*

Well, well, what do we have here? Seems as if your fella Sam decided that his life was worth more than his pride.

> *TOM hands the note to CECIL.*

It's a formal apology from Sam Childress. He apologizes for the insult and begs my forgiveness. Pudd'nhead? I think you have something of mine.

CECIL (*Reading the note*): You knew all along he wasn't coming.

TOM: Course I knew. Told ya, I only bet when it's a sure thing.

CECIL: How did you know?

TOM: Sam may be a good shot, but I am better, and Sam knows it. There is not another man within a hundred miles who can handle a pistol better than I. And while Sam's pride may have encouraged him to keep all previous engagements, I believe his will to live is stronger than his pride, ergo, his apology. You see, Pudd'nhead, when it comes to the science of human nature, I know what I'm talking about. Now gimme my money.

> PUDD'NHEAD *hands over the money.*

WILSON: You may be right about Sam, but you're wrong about everything else.

TOM: Is that right? Is that what you think? Chambers? Come here.

CHAMBERS: Marster?

TOM: Looka here, Pudd'nhead. See this here nigger? Big as a mountain, strong as an ox. This nigger was built for working. Chambers? Here.

> TOM *offers* CHAMBERS *his pistol.*

Take the pistol.

CHAMBERS: Marster?

TOM: Take the pistol.

CHAMBERS: What ya want me t'take it fer?

TOM: Don't ask questions, nigger, just take the pistol.

CHAMBERS: Ah cain't, Marster.

TOM: Take it.

CHAMBERS: Please, Marster.

TOM: You want me to smash your head like a grape? Is that what you want?

CHAMBERS: No, Marster.

TOM: Then take the pistol.

CHAMBERS: Please don' make me do dis.

TOM: I said take the pistol, you stupid nigger!

> TOM *swipes at* CHAMBERS. CHAMBERS *lets out a yelp but avoids the blow.*

Take it!

WILSON: That's enough, Tom!

TOM: I'm proving a point here, Pudd'nhead.

WILSON: He's not gonna take it.

CECIL: Not if he knows what's good for him.

WILSON: He knows what'll happen to him if he gets caught holding that pistol.

TOM: Come here, Chambers.

> *CHAMBERS cowers.*

Come on. I'm not gonna hit ya. I promise. Come here.

> *CHAMBERS moves closer.*

Listen to me. I want you to take the pistol, but you're not gonna get in trouble, okay? We're doing an experiment here. A scientific experiment. I want you to take it and I want you to see if you can fire it. Okay?

CHAMBERS: Please, Marster, please don' make me do dis, Marster.

TOM: You're gonna do it and that's all there is to it. Don't make me lose my temper cause you know what will happen if I lose my temper. Now take the goddamn pistol.

> *CHAMBERS reaches out, takes the pistol.*

Now hold it in your hand like you're gonna fire it.

CHAMBERS: Please, Marster.

TOM: Do it!

> *TOM hits CHAMBERS. In an instant, there is a flash of anger in CHAMBERS's eyes as he points the pistol directly at TOM. TOM smiles, amused. CHAMBERS realizes what he has done and is aghast. He lets out a yelp, drops the pistol as if the pistol were red-hot, then nurses his hand as if he had been burnt.*

See what I'm saying?

WILSON: That doesn't prove anything.

TOM: Why can't you hold the pistol, Chambers?

CHAMBERS: Please Marster, Ah don' know how. Mah han' ain't right. It don' fit. It's too slippery. Mah fingers are too big. Mah han' is too small. Please don' make me hold dat pistol ag'in.

ROWENA: Alright, Tom, leave him alone.

TOM: I was proving a point.

ROWENA: You proved your point, now leave him alone. Poor boy. Breaks my heart to see a nigger carrying on that away. Pudd'nhead? You coming to the party tonight?

WILSON: Wouldn't miss it.

ROWENA: Cecil?

CECIL: That was my last twenty dollars.

ROWENA: I'm going home and getting dressed.

WILSON: I'll walk that way with you.

ROWENA: And Tom, you ought to think about doing the same.

TOM: Don't worry about Tom. Tom can take care of himself. Cecil? How would you like to have a chance to win your money back?

CECIL: I ain't betting you no more, Tom.

TOM: The choice is yours.

> PUDD'NHEAD, ROWENA, and CECIL exit. TOM counts his winnings.

CHAMBERS: Marster Tom?

TOM: What is it?

CHAMBERS: Ya 'member mah mammy?

TOM: Your mammy?

CHAMBERS: Roxy by name, Marster Tom.

TOM: Yeah, I remember the ole wench. What about her?

CHAMBERS: She come back, Marster Tom.

TOM: She escape?

CHAMBERS: Nawsir. She say her Marster set her free befo' she died.

TOM: Well, good for her.

CHAMBERS: She say she wants t'see ya, Marster Tom. She say she wants t'have sight o' ya jes one more time befo' she die.

TOM: Who gave you permission to come and disturb me with the social attentions of niggers?

> TOM smacks CHAMBERS a couple of times.

CHAMBERS: Please, Marster Tom. Oh please!

ROXY *moves into the space. When* TOM *sees her, he stops beating* CHAMBERS.

ROXY: Mah lan', how you is growed, honey! 'Clah to goodness, Ah wouldn't a knowed you, Marster Tom! 'Deed Ah wouldn't!

TOM: Well, what d'we have here?

CHAMBERS: Kin Ah go, Marster Tom?

TOM: Go home. But stay close where I can find you if I need you.

CHAMBERS: Yassir.

CHAMBERS *runs off.*

ROXY: 'Clah to goodness, Ah wouldn't a knowed ya, Marster Tom! Does ya 'member me? Ole Roxy? Does ya know yo' ole nigger mammy, honey? Well now, Ah kin lay down en die in peace, cause Ah's seen't—

TOM: Cut it short and get to the point. What do you want?

ROXY: Ya heah dat? Jes de same ole Marster Tom, al'ays so gay en funnin' wid de ole mammy. Ah's jes as shore—

TOM: I said cut it short, goddamn it! What do you want?

ROXY: Please, Marster Tom, don' be short wid yo' ole nigger mammy.

TOM: I'll speak to you any way I damn well please. Now I'm gonna ask you for the last time. What do you want?

ROXY: Marster Tom, de po' ole mammy is in such hard luck dese days; en she's kinda crippled in de legs en cain't werk, en if ya could gimme a dollah—on'y jes one lil dol—

TOM: A dollar! Give you a dollar! Did hell freeze over and somebody not tell me about it? A dollar. Is that what you've come here for? Clear out! And be quick about it!

ROXY: Marster Tom, Ah nussed ya when ya was a lil baby, en Ah raised ya all by myself 'til ya was 'most a young man. En now you is young en rich, en Ah is po' en gittin' ole, en Ah come heah b'lievin' dat ya would he'p de ole mammy 'long down de lil road dat's lef' 'twix her en de grave.

TOM: I'll help you into the grave if that's what you want. You want me to help you into the grave? It'll be my pleasure.

ROXY: Ya ain't gwine he'p yo' ole mammy?

TOM: What did I tell ya? Now get away from me, you nigger wench, before I give you a boot in the ass.

ROXY: Lawd have mercy. Ah put boots on a barefoot nigger en what does he do? He tromples me wid 'em.

TOM: What? What did you say?

ROXY: T'ain't what Ah said. Tis what ya said en ya has said de word. Ya has had yo' chance, en ya has trompled it under yo' foot. When Ah give ya 'nother one, you'll git down on yo' knees en beg fer it.

TOM: When you give me a chance? You? Oh lawdy hab mercy on mah soul. Perhaps Ah better get down on mah knees right now!

ROXY: Perhaps ya better.

TOM: And if I don't?

ROXY: En iffen ya don', Ah's gwine as straight to yo' daddy as Ah kin walk, en tell him e'ry las' thang Ah knows 'bout you.

TOM: What do you know about me, you ole wench? That I was smacking around that boy of yours? Is that what you gonna run and tell my daddy?

ROXY: Nawsir. Dat jes ain't nothin' at all, 'longside o' what Ah knows.

TOM: What? That I was gambling? Is that it?

ROXY: Ah'm servin' up roasted ham en ya still chewin' on chitlens.

TOM: Then what do you know about me? Tell me.

ROXY: Ah knows dat yo' daddy tuck 'n' dissenhurrit ya frum his will. Ah knows dat. En Ah also knows dat iffen yo' daddy finds out what Ah knows 'bout ya, he'll take en bu'st dat will to flinders—en more, mind ya, more!

TOM: What more could he possibly do?

ROXY: Ya find out soon enuf.

TOM: Roxy, look, I'm sorry I was a bit short with you, but here. Here's your dollar—now tell me what you know.

TOM holds out a bill to ROXY. She doesn't take it.

ROXY: So, you a bit inner-rested now, wid yo' po' lil ole rag dollah. What ya reckon Ah's gwine t'tell ya mah secret fer? Ya ain't got no money. Ah's gwine t'tell yo' daddy. En Ah'll do it dis minute, too. He'll gimme five dollahs fer de news. En he'll be mighty glad t'do it too.

TOM: Wait, Roxy, listen to me. You're right, you and me, we're like old friends and we shouldn't quarrel. Let's talk. As one friend to another.

ROXY: Ya wanna talk? Meet me at de ole McVicker's place 'bout ten or 'leven tonight.

TOM: McVicker's place?

ROXY: De abandoned house next do' ta whar Pudd'nhead live. Meet me dere 'bout ten or 'leven en Ah'll tell ya everythin' Ah know. En don' let nobody see ya come in. En climb up de ladder, cause de sta'rsteps is broke down.

TOM: Why can't you just tell me now?

ROXY: Ah wanna give ya some time t'think. Ah want ya t'think on how Ah used t'nurse ya en tend t'ya en watch oveah ya when ya was sick. Ah want to give ya some time t'think on me en everythin' Ah done fer ya. Now gimme de money!

> *She takes the bill.*

En brang wid ya some food en some whiskey when ya come.

TOM: Whiskey?

ROXY: Good whiskey. De stuff dat Ah know yo' daddy keeps under lock en key.

TOM: You really starting to push your luck here.

ROXY: Don' worry. Ah promise ya, ya gwine git yo' money's werth.

TOM: En if not, I'm gonna take it outta your backside.

> *As ROXY and TOM exit, enter the twins, ANGELO and LUIGI. ANGELO is white, LUIGI is black. The twins are followed by JUDGE HOWARD, ROWENA, JUDGE DRISCOLL, CECIL, and PUDD'NHEAD. They are being attended to by CHAMBERS.*

> *The twins are performing for the assembled group. They sing the last phrase from Stephen Foster's "Old Black Joe."*

ANGELO and LUIGI:

> *I'm coming, I'm coming, for my head is bending low,*
> *I hear their gentle voices calling "Old Black Joe."*

> *The group applauds, the twins take a gracious bow.*

DRISCOLL: My God, they do look alike, don't they?

ROWENA: Of course they do. Spitting images of each other.

CECIL: Like one man looking in a mirror.

WILSON: I don't think they look anything alike.

CECIL: Pudd'nhead?

DRISCOLL: Wilson? How can you say such a thing? Can't you see them standing there?

WILSON: I can see them and I think they look different.

ROWENA: They're European, Pudd'nhead. Europeans naturally look different.

WILSON: That's not what I mean. I think one looks a little darker than the other.

DRISCOLL: It's the light, Wilson. The light in here in atrocious. Rowena, remind me at some point in time to get that light fixed.

HOWARD: Hold on a minute, Judge Driscoll. I agree with Wilson. I think I can tell these boys apart.

DRISCOLL: I don't see how that's possible, Judge Howard.

HOWARD: That's because you're not really looking at them, Judge Driscoll.

DRISCOLL: I'm standing here, they're standing there, I'd like to know what I'm doing if I'm not looking at them, Judge Howard.

HOWARD: You may be looking at them, but you don't actually see them. All you can see is what you think they are. You think they are a pair of Italian twins, therefore, that's all you can see. What you have to do, in this case, is look past what you think. You have to look past all of the trappings and all of the finery or lack thereof and see the essence of who these men are. That's what being a judge is all about. Once you learn how to see the who as opposed to the what, identification becomes simple.

   He points to LUIGI.

That one is Angelo.

ANGELO: I am Angelo.

LUIGI: And I am Luigi.

DRISCOLL: And I am impressed.

CECIL (*To HOWARD*): So much for your high flaunting theories.

DRISCOLL: Where'd you boys learn to sing like that?

ANGELO: We're musical . . .

LUIGI: Prodigies.

ANGELO: And we've made it a point . . .

LUIGI: To learn the music . . .

ANGELO: Of every place we've visited.

DRISCOLL: I understand that you boys are also of nobility.

LUIGI: Yes, we were pretty well-to-do back in Italy.

ANGELO: But when the war broke out, our father was on the losing side.

LUIGI: He and our mother paid with their lives.

ANGELO: Our estates were confiscated.

LUIGI: Our personal property seized.

ANGELO: And there we were, in Germany . . .

LUIGI: Strangers, friendless, and in fact paupers.

ANGELO: We were abducted, sold, and consequently placed among the attractions of a traveling museum in Berlin.

LUIGI: It took us two years to get out of that slavery.

ANGELO: When we escaped at twelve years of age, we were, in some respects, men.

LUIGI: We traveled everywhere.

ANGELO: Venice.

LUIGI: London.

ANGELO: Paris.

LUIGI: Russia.

ANGELO: India.

LUIGI: China.

ANGELO: Australia.

LUIGI: And now, we are here in the United States of America.

NANCY: 'Cuse me, Marster Driscoll, but de house is plum jam full o' people, en dey's jes a spi'lin' to see de gen'lemen!

DRISCOLL: I suppose we ought to not wait any longer. Anybody seen Tom around?

NANCY: Nobody, Marster Driscoll.

DRISCOLL: Chambers?

CHAMBERS: Ah ain't seen't him, Marster Driscoll.

DRISCOLL: Maybe he'll join us later. If not, you'll have to wait 'til the morning to meet my boy, Tom. Shall we join the rest of the party?

ANGELO: Let's join . . .

LUIGI: The rest of the party.

All exit as TOM joins ROXY in the haunted house.

ROXY: Whar's mah food?

TOM: Brought you some corn pone.

ROXY: Whiskey?

TOM: Tell me what you brought me here to tell me first.

ROXY: Whiskey fust.

She takes the flask from him and takes a long drink.

TOM: God, it's filthy in here.

ROXY: What ya 'spect? Don' nobody live heah.

TOM: Looks like you're living here.

ROXY: Cain't 'ford to roos' no whar else. Had to roos' somewhar.

TOM: Least you can do is straighten the place up a bit.

ROXY: Cain't you nor God make me clean 'nother sumbody else's house.

TOM: I'm tired of messing with you, Roxy. I want you to tell me what you brought me here to tell me.

ROXY: Fust, ya tell me sumthin', Tom. Are ya afeard?

TOM: Afraid of what?

ROXY: Dis house.

TOM: Why would I be afraid of this house?

ROXY: Haunted house.

TOM: Is that right?

ROXY: Dats right. Dey say dis house is full o' ghosts. Full o' spirits o' folks frum de past who died en come back to make life a misery fer de folks who still living. Ya b'lieve in dat, Tom? Ya b'lieve in ghosts? Ya ever see a spirit befo'?

TOM: Never have.

ROXY: Never?

TOM: Nobody but niggers believe that nigger superstition.

ROXY: Den ya ought to b'lieve it cause you's a nigger.

TOM: What did you say?

ROXY: Ah said you's a nigger. You's bawn a nigger en raised a nigger 'til you's five months ole. You's bawn a nigger en a slave, en you's a nigger en a slave right dis minute.

TOM: That's what you brought me here to tell me?

ROXY: Dat's right. En if Ah opens mah mouf, yo' sweet white world will turn as black as a fresh-off-de-boat nigger at night.

TOM: Wasting my precious time over this nonsense . . . I ought to beat you 'til you learn some respect.

ROXY: Raise a han' to me, Ah'll tell Marster Driscoll everythin' en he'll sell ya down de river befo' you's two days older den what ya is now.

TOM: What you gonna tell him?

ROXY: De truth. Ah'll tell him dat you is mah son.

TOM: Your son?

ROXY: Dat's right. You's a nigger en Ah knows you's a nigger cause you's mah son. Mah baby.

TOM: That's good. That's funny. Yeah, that's a good one.

ROXY: Ah switched ya wid dat po' boy dat you's be'n a kickin' en a cuffin'. His name's Tom Driscoll, not you, en he's yo' Marster. En yo' name's Chambers, en you ain't got no fambly name, cause niggers don' have em!

TOM: That's it, you miserable old blatherskite. You're about to get the beating of your life.

ROXY: Set down, ya lil snot-nosed pup. Does ya think ya kin skyer me? It ain't in ya, nor de likes o' ya. Ah reckon ya'd shoot me in de back, maybe, if ya got a chance, fer dat's jes yo' style. See? Ah knows ya, thru en thru. En Ah'll tell ya sumthin' else. Ah don' mind gettin' kilt, cause all dis is down in writin' en it's in safe han's, too, en de man in St. Louie dat's got it knows whah to do iffen Ah gits kilt. Oh, bless yo' soul, if you puts yo' mother up fer as big a fool as you is, you's pow'ful mistaken, Ah kin tell ya! Ah said set down!

TOM: Look, Roxy, what do you want with me?

ROXY: Fust o' all, Ah wants ya t'stop calling me Roxy de same as if ya was mah equal. Chilluns don' speak to dey mammies like dat. You'll call me ma or mammy, dat's what you'll call me. Leastways when dere ain't nobody 'round.

TOM: You're not my mother. My mother died in childbirth.

ROXY: De white lady ya think was yo' momma died in chilebirth. Ya en e'rybody else think she was yo' momma but Ah's de woman what gave birth t'ya. She gave birth t'de udder boy en Ah tuck ker o' bofe o' ya. Den Ah seen't what type o' life was waiting fer ya as a nigger so Ah switched ya wid dat boy. Ah put his clo'es on yo' back en yo' clot'es onto his. Now e'rybody thinks dat you is de rich white gen'leman en him de nigger. But Ah kin put thangs back de way dey was. All Ah gots to do is open mah mouf . . .

TOM: Go ahead. Tell whomsoever you want. Nobody's gonna believe this thundering lie.

ROXY: Ya think Ah'm lying? Dat what ya think? Ya think Ah'm standin' here, lookin' ya in de eye en lying? Den turn yo' back on me en walk out dat do'. Go 'head. Turn yo' back on me, walk straight out dat do', en leave me heah iffen ya b'lieve dat Ah'm lying en dat nobody's gwine b'lieve me. Go 'head, Valet de Chambers, walk out de do' iffen dat's what ya b'lieve. Go 'head. Walk out de do'.

    TOM doesn't move.

Ah don' sees ya gwine no whar.

TOM: Look, Roxy . . .

ROXY: Mammy. Ah wants to hear ya call me Mammy.

TOM: Do we really have to . . .

ROXY: Say it or Ah'll be de one walkin' outta dat do' en ya won't see me ag'in 'til ya on yo' way down de river. Now say it.

TOM: Mammy.

ROXY: En don' ya ever forgit it ag'in, if ya knows what's good fer ya. If ya ever says Ah's lying ag'in, or if ya ever call me out mah name ag'in,

Ah'll tramp as straight to de judge as Ah kin walk, en tell him who you is, en prove it. Does ya b'lieve me when Ah says dat?

TOM: Yes.

ROXY: Yes what?

TOM: Mammy.

ROXY: Good. Now den, we's gwine 'scuss bidness, en dey ain't gwine to be no mo' foolishness. In de fust place, ya gits fifty dollahs a month; you's gwine to han' over half o' it to yo' ma. Plank it out!

TOM: I don't have any more money.

ROXY: Ah think ya do en iffen ya don', ya bes' t'find some quick or ya gwine find yoself in a worl' o' trouble.

TOM: All I have is forty dollars. That's it.

ROXY: Ah'll take half.

TOM: I can't.

ROXY: Why not?

TOM: I need it.

ROXY: Fer what?

TOM: None of your business for what.

ROXY: O it's mah bidness alright. Ya gwine make it mah bidness. Either dat or Ah'm gwine make it yo' daddy's bidness.

TOM: Listen. There's a man. I owe him.

ROXY: What man?

TOM: I made a bet.

ROXY: Gambling? Ya owe money fer gambling? How much?

TOM: Nearly three hundred dollars.

ROXY: Tree hunnred dollahs? Lawd Jesus. How is ya gwine to pay tree hunnred dollahs?

TOM: I don't know. I haven't figured it out yet.

ROXY: Cain't ya git it frum yo' daddy?

TOM: He find out I've been gambling again, he'll never put me back into the will. And the money he does give me is just enough to cover the interest on the money I owe.

ROXY: Interest? What's dat?

TOM: Money they charge you for owing money. Papa gives me fifty dollars a month. I pay thirty in interest. The three hundred stays even. I been trying to make it up by placing small wagers here and there. Playing poker, rolling bones . . .

ROXY: Dat's what got ya in dis mess in de fust place, ya fool.

TOM: I know that.

ROXY: Number one, ya gotta stop gambling, Chambers. Number two, ya gotta find a way to git mo' money frum someplace.

TOM: And how do you propose I do that?

ROXY: De new white folk dat jes come to town look rich.

TOM: The Italians?

ROXY: Ah seen't dem wid a oak chess dat look like it was fulla gold en jewels.

TOM: And what does that have to do with me?

ROXY: Dey ain't gwine hardly miss tree hunnred dollahs werth o' gold en jewels.

TOM: You're suggesting that I steal?

ROXY: En what's wrong wid dat? Ain't de white folks done stole frum us all our lives? Ain't dey stole mah labor, werkin' me frum kin to cain't without paying me a howyado or t'ank you? En heah Ah is now, broke down en cain't werk, alls Ah's axing fer is a lil money to buy some food en ta keep a place to roos' dat ain't haunted. If ya gots to steal frum de white folks what stole frum us to gimme dat, Ah don' ker. But Ah ain't gwine crawl up en die whist you's living like a king, Chambers. Ah ain't gwine do it. Ya unnerstand me?

TOM: Roxy? I want to know the truth.

ROXY: What did ya call me?

TOM: Are you really my mother?

ROXY: Look at me, Chambers. Look at me real hard. Look at mah face, look at mah eyes.

> TOM *looks into her eyes, then looks away.*

Now straighten yoself up. Make yoself presentable. Ya gots some werk to do.

*The twins enter followed by HOWARD, ROWENA, JUDGE
DRISCOLL, CECIL, PUDD'NHEAD, NANCY, and
CHAMBERS. The twins sing* "Old Black Joe".

ANGELO:

Gone are the days when my heart was young and gay,

LUIGI:

Gone are my friends from the cotton fields away,

ANGELO:

Gone from the earth to a better land I know,

LUIGI:

I hear their gentle voices calling "Old Black Joe."

ANGELO and LUIGI:

I'm coming, I'm coming, for my head is bending low,
I hear their gentle voices calling "Old Black Joe."

ANGELO:

Where are the hearts once so happy and so free?

LUIGI:

The children so dear that I held upon my knee?

ANGELO:

Gone to the shore where my soul has longed to go,

LUIGI:

I hear their gentle voices calling "Old Black Joe."

LUIGI and ANGELO:

I'm coming, I'm coming, for my head is bending low,
I hear their gentle voices calling Old Black—

*TOM enters. The music stops. All turn to see TOM. All except the
twins call out.*

ALL: Tom!

End of Act One

ACT TWO

WILSON addresses the audience.

WILSON: The strangers were a hit. The reception went well past eleven thirty that night, and before it had ended, the strangers had accepted invitations from almost everybody in town. But it was Judge Driscoll who had the good fortune to secure them for a tour of the town the next morning. It was Judge Driscoll who was to be the first to display them in public. The next morning they climbed into the Judge's buckboard and were paraded down the main street of town, with everybody flocking to the windows and sidewalks to see. And rightly so, cause Judge Driscoll was the closest thing to a town father Dawson's Landing ever had.

    TOM enters.

TOM: Wilson? What you doing here?

WILSON: Your father asked me to meet him here.

TOM: Who were you talking to?

WILSON: When?

TOM: Just now, when I walked up. Looked like you were holding a conversation. Who were you conversating with?

WILSON: Nobody.

TOM: Nobody?

    He looks around.

And you wonder why they call you Pudd'nhead.

    ROWENA enters.

ROWENA: Morning, Tom, Wilson.

WILSON: Morning, Rowena.

TOM: Hey sweetness. Went by your house this morning looking for you.

ROWENA: Well, I ain't there.

TOM: I can see that. Thought maybe you'd be up for taking a walk down by Jacob's Pond this morning.

ROWENA: A walk?

TOM: You know. Take a walk. Take in a little bit of nature.

ROWENA: Ain't it a little early in the day for all that?

TOM: Never too early in the day for taking in a little nature.

ROWENA: Your daddy asked me to make some mid-morning refreshments for him and the strangers.

TOM: My daddy ain't here right now.

ROWENA: I know that, Tom. But he's gonna be back at any moment.

WILSON: They should've been back long before now. Your father must be showing them strangers every single nail and board in this town.

ROWENA: How about I pour you a nice tall glass of lemonade while we wait?

TOM: I don't want no damn lemonade. I wanna take a walk.

ROWENA: Go ahead. Ain't nobody stopping you.

TOM: It won't work if I go by myself.

ROWENA: If you want me to go with you, you gonna have to wait 'til your daddy gets back. Now you want some lemonade or not?

TOM: I'll get it myself. I swear.

     TOM exits.

ROWENA: How about you, Pudd'nhead? You wanna lil something cool to drink?

WILSON: Thank you, Miss Rowena. Lemonade sounds fine.

ROWENA: Alright.

     She turns to exit, then stops.

You mind if I ask you something and I know it ain't none of my business . . .

WILSON: Go right ahead.

ROWENA: Who were you out here talking to?

     JUDGE DRISCOLL enters, followed by ANGELO, LUIGI, and CHAMBERS.

DRISCOLL: You see, gentlemen, Dawson's Landing began as a slaveholding town with a rich history of slave-worked grain and pork which formed the backbone of this country. The town is almost a hundred years old and growing. We're growing slowly, but we are, nevertheless, growing. Rowena, you ready for us?

ROWENA: Ready, Your Honor.

DRISCOLL: At this point, gentlemen, we'll take a break and refresh ourselves with some of the best lemonade this side of Mason Dixon supplied by none other than our own Rowena. Rowena?

ROWENA: Coming right out.

ROWENA exits.

DRISCOLL: That girl's gonna make some man a fine wife one day. Chambers?

CHAMBERS: Yassir?

DRISCOLL: Unhitch and water the horses.

CHAMBERS: Yassir.

DRISCOLL: When you get done, go inside and get yourself something to eat. But don't go nowhere. I want you to stay close, stay out here in front where I can find you.

CHAMBERS: Yassir.

CHAMBERS exits as TOM enters.

DRISCOLL: Morning, Tom.

TOM: We been sitting here waiting for you all morning, Daddy. Where you been?

DRISCOLL: Well, Tom, Dawson's Landing has many fine points of interest, all of which deserve special attention.

TOM: Exactly what points of interest are you talking about?

DRISCOLL: I showed them the new graveyard, and the jail, and where the richest man in town lives, and the Freemasons' hall, and the Methodist church, and the Presbyterian church, and where the Baptist church is going to be once we get some money to build it with. I showed them the town hall and the slaughterhouse, and I got out the independent fire company, in uniform, and had them put out an imaginary fire.

TOM: I'm sure they were thrilled.

DRISCOLL: They certainly appeared to be.

ROWENA and NANCY enter.

ROWENA: Your Honor, could I see you inside for a moment?

DRISCOLL: What is it?

ROWENA: There appears to be a problem.

DRISCOLL: What kind of problem? And where are the refreshments I asked you to bring? I'm sure these heah boys are parched dry.

ROWENA: That's just it, Your Honor. I wanna serve the lemonade but I can't seem to find any of your silverware.

NANCY: Ah didn't have nothin' to do wid it, Marster. Swear t'God, las' night, Ah put everythin' right back whar it belong.

DRISCOLL: It's probably just misplaced, Rowena.

ROWENA: If you say so. But I couldn't find any knives or teaspoons at my house this morning either. On top of that, I couldn't find any of my earrings, charms, or bracelets.

DRISCOLL: Excuse me, gentlemen.

DRISCOLL exits, followed by NANCY and ROWENA.

TOM: You think we might have been robbed?

WILSON: Robbed? I doubt it.

TOM: That's what it sounds like to me. This might be a case for you, Wilson. Ole Wilson here is a lawyer. Did he tell ya? He's a bona fide attorney. But he doesn't practice, hasn't had a chance to practice in the twenty-something-odd years he's been here in Dawson's Landing. Seems like nobody wants to be represented in the halls of justice by a man known as Pudd'nhead.

WILSON: I haven't practiced but I've kept up my studies. I've kept myself sharp by working as a notary.

TOM: In addition to working hoodoo. Ole Pudd'nhead here's got a scheme for driving plain glass window panes out of the market by decorating them with greasy finger marks.

WILSON: Actually, I believe you can read a man by looking at the markings on his hands.

ANGELO: You're versed in palmistry?

WILSON: I wouldn't consider myself to be versed. I'm more of a neophyte than anything else.

TOM: Neophyte, hell. Wilson can read your wrinkles as easy as reading a book, and not only tell you fifty or sixty things that's gonna to happen to you, but fifty or sixty thousand that ain't. Come on,

Dave, give us a show. Look at the marks on my hand and show the gentlemen what an inspired jack-at-all-science you are.

WILSON: Not now, Tom.

ANGELO: Actually, we know a little about palmistry ourselves . . .

LUIGI: We've seen it in our wanderings . . .

ANGELO: And we know very well what astonishing things it can do.

TOM: You ain't serious, are you?

LUIGI: Four years ago we had our hands read to us as if our palms had been covered with print.

TOM: You mean to say that there is actually something to it?

ANGELO: There's more than something to it. What was read of our characters was minutely exact. In fact, we could not have done better ourselves. During that reading, two or three memorable events from our past were laid bare. And these were things which no one but ourselves could have known about.

TOM: Well I'll be dipped. Let's see how well ole Dave here does. Come on, Dave. Give us a show.

WILSON: I have to warn you, I'm not an expert, and I don't claim to be one.

LUIGI: Show us, Mister Wilson. You can begin with me.

TOM: Wait. Don't look yet, Dave. Count Luigi, here's a paper and pencil. Set to paper one of them striking prophecies that you said came true. Set it to paper, then give it to me so I can see if Dave finds it in your hand.

LUIGI takes the paper and begins to write.

You see, I think all of this nonsense about reading wrinkles, telling the future, and reading the past is all rank sorcery. That's what I think. But we'll see how well you fare.

WILSON: Again, I don't claim to be an expert.

TOM: Nobody's suggesting that you are, Dave. Nobody's suggesting you are.

LUIGI folds the paper and hands it to TOM.

Now let's see how well you do.

WILSON starts to examine LUIGI's hand.

Well? See anything?

WILSON: Yes, in fact. (*To LUIGI*) But I don't think you would want me to divulge your uh ...

LUIGI: Please feel free to tell us all what you see, Mister Wilson. I promise, whatever you say will not be an embarrassment. Tell us.

TOM: Yeah, Wilson, tell us.

WILSON: Well, according to this, you have killed someone, but whether man, woman, or child, I can't quite make out.

TOM: Jesus.

LUIGI: Now, Mister Driscoll, why don't you read aloud what I wrote.

TOM unfolds the first paper and reads.

TOM (*Reading*): "It was prophesied that I would kill a man. It came true before the year was out." Christ. This beats the hell out of anything I've ever heard of. You saw that in his hand?

WILSON: As I said, I can generally detect when a past event is prominently recorded in the palm.

TOM: I've never seen such a damned thing in all my life. Just think of that. A man's own hand keeping a record of the deepest and fatalest secrets of his life? Goddamn. You know what that means? That means that a man's own hand could be his deadliest enemy. (*To LUIGI*) Why do you let a person look at your hand, with that awful thing printed on it?

LUIGI: I don't mind.

TOM: You don't mind?

LUIGI: I killed the man for a good reason, and I don't regret it.

TOM: And what reason did you have for killing the man?

LUIGI: He needed killing.

ANGELO: I'll tell you why he did it, cause he won't say himself.

TOM: Somebody tell me something.

ANGELO: He did it to save my life. We were staying at the palace in Brunei while visiting with the Sultan, when one night a native stole into our room while we were sleeping.

LUIGI: The native had heard rumors about a knife that had been in our family for two hundred and fifty years.

ANGELO: A knife polished like a mirror with edges like a razor and a handle made of solid ivory as thick as a man's wrist. The ivory is inlaid with precious jewels and is engraved with our family's coat of arms. Would you like to see it?

WILSON: I would love to see it.

LUIGI: The native who had stolen into our room had come to kill us and steal the knife for the fortune encrusted in its handle.

ANGELO: Luigi had it under his pillow. We were in two small beds which were placed side by side. There was a dim night light burning. I was asleep, but Luigi was awake, and he thought he detected a vague form nearing the beds. Luigi slipped the knife out of the sheath when suddenly the native rose between us. The native bent over me and with his right hand lifted a dagger and aimed at my throat. Luigi rose up behind him, grabbed his wrist from behind, pulled him backwards and drove the knife into the man's back.

> *CHAMBERS enters. He sits on the periphery of the space and unwraps something to eat.*

LUIGI: I killed the man, and while I am not proud of it, I am certainly not ashamed.

ANGELO: I'll get the knife and show you.

> *ANGELO exits. CHAMBERS bites into his sandwich.*

WILSON: And while he's doing that, let me take a look at the marks on your hand, Tom. Let's see what kind of secrets you have hidden away there.

TOM: Keep your goddamn hands off of me.

WILSON: Sorry.

TOM: I don't have any secrets . . .

WILSON: I said I was sorry.

TOM: So just stay away from me.

WILSON: What's the matter with you?

TOM: Nothing's the matter with me. What's the matter with you?

LUIGI: All he wanted to do was have a look at the creases in your hand.

TOM: There's nothing here for him to see. Nothing.

LUIGI: Look at him. He's blushing.

TOM: Well, if I am, it ain't because I'm a murderer.

WILSON: Tom, that was uncalled for.

TOM: That's what he is. A goddamn murderer looking for secrets in people's hands. But he won't find anything here. That's right. There's nothing here for either one of you to see. (*To CHAMBERS*) And what the hell are you looking at?

CHAMBERS: Nothin', Marster.

TOM: What are you doing out heah anyway? Who told you you could sit out heah? Did I say you could sit out heah?

CHAMBERS: Nawsir.

TOM: Then what the hell you doing sitting out here?

CHAMBERS: Nothin', Marster Driscoll.

TOM: Don't look like nothing to me. Looks to me like you gettin' ready to sit there and have yourself something to eat.

CHAMBERS: Yassir.

TOM: Can't you see us oveh heah having a conversation?

CHAMBERS: Yassir.

TOM: And what makes you think I wanna sit heah and watch a nigger eat?

WILSON: Tom, your father told him to . . .

TOM: I don't care what my daddy told him. I'm not gonna sit here and watch a nigger eat.

LUIGI: Then go inside.

TOM: Pardon me?

LUIGI: I said, if you don't want to sit here and watch him eat, go inside.

TOM: This ain't none of your business, Mister.

WILSON: Chambers, go around back and finish your lunch.

TOM: Don't you try to tell him what to do.

WILSON: When the judge comes looking for you, I'll tell him where you are.

TOM: That's my nigger, Pudd'nhead. I own that nigger. He answers to me and to nobody but me.

LUIGI: That's an illusion, to think that you own this man.

TOM: I understand that you're a stranger and all, and that as a stranger, you're unfamiliar with the going-ons in this here part of the world, but if I were you, I'd keep my nose outta other people's business.

LUIGI: If you were me, you would be a lot smarter and more compassionate.

WILSON: Count Luigi, please.

TOM: You're really starting to test the elasticity of my hospitality, Mister.

LUIGI: You don't own this man any more than I was owned by the men who enslaved me and my brother. They, like you, did what they could to change who we were in order to justify their brutality. They burned our estates, they murdered our parents, they tried to erase our culture by making us believe we were something other than what we actually were, but I never, for one moment, believed what they said I was and therefore, never became what they wanted me to be. And now when you look at me, what do you see? A man who was once a slave, a prince? I dare say that you see what I want you to see, Mister Driscoll, you see who I say I am, not what others say I should be.

TOM: I don't know what happened over there in Europe and I don't care. The only thing I care about is the law of the state of Missouri, and according to the law of the state of Missouri, this man belongs to me. He is mine 'til I say otherwise.

LUIGI: The law of the state of Missouri is a man-made law and any law made by man is flawed, Mister Driscoll.

TOM: Is that what you think?

LUIGI: That's what I know. That's what experience has taught me. The only law you can count on is the law of chance and the law of fortune. That's the only law I recognize.

TOM: You may want to rethink that position while standing foot inside the state of Missouri, Mister.

LUIGI: The circumstances could have been reversed. Fortune could have smiled upon him and frowned upon you. You could very well have been the slave and he, your master.

TOM: You calling me a nigger?

WILSON: He didn't say that, Tom.

TOM: Then what did he say? What you trying to say? You trying to call me a nigger or not?

LUIGI: Depends on your definition of the word nigger.

WILSON: Oh God.

TOM: If I had a gun I would kill you where you stand.

WILSON: Alright, that's enough.

LUIGI: Don't let the circumstances stop you from trying.

WILSON: Count Luigi . . .

TOM: I demand satisfaction.

WILSON: Tom!

LUIGI: And I am more than happy to assist you in your quest.

WILSON: Please . . .

LUIGI: Name the time and place.

WILSON: Both of you, stop it!

TOM: You will be notified of the time and place within the next twenty-four hours, sir.

LUIGI: And I will be there.

WILSON: There's no need to do this.

TOM: Chambers? Let's go.

CHAMBERS: Yassir.

TOM and CHAMBERS exit.

WILSON: You don't have to go through with this.

LUIGI: The man deserves to be taught a lesson.

WILSON: But you don't have to be the one who does it.

DRISCOLL enters, followed by ANGELO and ROWENA.

DRISCOLL: Count Luigi, I am so sorry.

LUIGI: For what? What happened?

DRISCOLL: It's all my fault.

ROWENA: We have been robbed.

ANGELO: And our knife, our knife has been stolen.

ANGELO, LUIGI, DRISCOLL, and ROWENA exit.

WILSON (*To audience*): I tried to stop Tom from getting tangled up with Luigi. I did everything I could to stop it, but it was like arguing with a couple of drunks. Luigi was drunk with his sense of righteousness and Tom was intoxicated with the fear of being discovered.

The duel was set for noon the following day. Meanwhile, rumors started going around about the ole abandoned McVicker's place. There was always talk about it being haunted, but it seems as if some folks had actually heard voices coming from there at night.

> *WILSON exits as TOM and ROXY enter. ROXY carries a burlap bag full of loot that she begins to rummage through.*

ROXY: What ya got to go git yoself all tangled up wid dat eye-talian fer?

TOM: He called me a nigger.

ROXY: En ya tuck offense.

TOM: Wouldn't you?

> *He considers what he has said.*

Never mind.

ROXY: Gettin' called a nigger ain't no reason t'fight a man, Chambers.

TOM: I'm gonna fight him and I'm gonna kill him.

ROXY: Chambers . . .

TOM: He suspects something. He suspects something about me.

ROXY: Dat man don' 'spect nothin' 'bout ya.

TOM: I think he can see who I really am. Why else would he call me a nigger?

ROXY: He was trying to git at ya. Ain't ya got no sense at all? Man don' 'spect nothin'. How could he 'spect sumthin' when Ah ain't said nothin' to nobody 'bout sumthin'?

TOM: What about the man in St. Louis?

ROXY: What man in St. Louie?

TOM: You said you put everything down in writing and left it with a man in St. Louis.

ROXY: Dat's right. En don' ya forgit it, neither.

TOM: Whether he suspects something or not, he called me a nigger and now I'm gonna kill him.

ROXY: Ya cain't go 'round callin 'tention to yoself, Chambers. Ya got to try en steer clear o' trouble, en ya got to try en act like ya white.

TOM: That's what I was doing.

ROXY: Anybody see ya las' night befo' ya went t'de party?

TOM: Nobody but Pudd'nhead.

ROXY: Pudd'nhead Wilson?

TOM: He saw me but he didn't know what he was looking at.

ROXY: How could he not know what he was looking at?

TOM: I was in disguise.

ROXY: What kinda 'skies?

TOM: I was dressed up like a girl. Just in case somebody saw me, it would throw 'em off my trail. Good thing, too, cause Pudd'nhead was looking right at me.

ROXY: Ah swear ya ain't got de sense dat God gave a goose.

TOM: He didn't know what he was looking at. He's a pudd'nhead.

ROXY: Don' ya b'lieve what de folks in dis town say 'bout dat man. Dey calls him a pudd'nhead, en says he's a fool, but dat man ain't no mo' fool den Ah is! He's de smartes' man in dis town.

TOM: Pudd'nhead Wilson?

ROXY: Watch yoself 'round him, Chambers.

TOM: He's a fool, Mammy.

ROXY: You de fool judging by what ya tuck to be treasure. Looka dis.

> *She tosses things out of the bag.*

Silverware, dull, tarnished, en pitted? Junk. Bracelet made outta tin? Junk. Earrangs made outta colored glass en paste? Junk. All o' it werthless junk. Ain't werth de time en effort it's gwine t'take t'throw it all 'way.

TOM: What about this?

> *TOM produces the jewel-encrusted, ivory-handled dagger.*

ROXY: 'Sit real?

TOM: Oh yeah. It's real alright. Handle made outta solid ivory. And see these stones? Every one of these stones have to be worth thousands. Not only is it real, but it's highly coveted.

ROXY: Coveted?

TOM: Men have lost their lives trying to possess this knife.

ROXY: Dats not good.

TOM: What's not good?

ROXY: Knife might be janxed.

TOM: Aww, Mammy, that ain't nothing but nigger sup . . .

ROXY: Niggah what?

TOM: Nothing.

ROXY: Niggah superstition?

TOM: There's nothing wrong with this knife.

ROXY: Ya bes' start paying 'tention to niggah superstition.

TOM: It's all rank sorcery. Got nothing to do with me.

ROXY: Ya change yo' tune when it's standin' wid all four feet in yo' chess starin' ya in de face wid blood on its mouf.

TOM: The only thing I believe in is what I can touch, what I can see, and what I can hold in my hand. This knife, I can see, touch, and hold in my hand so I'm gonna take this knife, and I'm gonna sell it. I'm gonna sell it to the man I owe the gambling debt to. He deals in precious stones and he deals in jewels, and he shows up every two weeks to collect the interest on the money I owe. Instead of giving him the money, I'm gonna give him the knife. I'm gonna give him the knife in exchange for my marker plus five hundred dollars. And then, I ain't gonna gamble no more, I swear. I'm gonna stop drinking, I'm gonna stop gambling, Daddy's gonna put me back into the will, and I'm gonna take care of you. I'm gonna get you outta this haunted house and I'm gonna find you a place to live. Nice place to live somewhere. But first I got a little business to take care of with that Italian. After that, everything's gonna be alright.

> ROXY and TOM exit as WILSON enters examining his glass slides. He addresses the audience.

WILSON: I started to think about Tom's theories about the sheep. About his ideas on breeding, systems of selection, and propagation. I started to ask myself, what if Tom was right? What if education and training had absolutely no influence upon our stations in life? What if a cabbage, born a cabbage, was destined to remain a cabbage and could never grow into a cauliflower? And if this was true, what impact did chance and fortune have upon our lives?

WILSON exits as CECIL and ROWENA enter.

CECIL: Tom? Are you here, Tom?

TOM enters with a pair of pistols. He is followed by CHAMBERS.

What ya doing? Everybody's waiting for you.

TOM: I have been vandalized.

CECIL: Vandalized?

TOM: Somebody snuck into the house last night, found my dueling pistols, and sabotaged them.

CECIL: You sure?

TOM: Course I'm sure. I know my pistols, Cecil. Look at this.

He hands the pistols to CECIL.

The saboteur was extremely clever. When I opened the pistol case this morning, the pistols appeared to be undisturbed. However, once I began to practice my aim, I noticed that the sights had been tampered with.

CECIL: Looks okay to me.

TOM: That's because you don't know what you're looking at. Rowena, take a look at this pistol and tell me what you see.

ROWENA: I don't know nothing about pistols, Tom. At least not that kind of pistol.

TOM: You don't need to know anything about pistols to know that these pistols have been tampered with. Feel it. Feel the weight. Feels a bit too heavy. The balance is off. The weight is wrong, the trigger guard is too small, it doesn't feel right in my hand.

DRISCOLL and HOWARD enter.

DRISCOLL: Tom? Folks are waiting for you.

TOM: I know that, goddamn it. Why does everybody keep telling me that?

DRISCOLL: Chambers? Get that outta here. Cecil? Rowena? If you please.

CHAMBERS exits followed by CECIL and ROWENA.

DRISCOLL: You been drinking again, Tom?

TOM: No, sir. I swear. Didn't touch a drop.

DRISCOLL: Then you want to explain to me why you're not out on the field?

TOM: I'm not quite sure.

DRISCOLL: Ever since you were fifteen years old, you fought every man who looked at you sideways and now you sit here and cower in the face of an Italian? You worthless dog, you. You cur. What have I done to deserve this? Judge Howard? Will you be my second?

HOWARD: Of course I will, Judge Driscoll.

TOM: What're you doing?

DRISCOLL: Somebody has to defend the best blood of the Old Dominion and that somebody is clearly not you. And to think, I had considered nullifying your disinheritance. What a fool I had been.

TOM: No, Daddy, wait. I can explain. You see . . . he's a confessed assassin.

DRISCOLL: Who?

TOM: Count Luigi. He's a murderer. He killed a man outside the field of honor. Wilson detected it in his hand by palmistry, and charged him with it. After being charged, he confessed.

DRISCOLL: Why didn't you say something about this before?

TOM: They begged us to keep the secret, then swore they would lead honorable lives while they were here. In exchange, we gave our word not to expose them.

> *WILSON enters.*

WILSON: Judge? The twins are about to declare Tom in default.

TOM: And there's something else I think you should know.

DRISCOLL: What's that?

TOM: My pistols have been stolen.

DRISCOLL: Your pistols?

TOM: These are not my pistols. Somebody came into the house last night, stole my pistols, and left these two pieces of junk in their place.

HOWARD: If this is true, score another theft to the list.

DRISCOLL: The list?

HOWARD: The Dobsons, the Pilligrews, the Ortons, in fact everybody that lives around about Patsy Cooper's has been robbed of little things like trinkets and teaspoons and small valuables that are easily carried off. Wilson thinks that the thief is a young girl.

WILSON: I spotted her the night of the party. It was a girl I had never seen before. But don't worry. We will catch her.

TOM: How?

WILSON: She made a mistake when she stole the dagger belonging to the twins. It's a very valuable dagger that I'm sure she'll try to sell right off. We've distributed a description of the dagger and posted a reward. Five hundred dollars for the dagger.

HOWARD: And five hundred for the thief.

WILSON: The thief will try to sell or pawn the dagger.

HOWARD: And we will have her.

WILSON: I give it three days.

DRISCOLL: I can't tell them apart. These pistols. They look exactly like your pistols, Tom.

TOM: I couldn't tell them apart either. Not at first. But that's evidence of the depth of this chicanery.

HOWARD: Should I round up another set of pistols?

TOM: Daddy?

DRISCOLL: Wilson, my boy tells me that Count Luigi is a confessed assassin. Is this true?

WILSON: A what?

TOM: He killed a man outside the field of honor. You were there when he confessed it.

WILSON: Yes, but . . .

TOM: But what? He confessed. Wilson was there. He heard it.

WILSON: It was an act of self-defense, Your Honor.

TOM: Self-defense? He stabbed the man in the back, Daddy.

DRISCOLL: Is that true, Wilson?

TOM: Count Luigi said that the man deserved to be killed, then he snuck up behind him and stabbed him in his back. Am I right, Wilson? Did he stab him in the back or not?

WILSON: It sounds a lot more diabolical than it actually was.

TOM: I believe the answer to the question is either yes or no. Did he stab the man in his back or not?

DRISCOLL: Wilson?

WILSON: Your Honor . . .

TOM: See? He can't deny it. The man is a confessed assassin. Now, I would be more than happy to meet a gentleman on the field of honor, but a confessed assassin . . .

DRISCOLL: Wilson, inform the strangers that neither I nor my son will meet them on a field of honor. However, let it be known that elsewhere, I shall be ready.

   DRISCOLL and HOWARD exit as ANGELO and LUIGI enter.

ANGELO: And what did he say?

WILSON: He said that Luigi was a confessed assassin and that neither his son nor he will fight a confessed assassin. Well, he said that he will not fight you on a field of honor. Elsewhere, he said, he will be ready.

LUIGI: What does that mean?

WILSON: It means he will try to kill you on sight.

LUIGI: But I have done nothing to him.

WILSON: I tried to explain.

LUIGI: My quarrel is with his son.

WILSON: I know.

LUIGI: So what am I supposed to do? Sit here and wait for him to seek me out?

WILSON: You could leave town.

LUIGI: Run? You want me to run from a judge who has bad judgment? No, Mister Wilson. I will not run.

WILSON: Then your only other option is to try to kill him before he kills you.

LUIGI: And if I refuse to participate in this senseless game?

WILSON: He's gonna try to kill you, whether you participate or not. The only other option you have is to leave town.

LUIGI: I will not leave.

WILSON: Then you must prepare yourself for the consequences.

    TOM enters into the haunted house. ROXY appears.

ROXY: You's alive.

TOM: Course I'm alive.

ROXY: Ah be'n worried sick dat ya was dead.

TOM: Dead?

ROXY: Dat ya lost de duel. Dat ya was shot thru de heart, dead en buried en Ah wouldn't know it. Dat Ah'd be sittin' heah waiting fer ya en de man frum St. Louie would show up t'git his money en ya wouldn't be heah. You'd be dead.

TOM: I might as well be dead. I'm as good as dead.

ROXY: What's wrong?

TOM: We can't sell the dagger. There's a reward. If I give it to the man from St. Louis, he'll get caught when he tries to sell it and I know he'll turn me in.

ROXY: Tole ya it was janxed. Didn't Ah tell ya dat? Dat knife ain't gwine cause nothin' but trouble fer anybody who tetches it.

TOM: It's like a bag of gold that's turned to dirt and ashes before my very eyes.

ROXY: We gotta think.

TOM: We've gotta get outta here. We can't be here when that man shows up.

ROXY: En go whar?

TOM: I don't know.

ROXY: Runnin' ain't gwine he'p us. We got t'figure 'nother way out.

TOM: What other way? There is no other way.

ROXY: Dere is one udder way.

TOM: What?

ROXY: Ya cain't sell de knife. Ya kin take en sell me.

TOM: What?

ROXY: Ya kin sell me t'de man frum St. Louie. Ah's werth six hunnred dollahs. Dat's what ya kin do. Ya kin take en sell me, en pay off yo' debts.

TOM: You're willing to be sold into slavery to save me?

ROXY: Ain't ya mah chile? En does ya know anythin' dat a mother won' do fer her chile? Dere ain't nothin' a white mother won' do fer her chile. Who made 'em so? De Lawd done it. En who made de niggers? De Lawd made 'em. In de inside, mothers is all de same. Ah's gwine t'be sole into slavery, en in a year you's gwine t'buy yo' ole mammy free ag'in. Dat's de plan.

TOM: I'm sorry, Mammy, but I can't . . .

ROXY: Say dat ag'in.

TOM: What?

ROXY: Mammy. Call me yo' Mammy.

TOM: Mammy.

ROXY: Say it en keep on sayin' it, Chambers. It's all dat a body kin want in dis worl', en it's mo' den enuf. When Ah's slav' 'round, en dey 'buses me, if Ah knows you's a sayin' dat, 'way off yonder somewhar, it'll heal up all de sore places, en Ah kin stan' 'em.

TOM: It wouldn't work, Mammy. I mean, how would we do it? You're forgetting that you're free.

ROXY: Don' make no diff'rence. White folks ain't partic'lar. De law kin sell me now if dey tell me t'leave de state en Ah don' go.

LOU'S VOICE (*from off*): Tom? You in heah?

ROXY: Who dat?

TOM: The man from St. Louis.

ROXY: Take en sell me, Chambers.

TOM: How?

LOU'S VOICE: Tom?

TOM: Up here. Climb the ladder cause the stairs are broken.

ROXY: Ya say you'll sell me cheap cause you's hard up en you'll find ya ain't gwine to have no trouble. Den ya draw up a paper, a bill o' sale, en put it 'way off yonder, in de middle o' 'nother state somewhar, en sign some names to it.

TOM: What if people start asking questions?

ROXY: Ain't nobody gwine to ax no questions if Ah's a bargain. Jes make sho he keep me somewhar close, Chambers. Ya heah me? Ya make him give ya his word dat Ah will not git sole down de river.

LOU: Tom, Goddamn it, where are ya?

TOM: In here.

ROXY: Nigger shouldn't be 'round when de white folks is 'ducting bidness. Call me when it's time to 'spect me.

ROXY *exits as LOU enters.*

LOU: Why the hell you wanna meet in this spooky-ass place fer? I heard there were demons and devils and shit like that up in heah.

TOM: Don't tell me that a big strong man like you is afraid of a demon.

LOU: You say you had something for me. I hope it's my money.

TOM: I wanna square up with you.

LOU: Three hundred in principal and thirty in interest for this month. That's three hundred and thirty dollars.

TOM: I got something even better than money.

LOU: Gold?

TOM: Black gold.

LOU: You know I don't deal in slaves.

TOM: She's a good one, Lou. Worth at least six hundred dollars. I sign her over to you, you give me three hundred and we'll call it even.

LOU: Not interested.

TOM: You can make your money back and then some.

LOU: What did I just tell you?

TOM: Tell you what. I'll sell her to you cheap. I'll give her to you for what I owe plus one fifty, only cause I'm hard up heah. Now that's a good deal. Can't beat it. What d'ya say?

LOU: What kind of nigger? Carpenter? Blacksmith? House nigger? Field nigger, what?

TOM: Wet nurse. I know you can sell her for at least six hundred. Folks in St. Louis always looking for a good wet nurse.

LOU: I do know a man from Kentucky. He's got a family . . .

TOM: Kentucky?

LOU: Might be interested.

TOM: Down the river?

LOU: You sound like a nigger when you said that. Course it's down the river. Where did you think Kentucky was?

TOM: I'd rather you sold her locally, Lou.

LOU: If I take her, I'll sell her wherever I can. Now where is she? Let's have a look at her.

TOM: I gotta know about this man first.

LOU: What man?

TOM: The man from Kentucky.

LOU: What you need to know about him?

TOM: Is he a good man?

LOU: Is he a what?

TOM: A good man. Does he mistreat niggers?

LOU: Hell, I don't know.

TOM: I have to know, Lou.

LOU: What you concerned about it for? You attached to this nigger or something?

TOM: You could say that.

LOU: Soft on the eyes, is she? Know how to make a man happy?

TOM: She nursed me when I was little. The only mammy I've ever known. That's why I've got to make sure she doesn't go to somebody who's gonna mistreat her.

LOU: I don't think he's a cruel man if that's what you mean.

TOM: But is he a kind master?

LOU: Yeah, Tom, he's a kind master. One of the kindest. Now where is she?

TOM: Roxy? Get in heah.

        ROXY enters.

ROXY: Yassir, Marster Driscoll.

TOM: Here she is. One of the finest mammies on this side of Mason Dixon.

LOU: Kinda old, ain't she?

TOM: Not that old. Maybe around forty.

LOU: Look at dem arms. Lil bony. Looks a lil beat down to me.

TOM: She's not a field nigger, Lou. She's not supposed to be out picking cotton and tobacco. She's a mammy.

LOU: Alright. Open ya mouth and let's have a look.

TOM: Won't find anything rotten in there. No sir, she's been well taken care of.

LOU: Turn around.

>ROXY *slowly turns for inspection.*

She ever been sick?

TOM: Not a day in her life.

LOU: Can she cook?

TOM: Like a chef from Paris. But as I said, she's a mammy and I want her to be used as a mammy.

LOU: Yeah, yeah, I hear ya talking. Open your shirt. Let's have a look.

TOM: What?

LOU: She's supposed to be a nurse. I wanna see her tits.

>ROXY *opens her shirt for LOU, who continues to inspect her.*

You got papers on her?

TOM: At the house. I can get them for you later tonight.

LOU: I'll take her for an even trade.

TOM: Even trade?

LOU: That's right. I'll take her off your hands for ya and in return, I'll give you your marker and we'll call it even.

TOM: I can't do that.

LOU: Then give me my money. Three hundred and thirty dollars.

TOM: You're robbing me, you know that, Lou? It's like you're sticking a gun to my head.

LOU: You the one who stuck the gun to your head when you sat down to play poker and didn't have enough to cover your losses. So what you gonna do? You gonna give me the wench or you gonna give me my money?

TOM: The wench plus fifty.

LOU: You don't seem to understand, Tom. There is no negotiation heah. This is a take-it-or-leave-it proposition. And I suggest you take it before the wind blows and my streak of kindness evaporates.

TOM: Alright. Even trade.

LOU: That's my boy. When do I get the papers?

TOM: Tonight. Around nine?

LOU: You got yourself a deal. (*To ROXY*) Come on, nigger. If you got any belongings, you better get 'em if you wanna take 'em with ya cause you going with me.

TOM: How 'bout you take her later? When you come back to pick up her papers.

LOU: Don't try none of your shenanigans with me, Tom, cause I'll go straight to your daddy.

TOM: Nine o'clock. We'll be here.

LOU: See you then.

> *LOU exits.*

ROXY: How ya git yoself mixed up wid such a evil man?

TOM: He had money, I needed money.

ROXY: Who he gwine t'sell me to?

TOM: What makes you think he's gonna sell you?

ROXY: He ain't de kind o' man who keeps slaves, en he ain't de kind o' man who buys sumthin' without knowin' how he gwine sell dat sumthin' dat he bought, so who is he gwine sell me to or did ya sell me without findin' out furst?

TOM: There's a man.

ROXY: A man?

TOM: With a family.

ROXY: Whar's dis man frum?

TOM: St. Louis.

ROXY: En dat's whar I'm gwine? St. Louie?

TOM: That's where you're going. St. Louis.

ROXY: Good. Now yo' debts is paid off, Chambers, ya got to swear to me dat frum dis day forward ya gwine walk as straight as string.

TOM: I swear.

ROXY: Ya got to swear dat ya ain't gwine gamble no more en ya ain't gwine drink.

TOM: I swear, Mammy.

ROXY: En now dat ya ain't got to pay interest to dat man no more, ya kin save de money dat yo' daddy gives ya 'til ya git enuf t'come git me en buy me back.

TOM: I will, Mammy.

ROXY: Now gimme sumthin' o' yourns.

TOM: Something like what?

ROXY: Sumthin' so Ah kin 'member ya. Sumthin' Ah kin hold in mah han' en 'member de reason Ah's doing dis.

TOM: Here's my ring. You keep it safe.

ROXY: Ya come en git me, Chambers.

TOM: I will, Mammy. I swear. I'll come get you just as soon as I can.

TOM and ROXY exit as WILSON enters and addresses the audience.

WILSON: Even though the twins managed to keep to themselves over the next few months, they flat out refused to leave town. This meant that a final showdown between them and Judge Driscoll and Tom was inevitable and believe me, there was a lot of very unpleasant speculation about what was gonna happen when that showdown finally occurred. Me, I spent my days wracking my brain trying to figure out why my plan to catch the thief and recover the stolen knife had failed.

NANCY enters and watches WILSON.

I was sure that the culprit was the young girl I had seen, but I couldn't figure out why she hadn't tried to sell the knife.

WILSON notices NANCY watching him.

Nancy, sorry. I was just ... thinking through some things.

NANCY: S'alright, Marster Wilson. Don' lemme stop ya.

She goes about her business.

WILSON: You think I'm crazy, don't you?

NANCY: Nawsir. Ah ain't think no such thang.

WILSON: You can tell the truth, Nancy. I don't mind. A man standing here talking to himself, you must think I'm one of the craziest white men you've ever seen in your life.

NANCY: Nawsir. Fack be tole, Marster Wilson, Ah think ya one o' de smartes' men in dis town.

WILSON: Thank you, but I was not fishing for a compliment.

NANCY: En Ah warrn't giving 'way free fish. Fack be tole, Marster Wilson, Ah think ya one o' de few mens in dis town who unnerstand de whole world en mos' thin's in it.

WILSON: Even though you found me here, alone, talking to myself?

NANCY: Ah figure dat when sumbody talk to deyself, dey keeping de bes' company dey kin keep. 'Sides, chilluns talk to demself all de time en nobody call dem pudd'nhead.

WILSON: Children have freedom and imagination.

NANCY: Yassir. Chilluns kin see thangs dat grown folks cain't. En Ah b'lieve dats what ya kin do. Ya see a whole lot o' thangs dat most folks in dis town cain't. En dey call ya pudd'nhead. Nawsir. De way Ah see it, ya may be many thangs but a pudd'nhead ain't one o' 'em.

Enter DRISCOLL, TOM, and HOWARD.

TOM: I'll tell you why your plan didn't work, Wilson. Your plan didn't work because there is no knife.

HOWARD: No knife?

DRISCOLL: What d'you mean, no knife?

WILSON: He described it in such detail . . .

TOM: Maybe he was describing a knife he had seen in a book. Or maybe at one point in time he actually did own a knife like the one he described. Maybe he was describing a knife that they had when they came to town and maybe they still have it.

HOWARD: Now that makes sense.

TOM: Course it does. They described the knife in perfect detail because it's a knife that they own but it was never stolen.

HOWARD: Makes sense to me.

TOM: That's the reason your plan didn't work, Wilson. The knife was never stolen in the first place.

WILSON: I find that hard to believe.

HOWARD: I'm bound to say that I put it up the way Tom does. They never had the knife, or if they had it, they still got it.

DRISCOLL: Certainly would explain the reason it hasn't surfaced.

WILSON: I can't believe I've been played upon.

TOM: Not only that, but rumor going on around town says that the twins are not identical. That one is a little darker than the other.

HOWARD: I knew it. I knew it all along.

TOM: If you find your mysterious young girl, Wilson, and if she doesn't have the knife, go search the twins. If I were a betting man, I'd bet that you'd find it on them.

DRISCOLL: If you were a betting man?

TOM: I don't gamble anymore, Daddy. Haven't gambled for months now. Don't have the urge.

DRISCOLL: That makes me very happy.

TOM: Happy enough to increase my allowance?

DRISCOLL: We've been down that road, Tom.

TOM: But we didn't go far enough. I need more than fifty dollars a month.

DRISCOLL: For what? What do you need more money for?

TOM: You have disinherited me, Daddy. Without an inheritance, I might as well be an orphan, and I have to start planning for my future.

DRISCOLL: Judge Howard?

HOWARD: Tom, your father and I spent the morning rewriting his will. He has reinstated your claim to the estate. You are the only heir and the only beneficiary.

TOM: Yes! Thank you.

DRISCOLL: Son, I'm proud of the way you've conducted yourself over the past few months and I'm proud of the way that you walked away from the challenge presented to you by that Italian assassin.

TOM: I can't tell you how happy this makes me.

DRISCOLL: If only your dearly departed mother could see you now. I'm sure her heart would burst with pride.

TOM: Daddy, I have to ask you for one more thing.

DRISCOLL: Whatever you want.

TOM: I want you to give me your permission to sell Chambers.

DRISCOLL: Chambers?

TOM: I promise that I will do everything I can to find a good home for him.

DRISCOLL: You want to sell Chambers?

TOM: He's useless. He's lazy. He serves no purpose around here.

DRISCOLL: Is that the only reason?

TOM: It's reason enough.

DRISCOLL: I will not allow the selling of a slave, any slave, for no good reason.

TOM: Then allow me to set him free.

DRISCOLL: What?

TOM: He's served this family well. He's served us for years. We should give him something in return. There's no reason to keep him here.

DRISCOLL: I am not in the business of giving away my investments, Tom.

TOM: Don't you feel any sense of responsibility towards him?

DRISCOLL: Course I do. That's why I won't allow him to be sold without good reason.

TOM: That's not what I mean, Daddy.

DRISCOLL: Then what do you mean, Tom?

TOM: You can't deny the fact that he resembles you.

DRISCOLL: Of course he resembles me. Most of my slaves resemble me.

TOM: You remember Roxy?

DRISCOLL: Yes. Fine gal. Very pretty.

TOM: Roxy was his mammy.

DRISCOLL: I know that, Tom.

TOM: You spent time with Roxy.

DRISCOLL: That was my God-given prerogative.

TOM: Some men might say that you were the father of the baby Roxy had.

DRISCOLL: No, Tom, you're confused. You see, I fathered a slave, yes, of course, I have fathered many slaves. Most men who own slaves father slaves. It's the easiest way to increase your holdings, especially when your bucks aren't performing as they should. But even though you may father a slave, no one would ever consider you to be the father of that slave because fathering a slave means something completely different than being a father of that slave.

TOM: I don't understand the difference.

DRISCOLL: Come on, Tom. You know the difference. You've studied animal husbandry at Yale. I know you did cause I paid the bill. When you father something, something like a slave, all you're doing is supplying a seed much the same way you would hire out a horse or a bull for stud. But being a father, now that's something completely different. Being a father implies all sorts of familial ties. It means you guard and protect and teach your young. It means passing on to your progeny everything valuable, from your house and land, to your knowledge, your history, your customs, and morals, all of which I am passing on to you. Make no mistake about this, Tom. There's a huge difference between fathering and being a father.

TOM: I don't understand any of this. I don't understand why whites and niggers were even made in the first place. I mean, what kind of crime did that first uncreated nigger commit so that the curse of birth was decreed to him? And why is this difference made between white and black?

DRISCOLL: Niggers were created to serve us, Tom. You know that.

HOWARD: It's in the Bible.

TOM: No Bible that I've ever seen. And anybody who says different has made the Bible lie. What kind of sin must that be? To make the Bible lie.

DRISCOLL: What's the matter with you, boy?

CHAMBERS *enters.*

CHAMBERS: Marster Tom? Sumbody dropped off dis heah fer you.

TOM: What is it?

CHAMBERS: Ah dunno. Looks like a rang, sir.

DRISCOLL: A ring?

CHAMBERS *hands a ring to TOM.*

Your ring?

TOM: I must of lost it someplace. Thank you, Chambers.

CHAMBERS: Yassir.

CHAMBERS exits.

TOM: Gentlemen, if you would excuse me.

DRISCOLL: Tom, I don't know what wild hair has crawled up your ass but that boy has served us well. I will not get rid of him for no good reason.

TOM exits.

HOWARD: I told you that you shouldn't have sent him to a northern university. You should have kept him south, in the Old Dominion.

HOWARD, WILSON, and DRISCOLL exit as TOM and ROXY enter.

TOM: Mammy? You in heah?

ROXY: Ah's heah. Ya git mah message?

TOM: What're you doing here?

ROXY: What do ya think Ah'ma doing heah?

TOM: I don't know. Everything all right?

ROXY: He sells a pusson down de river, den ax dat pusson iffen everythin's alright.

TOM: What do you mean?

ROXY: Ya cain't lie to me, Chambers, so don' even try.

TOM: Mammy, listen to me. I tried not to do it. I fought against it with everything I had.

ROXY: Fought against selling me down de river?

TOM: Fought against who I am, Mammy. It's my inheritance. It's what my father has passed on to me. My daddy is a slave owner as was his daddy and his daddy and his daddy before him. The white blood in my veins has been debased by five generations of slave owning. That's five generations of brutality. Five generations of cruelty, of irresponsible power and abuse. All of it, poured all into me, into my veins. And I did everything I could to fight it. I even asked the man and he told me that the man he was gonna sell you to was a kind man. That's what he told me, Mammy. That's what he told me.

ROXY: Warrn't him dat was de problem. De problem was de wife. De wife was cruel.

TOM: Mind if I turn up the light?

ROXY: Leave de light as tis. A pusson dat is hunted don' like de light.

TOM: Hunted?

ROXY: What ya think? Ya think dey jes found it in dey hearts to set me free? Dat what ya think? Ah said dey was kind, not crazy.

TOM: You run off?

ROXY: Ah al'ays did say ya was quick wid de wit.

TOM: You shouldn't have come here, Mammy.

ROXY: Whar else was Ah 'posed to go?

TOM: If they track you here, they're gonna wonder why you didn't run to a free state.

ROXY: Ah had no whar else t'go.

TOM: They're gonna know something's wrong. They're gonna know that we were in cahoots together.

ROXY: Den we got t'fix it. We got t'make it right befo' dey git heah.

TOM: How are we supposed to do that?

ROXY: Ah tell ya how. You's gwine go to yo' daddy en git de money, en buy me free ag'in.

TOM: And what am I supposed to tell him I want this money for?

ROXY: Ah don' ker what ya tell him, but ya gwine git de money, cause if ya don', Ah'll go to yo' daddy myself, en den he'll sell ya down de river, en ya kin see how ya like it.

TOM: What d'ya got tucked under your arm?

ROXY: Nothin'.

TOM: Is that my knife?

ROXY: Warrn't yo' knife t'begin wid. It was never yo' knife. It's de knife ya stole.

TOM: What do you think you're doing with it?

ROXY: Dey come heah en find me, Ah ain't gwine back.

TOM: You think you're gonna fight somebody?

ROXY: Too ole t'fight. Dey ketch me, Ah's gwine to kill myself.

TOM: You're not gonna do no such thing.

ROXY: Ah ain't gwine back.

TOM: Give me that.

> *He takes the knife from her.*

ROXY: Ah ain't gwine back, Chambers.

TOM: Don't worry. I'll get the money.

ROXY: Ya gwine tell him?

TOM: You out of your mind?

ROXY: Den how ya gwine git de money?

TOM: I'm gonna rob the old skinflint.

> *WILSON enters.*

WILSON: The most striking characteristic I remember of that year was an inordinate amount of funerals. It seems like every morning we were greeted with the news of another passing. I always thought that one should endeavor to live so that when one dies, even the undertaker will be sorry.

> *TOM enters in the guise of a young girl. WILSON watches as DRISCOLL enters. TOM and DRISCOLL are unaware of WILSON.*

DRISCOLL: Don't move or I'll blow a hole in you big enough to put my fist through. Well, what do we have here? I knew I'd get ya sooner or later. Just couldn't stay away, could ya? The only question I have is why? Who are you? And what's a pretty little thing like you doing out heah robbing folks?

> *TOM turns.*

TOM: You wanna know who I am?

DRISCOLL: Tom?

TOM: I'll tell you who I am. I am a ghost. A haunt.

DRISCOLL: What are you doing?

TOM: A spirit from the past who has returned to make your life a living hell.

DRISCOLL: You're robbing me?

TOM: I am all of your past sins and transgressions, Daddy.

DRISCOLL: You're the thief, you goddamn dog.

> DRISCOLL *charges TOM. In a flash, TOM takes out the dagger and stabs DRISCOLL under the ribs. They hold for a moment.*

> DRISCOLL *falls to the floor as TOM hears a sound. He panics and exits just as NANCY enters.*

NANCY: Marster Driscoll? Zat you?

> NANCY *spots DRISCOLL's body and screams.*

WILSON (*To audience*): The judge was found murdered by the dagger belonging to Count Luigi, the same dagger everyone believed that the count had in his possession the entire time. And because of the feud between the judge and the count, everyone assumed that the twins, who were known to be confessed assassins, had murdered the judge. The twins were arrested and charged with murder. They, of course, claimed to be innocent, and because Dawson's Landing was a sleepy little town and because we, after all, do live in a civilized democratic society, it was decided and agreed that the twins should be given a fair trial before they were hanged.

> TOM *enters with LOU.*

LOU: Heard about your father. Tough break.

TOM: Yeah. The grief is overwhelming.

LOU: I'm sorry for your loss but that nigger you sold me ran away.

TOM: That's what I heard.

LOU: Is that what you heard?

TOM: That's what I heard.

LOU: Let me tell you what I heard. I heard that she was spotted not too far from here. Is that true?

TOM: This is the only home she's ever known, so it would make sense that if she ran away, she would try to come back here.

LOU: I want her back, Tom.

TOM: I know you do.

LOU: And you're gonna deliver her to me. And it's gonna be real soon or I'm going to the law.

TOM: How about I buy her back from you? Then she becomes my problem.

LOU: How much?

TOM: Four hundred?

LOU: Not nearly enough to keep me quiet.

TOM: Four hundred plus a young buck? Chambers! Get in heah!

> *CHAMBERS enters.*

CHAMBERS: Yassir?

TOM: He's young, healthy.

LOU: Come here, boy. Open your mouth. Let's have a look.

> *CHAMBERS complies.*

Turn around.

> *CHAMBERS turns.*

What's the catch?

TOM: No catch. I'll give him to you plus four hundred in exchange for the wench.

CHAMBERS: What Ah done done, Marster?

TOM: Shut up, nigger.

CHAMBERS: But, Marster Tom . . .

TOM: I'm not gonna tell you again.

LOU: You must really like the old wench.

TOM: Sentimental value. So what d'you say? Four hundred plus the buck?

LOU: You got yourself a deal.

TOM: I'll get the papers.

LOU: No rush. I'm not going anywhere anytime soon. I decided to hang around for the spectacle. I ain't never seen an Italian get lynched before. I seen plenty of niggers do a rope dance, but an Italian, I think that's worth hanging around for a few days.

> *WILSON enters as LOU, TOM, and CHAMBERS exit.*

WILSON: I started to believe that maybe the twins' claim of innocence had some validity to it. When they were arrested, their hands and clothes were carefully examined and not a single bloodstain was found. But at the scene of the crime, blood was everywhere. On the floor, on the walls, there were bloody finger marks on the dagger that were just as clear and precise as words written in a book. I matched the marks found on the dagger against the marks that I had for the twins and you know what? They didn't match, and this was the riddle. But then I remembered Nancy saying that she thought she had seen a girl in the room that night and she described what sounded like the same girl I had seen months earlier, so I started matching the finger marks from the dagger against the finger marks of all of the girls and women in Dawson's Landing.

    HOWARD enters.

HOWARD: Looks like you haven't slept for days. Any luck?

WILSON: I've gone over every ridge, loop, and spiral of every hand and finger mark of every girl and woman in town and nothing even comes close.

HOWARD: It's about time for us to start moving towards the courthouse.

WILSON: I need more time.

HOWARD: There is no more time.

WILSON: Just another couple of days.

HOWARD: I'm sorry, Wilson.

    TOM enters with CECIL, ROWENA, and CHAMBERS.
    CHAMBERS carries the portable bar.

TOM: Morning, Wilson, Judge Howard. How goes it?

HOWARD: Fine, Tom. How you holding up?

TOM: Holding steady, Your Honor, holding steady. You remember my ole nigger mammy, Roxy?

HOWARD: Yeah, I remember Roxy.

TOM: A few days ago, I had the opportunity to purchase Roxy, which I promptly did. Then just as promptly, I set her free and gave her the option of staying in the quarters at the house for as long as she pleases. Having my ole mammy back has given me my only measure of comfort in this time of difficult sorrow.

HOWARD: It's good to know that you've found a bit of consolation.

TOM: And what about you, Dave? Gone back to your obscure hobby of collecting finger marks on pieces of glass for consolation, have you?

WILSON: Actually, I'm trying to discover who murdered your father.

TOM: We know who murdered my father. The murderer and his accomplice are sitting in jail and both will hang by sundown. Why you choose to defend them, I will never understand.

WILSON: I choose to defend them because I'm trying to bring justice to Dawson's Landing.

TOM: Justice? There is no such thing as justice. If there was justice, I wouldn't have to purchase a woman who was like a mother to me from a man who's selling her on an open market. If there were justice, my father would be here and alive today.

HOWARD: Tom?

TOM: My apologies, but I am clearly grief-stricken. Chambers? Libation.

      CHAMBERS begins to openly weep as he opens the portable bar.

HOWARD: Drinking again, Tom?

TOM: That's what a libation is, Judge Howard.

HOWARD: I thought you had quit.

TOM: I started again when an Italian tried to cut my father's heart out.

HOWARD: What's the matter with Chambers?

TOM: He's a little down in the mouth because he's about to leave us.

HOWARD: Is he sick?

TOM: He's sold.

HOWARD: You sold Chambers?

TOM: He was no longer of any use to me. And I used the money I got for Chambers to purchase Roxanne. How's that for justice, Pudd'nhead?

      CHAMBERS hands TOM a glass containing a shot of whiskey.
      TOM knocks it back, then hands the glass back to CHAMBERS.

WILSON: You shouldn't take my defense of the twins personally, Tom.

TOM: I don't. In fact, to let you know that there are no hard feelings, let's have a drink together. You and I. Chambers? Pour a drink for Mister Wilson here.

WILSON: I'd rather not.

TOM: To show that there are no hard feelings.

WILSON: I don't drink, Tom.

TOM: On most occasions, but this is a special occasion. To the first case of Attorney Pudd'nhead Wilson. May you meet with the same success of all your previous endeavors. Chambers?

CHAMBERS offers the glass to WILSON.

Come on, Wilson, take it. Have a drink with your old friend, Tom.

CHAMBERS holds the glass at arm's length, eye level to WILSON. WILSON stares at the glass for a long moment. As CHAMBERS holds the glass, WILSON begins to inspect it closer.

WILSON takes the glass, careful to touch only the bottom of the glass and the rim. He downs the whiskey but keeps the glass.

TOM: There. No hard feelings?

WILSON: No hard feelings.

TOM: See you in court, Counselor.

TOM exits followed by ROWENA and CECIL.

CHAMBERS: Marster Wilson? May Ah have dat dere glass back, sir?

WILSON: I need to keep the glass, Chambers.

CHAMBERS: What Ah'm 'posed to tell Marster Tom?

HOWARD: Tell Tom that I took it. If he wants it back, tell him to come see me.

CHAMBERS: Yassir.

CHAMBERS exits.

HOWARD: What is it?

WILSON: The marks. The finger marks. They're on this glass.

HOWARD: What finger marks?

WILSON: The ridges, loops, and spirals. They look like they're the same.

HOWARD: How?

WILSON: I don't know how, but they're here on the glass. That means it's either Chambers or it's Tom. Those are the only two who handled the glass. But I can check. I can check to make sure. I have both of their finger marks on record.

HOWARD: How long is it gonna take?

WILSON: Not long.

HOWARD: I have to get to the courthouse. I'll delay as long as I can but you get there.

HOWARD exits. WILSON addresses the audience.

WILSON: Well, I was right about the ridges, spirals, and loops. I had found a match but I became even more confused. The marks on the knife matched the marks I had for Chambers as a baby, but they didn't match the marks I had for Chambers as a young man. I didn't think finger marks could change, but it clearly appeared as if the marks of Chambers had changed after his infancy. When I checked Tom's finger marks, I became even more confused because it appeared as if the exact same thing had happened to Tom. How could the finger marks of both men change at the same time? That's when it slowly began to dawn on me what had happened.

Enter HOWARD in robes, LUIGI and ANGELO, CHAMBERS, CECIL, ROWENA, NANCY, ROXY, and TOM.

HOWARD: Order! Order! Come to order! Is David Wilson heah?

WILSON: Here, Your Honor.

HOWARD: Are you ready?

WILSON: Ready, Your Honor.

HOWARD: Let's get under way.

WILSON: Your Honor, ladies and gentlemen, I think everybody here would agree that the person whose hand left the bloodstained finger marks upon the handle of the knife that killed Judge Driscoll is the person who committed the murder.

HOWARD: I think everybody would agree to that.

WILSON: I intend to prove that it was not Count Luigi, nor was it Count Angelo who left those bloodstained finger marks. Not only that, but I also intend to reveal the identity of the person who did leave the finger marks, and that person, the true murderer of Judge Driscoll, is sitting in this courtroom, at this very moment. Throughout the course of this trial, I intend to prove . . .

HOWARD: Goddamn it, Wilson! Do you know who did it or not?

WILSON: Yes, Your Honor, I do.

HOWARD: Then why don't you tell us, for God's sake.

WILSON: The person who left the finger marks on the knife, the murderer of Judge Driscoll, is none other than the slave, Valet de Chambers.

HOWARD: Chambers?

CHAMBERS: No, Lawd have mercy, Ah didn't do it. Ah swear! Ah warrn't no whar near dat house when dat man was kilt.

HOWARD: Take the nigger away.

CECIL: No, uh uh. This nigger ain't going nowhere. We got plans for this nigger that involves that big oak tree in the center of the square.

ROWENA: Yeah, let's take the nigger to the oak tree.

CECIL: Oak tree.

CECIL and ROWENA: Oak tree! Oak tree!

WILSON: Hold it. You got the wrong man.

HOWARD: You said it was Chambers.

WILSON: But the man you have there is not Chambers. Everybody calls him Chambers because when he was five months old, somebody took him out of his cradle and put him into the cradle that belonged to Chambers. And the person who did that is also in this room.

ROXY (*To NANCY*): 'Cuse me, but Ah gots to go.

ROXY makes her way to the exit.

HOWARD: Goddamn it, Wilson, will you please just tell us who killed Judge Driscoll?

WILSON: The real Valet de Chambers, the murderer of Judge Driscoll, is a man we all have falsely called Thomas à Becket Driscoll.

CECIL: Tom Driscoll?

TOM: That's a lie and I'd like to see you prove it.

WILSON: I certainly will. Give me your hand. Allow me to record your finger marks.

TOM looks at his hands for a long moment before sinking to the floor.

There is no need. He has confessed.

ANGELO: What about us?

LUIGI: Can we go?

ANGELO: Please.

LUIGI: Please. Can we go?

HOWARD: You are free to go.

> *The twins bolt.*

HOWARD: I dare say that all of these years, we were wrong about you, Wilson. You proved yourself to be a man of intellect and a man of wisdom. And we called you Pudd'nhead. Can you find it in your heart to forgive us?

WILSON (*To audience*): And that was it. In a single moment, I, David Wilson, slew the giant Goliath, the champion of the Philistines. I had discovered the answer to the riddle that nobody else could figure out. I had become a hero.

ROWENA: What about Tom?

HOWARD: According to Wilson, he's a nigger.

ROWENA: A nigger?

CECIL: I was best friends with a nigger?

ROWENA: You? What about me?

WILSON (*To audience*): All I was trying to do was solve the mystery of the murder.

ROWENA: I once took a walk with him down by the pond.

CECIL: Once? How about every day two or three times a day?

WILSON (*To audience*): I didn't care about bloodlines and who was the father of who. Those things just didn't concern me.

ROWENA: What you gonna do about this, Your Honor?

WILSON (*To audience*): Or at least I thought they didn't.

HOWARD: There's only one solution to a problem like this.

CECIL: Oak tree?

HOWARD: Oak tree.

ROWENA: Yeah, let's take the nigger to the oak tree.

> *LOU enters.*

LOU: Wait a minute, Your Honor, hold the boat. I put out good money for a slave. Are you telling me that the slave I bought ain't a slave at all but a free man?

HOWARD: That's exactly what I'm telling you.

LOU: Then what am I supposed to do? I'm out dern near six hundred dollars and I can't even sue the man who sold me the slave cause the man who sold me the slave ain't even a white man. He's a nigger and I can't sue a nigger cause a nigger can't be sued.

HOWARD: What you want me to do?

LOU: You the judge, you figure it out. I am owed either six hundred dollars in cash or six hundred in flesh. How I collect makes no difference to me. But I got a legal bill of sale here, Your Honor. Says I am the legal owner of one male Negro slave named Valet de Chambers. But according to you, there ain't no slave named Valet de Chambers.

HOWARD: I never said that. I said that the man you thought you bought is a white man. However, there is a slave named Chambers.

LOU: He's mine, Your Honor. I own him. Says right here.

HOWARD takes the bill of sale and examines it.

HOWARD: That's what it says alright.

LOU: According to the law of the great state of Missouri, it is your duty, as judge, to turn that slave over to me.

CECIL: We turn him over to you, what you gonna do with him?

LOU: I'm gonna sell him and get my money back.

HOWARD: Where you gonna sell him?

LOU: The only place I can get full price for him. Down the river.

Everyone except WILSON exits.

WILSON (*To audience*): Tom was immediately pardoned, chained to the back of a wagon, and was on his way down the river before nightfall. Roxy was caught and taken to jail. The next morning, the twins had packed up and were on their way out of town, bound for Europe, vowing never to return to the States again. Unfortunately, Roxy wasn't as lucky. You see, nobody had a financial stake in Roxy's well-being and since making a white man a slave was considered to be a crime worse than murder, about the same time that the twins were boarding a ship for their return voyage, Roxy was pulled from the jail and was carried to the outskirts of town where she was tied to a tree. A slow fire was set under her feet.

NANCY enters.

From what I understand, she burned for the better part of three hours before she died.

NANCY: Is it de fire dat ya afeard o'?

WILSON: But that was not my fault.

NANCY: No need to be afeard o' de fire. Dat fire ain't gwine take up legs
en walk. Dat fire gwine stay right whar it belong jes as long as we
stay whar we belong.

WILSON (*To audience*): Justice had been served. I mean, consider the real
Tom Driscoll.

   CHAMBERS and HOWARD enter.

The real Tom Driscoll had suddenly found himself rich, white, and free.

CHAMBERS: What ya mean, Marster Wilson? Marster Howard, what he
talkin' 'bout?

HOWARD: First of all, you have to stop calling us Master.

CHAMBERS: Yassir.

HOWARD: And stop saying that.

CHAMBERS: Stop saying what, Marster?

HOWARD: Yassir. Stop saying that. I don't want you to say yassir anymore.

CHAMBERS: Yassir. Ah'll stop.

HOWARD: You're a white man, Chambers.

CHAMBERS: White man?

HOWARD: You're white, rich, and free.

CHAMBERS: Yassir. Ya 'most had me dere, Marster Howard. Rich, white,
en free. Yassir. Mah mind went places it ain't never be'n befo'.

WILSON: It's true. Your name is Tom Driscoll.

CHAMBERS: Tom Driscoll?

WILSON: You were born to Judge Driscoll and his wife.

CHAMBERS: But Ah don' wanna be Tom Driscoll. Ah wanna be who Ah is
en Ah be Valet de Chambers.

WILSON: You are a free man, Tom. Don't you want to be free? Don't you
want to be able to come and go as you please?

CHAMBERS: Ah don' rightly know, Marster.

WILSON: Don't you want to be able to sleep in a nice bed upstairs instead
of sleeping on a pallet out back?

HOWARD: Don't you want to be able to sit in the dining room with your friends and engage in stimulating conversation for dinner instead of eating leftovers out back in a dark, cold shack?

CHAMBERS: Everybody else git set free too?

WILSON: Everybody else?

CHAMBERS: Nancy. Big Jim.

WILSON: No, Tom. I'm sorry.

CHAMBERS: Ya said Ah kin set wid mah friends.

HOWARD: I meant your white friends, Tom.

CHAMBERS: Ah ain't got no white friends. All Ah got lef' is Nancy en Big Jim.

HOWARD: Nancy and Big Jim are niggers, Tom. They are slaves.

CHAMBERS: Ah'm a nigger. Ah'm a slave. En Ah ain't got nobody else. Mah mammy, Roxy's, gone.

HOWARD: Roxy was not your mother, Tom.

CHAMBERS: On'y mother Ah ever knew.

HOWARD: But she did a bad thing, Tom. Don't you see that? She ruined your life for you. She deserved what she got.

CHAMBERS: What she do?

WILSON: She made you a slave, Tom. That's the reason they did that god-awful thing to her. She made you a slave.

CHAMBERS: What 'bout folks dat made her a slave? Ya gwine find dem en tie dem to a tree too? What 'bout de folks dat made Big Jim a slave? En Nancy a slave?

HOWARD: You're confusing the issue here.

CHAMBERS: Sorry, Marster Howard. Ah don' mean to upset you.

HOWARD: Will you please stop calling me that?

CHAMBERS: Yassir.

HOWARD: You're a white man, Tom.

WILSON: You're rich, you're white, and you're free.

CHAMBERS: Wid all respect, sir, Ah may be free but Ah don' know how ya kin say Ah's white. All ya got to do is look at me en tell dat Ah ain't white. Nobody gwine b'lieve dat Ah's white. Listen to mah voice.

Look at mah han'. Dat han' is not de han' o' a white man. Look at mah face, mah arms, mah legs. Dat's de face, arms, en legs o' a nigger. Ya kin set me free, sho, ya kin make me rich, 'preciate it, but ya cain't make me white, Marster Howard. Ah's a nigger, thru en thru, dat's de one thang 'bout me dat cain't you or nobody else ever change.

NANCY: De way Ah look at it, ya cain't jes up en kill half a dog.

WILSON: All I wanted to do was solve the riddle.

NANCY: Ya kill half de dog en de udder half dies, ya gwine be 'sponsible fer de dead half jes de same as if ya had kilt dat half instead yourn own.

WILSON: It wasn't my fault.

HOWARD: You shouldn't let it bother you. You did a good thing, Wilson. You're a hero.

WILSON: Then why don't I feel like a hero?

HOWARD: Tell you this. Bet you nobody's ever gonna call you a pudd'nhead again.

NANCY: De mo' Ah think 'bout it, de mo' Ah think Ah was wrong 'bout you.

HOWARD: You turned out to be the smartest man in this town.

NANCY: Ya ain't no better den de rest o' 'em.

HOWARD: Come on in, Wilson.

NANCY: Fack be tole, ya ain't nothin' but a pudd'nhead.

WILSON: I brought order and I brought justice back to the world.

NANCY: Is that right?

WILSON: That's right.

NANCY: Pudd'nhead Wilson.

  Lights fade.

END OF PLAY

FREE MAN OF COLOR

PRODUCTION HISTORY

Free Man of Color was commissioned by Ohio University, Robert Glidden, president, and originally produced by Victory Gardens Theater, Chicago, Illinois, Dennis Začek, artistic director, Marcelle McVay, managing director. This world premiere production was in association with the Ohio University Bicentennial Celebration, Athens, Ohio, January 16–February 29, 2004. The production was directed by Andrea J. Dymond, with set design by Tim Morrison, costume design by Michelle Tesdall, lighting design by Mary McDonald Badger, and sound design/original composition by Joe Cerqua. Rita Vreeland was the production stage manager.

Robert Wilson	Gary Houston
John Newton Templeton	Anthony Fleming III
Jane Wilson	Shelley Delaney

Free Man of Color was the recipient of the 2005 Joseph Jefferson Award for Best New Work.

Free Man of Color, titled *Freed,* was produced Off Broadway by Penguin Rep Theatre (Joe Brancato, artistic director, and Andrew M. Horn, executive director) in association with Chase Mishkin, June 11–July 3, 2010, at 59E59 Theatres. The production was directed by Joe Brancato. Set design was by Joseph J. Egan, costume design by Patricia E. Doherty, lighting design by Martin E. Vreeland, and sound design by Chris Rummel. Zachary Spitzer was the production manager, and C. Renee Alexander was the stage manager.

Robert Wilson	Christopher McCann
John Newton Templeton	Sheldon Best
Jane Wilson	Emma O'Donnell

Free Man of Color was produced by the Colony Theatre Company, Burbank, California (Barbara Beckley, artistic director, and Trent Steelman, executive director), August 14–September 12, 2010. The production was directed by Dan Bonnell, with set design by David Potts, costume design by A. Jeffrey Schoenberg, lighting design by Chris Wojcieszyn, and sound design by Cricket S. Myers. Leesa Freed was the production stage manager.

Robert Wilson	Frank Ashmore
John Newton Templeton	Kareem Ferguson
Jane Wilson	Kathleen Mary Carthy

(*above*) Gary Houston as Robert Wilson, Anthony Fleming III as John Newton Templeton, and Shelley Delaney as Jane Wilson in the Victory Gardens Theater production of *Free Man of Color. Photo by Liz Lauren.*

(*right*) Shelley Delaney as Jane Wilson and Anthony Fleming III as John Newton Templeton in the Victory Gardens Theater production of *Free Man of Color. Photo by Liz Lauren.*

Kareen Ferguson as John Newton Templeton, Kathleen Mary Carthy as Jane Wilson, and Frank Ashmore as Robert Wilson in the Colony Theater Company production of *Free Man of Color. Photo by Michael Lamont.*

Sheldon Best as John Newton Templeton, Christopher McCann as Robert Wilson, and Emma O'Donnell as Jane Wilson in the Off-Broadway production of *Free Man of Color. Photo by John Quilty.*

Characters

John Newton Templeton	Twenty-year-old ex-slave.
Robert Wilson	Middle-aged white university president.
Jane Wilson	ROBERT'S somewhat younger wife.

Time: 1824–1828

Place: Athens, Ohio

FREE MAN OF COLOR

A play in two acts

ACT ONE

SCENE ONE

On stage are two chairs left and right. ROBERT WILSON sits in one of the chairs, JOHN NEWTON TEMPLETON sits in the other. A very rustic rendition of "Amazing Grace" plays in the background.

When the music ends, WILSON stands.

WILSON (*To audience*): Most distinguished assembled guests, trustees, gentlemen, at this point in the program, I present to you John Newton Templeton. The topic on which he will speak to you today is titled "The Claims of Liberia." Mister Templeton.

>*WILSON exits.*

JOHN (*To audience*): Non solum verba falsa sunt mala ipsa, sed etiam malo infligunt animam.

For those of you who don't know, that was not "The Claims of Liberia." It was Latin. Plato. Roughly translated, it means, "False words are not only evil in themselves, but they inflict the soul with evil." That's what I was thinking on that day in 1828 when Reverend Wilson introduced me. I was thinking about my soul. Reverend Wilson was the president of Ohio University, and judging by the look on his face, he and the seventy-five other assembled guests had fully expected to hear me speak on "The Claims of Liberia" because at one point in my life, I had been claimed by Liberia. 1828. Thirty-four years before the end of slavery, I stood with my graduating class and wondered about my soul.

>*WILSON enters. He has been traveling.*

WILSON: Here we are. I know it's a little different than what you're used to, but we consider it to be a good home. Wife? (*He listens. There is no answer.*) I hope she's feeling better. She hasn't been in what you would call the best of health.

JOHN: Sorry to hear that.

WILSON: Have to be careful nowadays. We've had our share of the cholera. Yellow fever. Scarlet fever and smallpox. (*He calls through the window.*) Wife! (*No answer.*) I hope she didn't walk into town again. Woman has a stubborn streak in her. Won't let anybody do anything for her. I usually have a friend check on her while I'm gone. Make sure she's all right, drive her into town if she needs it, but she'd rather walk and it's too far to walk. Town is that way, north, about four miles. We'll go in tomorrow.

JOHN: Tomorrow?

WILSON (*Calling*): Wife?

JOHN: What about my papers?

WILSON: Your papers?

JOHN: I need to get my papers in order.

WILSON: We'll take care of that tomorrow, when we go into town.

JOHN: The law says—

WILSON: I know what the law says. Don't worry about the law. The law is my concern. The only thing I want you to be concerned about is your studies. You will begin your studies with nine other students and you will be treated the exact same as everyone else. Is that clear?

JOHN: Yes, sir.

WILSON: You clear on what will be expected of you?

JOHN: Yes, sir.

WILSON: Let's go over it again. How do you plan to start each day?

JOHN: With prayers at sunrise.

WILSON: Breakfast?

JOHN: Breakfast by six.

WILSON: Followed by . . .

JOHN: Morning recitations.

WILSON: Then comes?

JOHN: Morning lecture, then study until noon. Dinner will be from noon to one-thirty, after which we begin afternoon recitations, followed by afternoon lecture and study until supper. Supper is at five-thirty, followed by a half-hour of relaxation and then evening debate.

WILSON: Good, John. Very good. Now, your first year will consist of the study of mathematics, science, and philosophy. Your second year will consist of the study of Latin, Hebrew, and Greek. In your third year, you will be expected to apply for admission into the Athenian Literary Society in addition to continuing your studies in Greek. And in your fourth year, you will prepare for your comprehensive exams.

JOHN: Yes, sir.

WILSON: Tell me something, John. Why do you think it's important that you study Greek?

JOHN: Why?

WILSON: That's right. Why? Why Greek?

JOHN: Greek is an important language, sir.

WILSON: Is that your answer? Greek is an important language? That's not an answer, John. That's circular logic based upon the original premise. "Why is the horse white? Because it's a white horse." Does that make sense? No. All you did was chew my question and then feed it back to me in the form of an answer, but that's not an answer. You haven't added anything to it. Nothing but your own saliva and I do not care for the taste of your saliva, John. Now let's try it again. Why is it important that you study Greek?

JOHN: I don't know.

WILSON: Didn't you study Greek at Ripley?

JOHN: Yes, sir.

WILSON: Didn't they tell you why you were studying Greek?

JOHN: They said it was important.

WILSON: Of course it's important, John. I want you to tell me why it's important.

JOHN: It's important for us to understand our language?

WILSON: Not unless you consider language to be the end, and language is not the end, it's merely a means to the end. Think about the white horse. Can you ride the words "white horse"? Will those words carry you to the store? Do you have to feed those words? No, those words are merely a representation of the thing itself. Those words do not have a heartbeat, those words will not leave filth in the middle of the road. Our goal is not to understand the words, John. Our goal is to understand all of the things the words represent. Have you ever studied the Bible?

JOHN: Of course I have.

WILSON: In what language did you study the Bible?

JOHN: English.

WILSON: Are you suggesting to me that Matthew, Mark, Timothy, and Samuel wrote their testaments in English?

JOHN: No, sir.

WILSON: In what language did they write?

JOHN: They wrote in Hebrew, sir. And Greek.

WILSON: That's right. And unless you are studying the Bible in Hebrew and Greek, you're not studying the Bible. You're studying what somebody else has said the Bible says, and while King James may have been a very honest man, I'd rather not stake my soul and the souls of all men on his judgment. That's the reason the study of Greek is so important, John, that's why the study of Hebrew and Latin is important, so that we may study the actual word of God in its original form. Remember, only by studying the origins of a thing, can one discern that thing's true meaning.

JOHN: Only by studying the origin of a thing—

    JANE enters. She stops and surveys the situation.

JANE: What's this?

WILSON: This is John Templeton. I'm sorry, John *Newton* Templeton. John, this is Misses Wilson.

JOHN: Pleased to meet you, ma'am.

JANE: You promised we were not going to do this.

WILSON: Do what, dear?

JANE: Take in runaways.

WILSON: He's not a runaway. He's a free man.

JANE: Legal free or liberated free?

WILSON: Legal free and he's here to go to school.

JANE: School?

WILSON: John, why don't you go out and get the rest of our things.

JOHN: Yes, sir.

    JOHN exits.

JANE: Robert, what're you doing?

WILSON: Reverend Hopkins come by while I was gone?

JANE: Course he came by, every day he came by. Can't get rid of the man.

WILSON: I asked him to check on you while I was gone.

JANE: And I told you that I don't need anybody to check on me. Now I would like to know what that boy is doing here.

WILSON: He was at Ripley with Reverend Williamson. The boy is smart, Jane. He knows philosophy, mathematics, basic Greek, and Latin. And the boy is strong. He had never ridden a horse before in his life, not until he got on one to come here. But after the first day, he was riding like a professional.

JANE: You taught him how to ride?

WILSON: First thirty miles to Hillsboro were kind of hard on him. But after I showed him a few things he got the hang of it. By the time we could see the first of the seven hills of Athens, he was riding like he had been born in the saddle.

JANE: What is he doing here, Robert?

WILSON: I told you. He's here to go to school.

JANE: You going up against the law for him?

WILSON: Nothing in the law that says that he can't be here.

JANE: And that's the reason you're doing it? Because nothing says you can't?

WILSON: We minister to everyone else in this world.

JANE: We minister to colored.

WILSON: Never with substance. We preach to them, sure, we offer them the word of God, but never has anyone offered them the means by which they can obtain that word on their own.

JANE: Where's he supposed to live while he's here?

WILSON: I thought he could stay here with us for a while.

JANE: Where here?

WILSON: Spare room.

JANE: We don't have a spare room.

WILSON: The room isn't being used, Jane. He can sleep there. Won't be for long. Only a month or so.

JANE: A month?

WILSON: After folks get used to the idea of him being around, we can move him into the edifice with the other students if you like.

JANE: With the gentleman from Virginia? The two gentlemen from Kentucky? You think that these men are going to sleep in the same room as a black?

WILSON: Won't be the same room.

JANE: Under the same roof. You expect these men to share a roof with a black who is not washing their clothes and serving them dinner? Is that what you're asking me to believe?

WILSON: If it doesn't work out, we can find him a room in town someplace, I don't know. The where of the matter is not important at this point.

JANE: The where of the matter is the most important. Everything in this world revolves around the where.

WILSON: If you don't want him here and if he has a problem in the edifice, we'll find a room for him in town.

    JOHN enters with saddlebags.

JANE: Is he registered?

WILSON: We'll take care of that tomorrow.

JANE: Does he have money to register?

WILSON: The university is sovereign. As long as he's in our charge, he's not subject to local ordinances.

JANE: Nobody in town is going to put him up unless he's registered.

WILSON: Why must you see darkness wherever you look?

JANE: Because my life has been shrouded in darkness. I've lived in darkness for so long, it's become a friend of mine, the only companion I have.

JOHN: Pardon me, sir, but if you would tell me where to unhitch and water the horses, I'll take care of it.

WILSON: I'll take care of it, John. You get yourself cleaned up, get yourself something to eat.

JANE: Folks in town are not going to want him here unless he's registered, Robert.

WILSON: Folks in town don't have a say in the matter.

JANE: You can't continue to ignore who these people are and what they believe in.

WILSON: I don't care what they believe in. John will be here whether they like it or not. My charge doesn't come from the folks in town. I receive my charge from the trustees and the state legislature. I answer to them and after them, I answer only to God. I do not have to answer to a bunch of provincial merchants, landowners, and pig farmers.

JANE: You may not have to answer to them. But we do have to live with them.

WILSON: I think we've been very charitable neighbors.

JANE: When it benefits you. You won't consider anything that doesn't benefit you or the university.

WILSON: I've considered many proposals.

JANE: What about the tent?

WILSON: I have no objections to that tent.

JANE: Within the square?

WILSON: Anyplace outside the gates.

JANE: Outside the gates.

WILSON: It's for the amusement and entertainment of the locals. If they want to be amused and entertained by abominations, they can erect as many circus tents as they please. Anyplace outside of the square.

JANE: There's nothing evil about the circus, Robert. They come in, they set up their tents, they tell stories. You go there and listen to stories about people and places far away from here. That's all it is. It's a diversion. It might be nice to have a bit of diversion around here.

WILSON: My students do not need diversion. My students need earnest, uninterrupted study.

JANE: There are people here other than your students.

WILSON: What people. Who?

JANE: People.

WILSON: I want you to tell me whose need for entertainment and diversion you think is more important than the education of my students.

JANE: Nobody's. I'm sorry I brought it up.

WILSON: Draw some water for the boy so he can get cleaned up. And he needs something different to wear. Look around and see if we've got some clothes that'll fit him. Shirt, pants, maybe a hat.

JANE: There's nothing here that will fit him.

WILSON: Why don't you look see?

JANE: I don't have to look see. I know. There is nothing here that will fit him.

WILSON: Draw him some water so he can get cleaned up. I'll be back in a bit.

WILSON exits.

JOHN: If it's all the same to you, ma'am, I can draw my own water.

JANE: Of course you can. You can and you will. I will not draw water for you while you're in this house.

JOHN: No, ma'am.

JANE: Wash basin is in there under the table.

JOHN: Yes, ma'am.

He moves to exit. He stops.

JOHN: I didn't come here to cause trouble, ma'am. Reverend Wilson asked me if I wanted to come here and go to school. He said he was looking for young men of high moral content; young men who would eventually serve in honor of the public good. I believe I am such a man. Reverend Wilson also believes that I am such a man, and I am grateful that he's given me the chance to prove it.

JANE: So . . . you want to serve the public good.

JOHN: Yes, ma'am.

JANE: And just how do you plan to do that . . . what's your name again?

JOHN: John, ma'am.

JANE: John what?

JOHN: John Newton Templeton.

JANE: Just how do you plan to serve the public good, Mister John Newton Templeton?

JOHN: I'm not quite sure, ma'am. I thought that maybe I'd become a preacher like the Reverend. Spread the word of God. Maybe one day, even open my own school. School for colored. That's what I'd like to do.

JANE: That's very sweet of you. Tell me something, Mister John Newton Templeton, you born free? Or is liberation a relatively new experience for you?

JOHN: I was freed when I was seven, eight years old, ma'am.

JANE: You don't remember the day?

JOHN: I remember the day. It was June 17th, 1813. That was the day the good Reverend Marster Thomas Williamson of Spartanburg, South Carolina, died. Yes, ma'am, I remember the day. What I meant to say was, I don't know how old I was on that day. I was born the winter of 06–07. Don't know which month, all I know is that I was born during a hard snowfall, which is rare for South Carolina. That would've made me seven, maybe eight years old on the day that me, my momma, and my daddy were freed. Yes, ma'am, I remember the day. Just don't know how old I was on that day.

JANE: What're you doing here?

JOHN: I believe I just told you, ma'am. I come here to prove myself.

JANE: You didn't come here, Mister John Newton Templeton. You were brought here. What I'm trying to figure out is if you know the reason you were brought here cause it sounds like you don't know.

JOHN: All right then. I was brought here to prove myself. Reverend says that I'm special, because of my birth. Reverend says that if I came here, I'd be treated the same as everybody else. I'd like to believe that I'm at least as good as most men. Better than some. Not as good as others.

JANE: You probably think you're pretty smart, don't you?

JOHN: Smart?

JANE: Intelligent.

JOHN: I would like to think I possess a modicum of intelligence, yes.

JANE: You don't sound so smart to me. Not so smart at all. See, your desire to prove yourself only put you in a place where you could be seen. But that is not the reason you were brought here, and make no mistake, you were not only brought here but brought here for a reason. You were chosen, Mister Templeton. Out of all the rest of them out there, they chose you. You might as well had been standing on the block. "How about dis one chere?" "Issy healthy?" "Healthy as a mule, looka him kicking." "How 'bout his mind? Issy crazy?" "Nope, dis here nigger has a nice, even temperament. Look at dose eyes. Who can resist dose puppy dog eyes?" Yes, sir, Mister Templeton, they fished you out of a lake of misery. And I bet you thought you were pretty lucky, when they pulled you outta that putrid lake. But what you should've done before patting yourself on the back for being so lucky, what you should've done was ask the reason why. If you knew the reason why, that lake of misery you were swimming in might not have looked so bad.

JOHN: I know the reason why.

JANE: Do you? You come here to be a houseboy? That the reason you're here?

JOHN: I come here to prove to this world that the colored race is capable of climbing to the same heights—(*He stops himself.*)

JANE: Same heights as white?

JOHN: Yes, ma'am. Same heights as white.

JANE: Is that what you believe? Or is that what somebody told you?

JOHN: That's what I believe.

JANE: And you think that's the reason Reverend brought you here? To prove that colored is as good as white?

JOHN: I know that's the reason he brought me here.

JANE: Is that what he said to you?

JOHN: Is that what he said to me?

JANE: Did he come out and say those words? That he brought you here to prove that colored was as good as white?

JOHN: Maybe not those exact words.

JANE: Then you didn't hear him say it.

JOHN: Didn't have to hear him say it exactly. I know what's in his heart, what's in his mind.

JANE: So, you supernatural on top of everything else? You able to look inside a man's heart and his mind? That's quite a trick. With skills like that, what you need to go to school for?

JOHN: Don't have to be supernatural to divine what's in a man's heart. All you have to do is listen to him speak. I know what he believes.

JANE: You know what? You remind me a little bit of my youngest boy, David. He was ignorant, you're ignorant. Just a fool. No idea of what's going on around them. Huge wheels turning, grinding the world into shattered bits of bone and shredded flesh. And you, like him, are ignorant, oblivious to the sounds, the screams. Tell me something, Mister John Newton Templeton. What would happen if you found out that the reason you were brought here was different than the reason you think? What would that do to your intelligent colored thinking?

JOHN: I don't understand your meaning.

JANE: You think you as good as white?

JOHN: I've studied Latin, Greek, and many of the classics in the canon.

JANE: I asked if you thought you were as good as white.

JOHN: That depends.

JANE: Depends on what?

JOHN: Depends on what you mean by "good."

JANE: Are you trying to play a word game with me? Is that what you're trying to do?

JOHN: I'm trying to understand your meaning, ma'am.

JANE: I asked if you thought you were as good as white. It's not a very complex question.

JOHN: I believe that, given the chance, I can achieve anything that a white man can achieve. And that's the reason I'm here. To prove that I'm a man of high moral content. A man who is capable of serving in honor of the public good.

JANE: Oh, you will serve. Make no mistake about that. I'm sure you will serve nicely.

JANE exits.

JOHN (*To audience*): I hated that woman. Every time I looked at her, I kept visualizing my fingers wrapped around her throat, and you don't have to tell me: I know, that was not a very good visualization. So I made up my mind to stay as far away from her as possible. I started to think of the many ways I was going to avoid her. Unfortunately, I wasn't able to think quite fast enough.

WILSON enters.

WILSON: One thing you have to understand about the others, particularly the gentlemen from South Carolina as well as the gentlemen from Virginia and Kentucky: they've never been around anybody like you before. I mean, they've been around plenty of blacks, but they were always blacks that they or somebody else owned. You can understand, it must be very difficult for them.

JOHN: I can imagine.

WILSON: And sleep is a very important part of a man's life, John. Even God had to rest. If these men are unable to sleep in the same room . . .

JOHN: Under the same roof. Not the same room. We'd be sleeping under the same roof.

WILSON: Under the same roof, you're right. These are their shortcomings, John. You have to understand.

JOHN: What about me? They need to rest, what about me? I need rest too.

WILSON: Haven't you been resting comfortably here in the house?

JOHN: Course I have.

WILSON: Then what's the urgency? You've been comfortable here in the house, we've been comfortable having you here. There's no problem. There's no urgency.

JOHN: I should be in the edifice with the other men.

WILSON: Of course you should be. Unfortunately, the world is full of should be's, John. And it wouldn't be so bad to live here in the house with Jane and me. In fact, Jane would like it, to have somebody else around. She needs somebody to keep her company. Somebody to drive her into town when she needs it.

JOHN: No, sir, it wouldn't be right.

WILSON: What wouldn't be right?

JOHN: You said if I came here, I'd come here as a charity student and that charity students didn't have to pay.

WILSON: That wouldn't change. You still wouldn't have to pay.

JOHN: If I was in the edifice, I'd be with other men, some of whom also didn't have to pay. But living here in the house with you and Misses Wilson, I wouldn't feel right, not paying. I'd at least want to pay for my room, pay for my meals.

WILSON: All right. You stay here with me and Misses Wilson, and in exchange, you can do a little work around the house. What do you think about that? Cut wood, clean squirrels, rabbits, serve dinner, that sort of thing.

JOHN: Like a houseboy?

WILSON: That's an unfortunate way to put it.

JOHN: Unfortunate but true. I'd be a houseboy.

WILSON: I'd prefer not to use that terminology, John. I'd prefer to look at it a bit differently. We'll call it something else. Something a bit kinder.

JOHN: Something like what?

WILSON: Student servant. That's what you'll be. You'd be a student servant.

JOHN: Just because we call it something different doesn't change the fact of what it is.

WILSON: We're not trying to change the fact of what it is. We're calling it something different because it will be something different. If you were a houseboy you would do exactly as I told you to do when I told you to do it. If you were a houseboy, you would follow my orders, without question or hesitation, or face severe consequences. But that's not who you will be, John. You will be a student servant, almost like one of the family. Student servant means that you're a student, first and foremost. Your primary duty will be to attend classes and to keep up with your studies. Student servant means that you and I together will decide what your secondary duties will be. If you don't find cutting wood and serving dinner to be acceptable, we'll find something else for you to do. Something that you do find acceptable. Like taking care of the horses. You said you liked being around horses. What do you think about that? You can take care of the horses and we could continue your riding lessons. You and I, we could go out once a week riding. What do you think?

JOHN: That would be nice. Yes.

WILSON: Then it's settled. You'll stay here in the house with us and in exchange, take care of the horses. Now tell me something. Elections coming up. If you were allowed to vote, whom would you vote for?

JOHN: Sir?

WILSON: I'm sure you've kept up with politics and must have formed an opinion on this debacle of an election.

JOHN: No, sir.

WILSON: No, you haven't formed an opinion or no, you don't keep up with politics?

JOHN: No, I haven't formed an opinion.

WILSON: We're talking about the future of the United States of America here, and you haven't formed an opinion?

JOHN: I learned a long time ago not to waste my time thinking about what I would do in a situation that I know will never happen. Why should I waste my time thinking about who I would vote for in a world in which I cannot vote?

WILSON: But that's where you're wrong. You can vote, John. However, at this point in time, you're not allowed to vote. There's a difference.

JOHN: None that I can see.

WILSON: Can't vote means that you're physically or mentally unable to vote. Not allowed to vote means that you're physically capable of voting, but just not permitted. Understand?

JOHN: Physically capable . . .

WILSON: But not permitted.

JOHN: What would happen if I went into town and tried to vote? Would somebody block my way?

WILSON: Probably.

JOHN: Would I be beaten?

WILSON: Most likely.

JOHN: Killed?

WILSON: You're drifting from the point, John.

JOHN: I thought the point was whether or not I was physically capable of voting. If somebody blocked my way, beat me, and tried to kill me, I would say that I would not be, at that point in time, physically capable, so not only am I not allowed, but I can't.

WILSON: All right. Let's put it this way. If you were allowed and if you could, who would you vote for?

JOHN: I don't know, sir. I think they're both very fine gentlemen.

WILSON: But they're nothing alike. Adams is the son of a Federalist. He was born with a silver spoon in his mouth. His daddy was president and some think that makes him qualified to be president too. Jackson is a military hero. No silver spoon here, no, sir, he was born with a shovel in his hand. Jackson is a self-made man who never asked anybody for anything. If you could choose between the two, which one would you choose?

JOHN: All things being equal, I imagine that if I could vote, I would vote for that Mister Adams fella.

WILSON: Adams? Why Adams?

JOHN: He's against slave owning. His daddy was against slave owning.

WILSON: So you do know something about the candidates.

JOHN: All I know is that Mister Adams is against slave owning so if I had to choose, I would choose him.

WILSON: That all you know about the man? That he's against slave owning?

JOHN: Isn't that enough?

WILSON: To make a decision like that based upon a single issue is selfish and irresponsible, John. The future of a nation cannot rest upon a single issue.

JOHN: What other issues are there?

WILSON: I thought you said you kept up with politics.

JOHN: I never said that. You said that.

WILSON: There are plenty of issues, John. There's the issue of the Monroe Doctrine; is it good policy or merely a prelude to war? There's the question of the Twelfth Amendment; should the House of Representatives be deciding who our next president should be? And Andrew Jackson is one of the founding members of the ACS, did you know that?

JOHN: The ACS?

WILSON: American Colonization Society, John. They want to do great things for you and your people.

JOHN: They want to ship us all back to Africa.

WILSON: That was a very uninformed and uneducated opinion. What the ACS wants to do is establish a civilized, democratic, Christian society where your people can live sovereign. A place where your people can rule themselves, John. A place where your people can determine their own destiny. A place that looks a lot like America.

JOHN: Why should the colored of America have to leave America in order to live in a place that looks like America?

WILSON: Why should the colored of America be any different than all the other people of this world? Men have had to roam the face of this earth in search of a place to call home for thousands of years.

My father did it. When the English came to Ireland, they took my father's land, they burned his house, they tried to relocate him and my mother to some remote strip of barren land that couldn't even yield a single potato or carrot. He tried to fight and when it became clear that he couldn't win, he and my mother stole upon a ship bound for America. I was born one year later in Lincoln County, North Carolina. And my father was not the only man who has had to do this. World history is replete with people searching for the land of promise, a place to call home. Think of Moses. Exodus, chapter 3, verse 10, and God said to Moses, "Come, I will send you to the Pharaoh that you may bring forth my people, the sons of Israel, out of Egypt." To say that all the ACS wants to do is send your people back to Africa reveals your ignorance, John. What the ACS wants to do is to free your people from bondage.

JOHN: Perhaps I should study the issue a bit more.

WILSON: Perhaps you should. Your master freed you at a very young age, but only through training and education will you be able to retain your freedom.

    JANE enters.

JANE: Tent's going up on the green. Half the town's turned out to see it. They say they have women who do trick riding, bareback and saddled. That's what I wanna see. Women on horseback. I'll tell you, there hasn't been this much excitement around here since Misses Mavis' cow gave birth to that two-headed calf.

WILSON: Abominations.

JANE: Pardon me?

WILSON: All of it's an abomination.

JANE: Have to admit, the two-headed calf was a bit strange. I want to thank you again for allowing them to put up the tents.

WILSON: I asked you not to thank me.

JANE: Now, Robert, there's no need to be shy. You did a good deed, and I believe in giving credit where credit is due.

WILSON: It wasn't a good deed.

JANE: I know you were against the idea. . . .

WILSON: Still am. Nothing's changed.

JANE: Whenever a man goes against what he believes in order to make somebody else happy, it should be recognized.

WILSON: I didn't do it to make anybody happy.

JANE: You made me happy.

WILSON: That's not the reason I did it.

JANE: Whatever reason you did it, I want to thank you.

WILSON: It was Miller. He wouldn't give John his papers. He said he
had to pay a five hundred dollar bond and nobody has five hundred
dollars. I told him, I said the university is a sovereign entity. As long
as this boy is in the charge of the university, we didn't need to pay a
bond, but he wasn't having it. Said the way he read the law, the boy
has to pay his bond, whether he's in the charge of the university or
not. Finally, I asked him, what would happen if the university allowed
the circus to put up its tents on the green. And you know what he
said? He said that if we allowed the circus to put up its tents on the
green that he might be inclined to read the law the same way I read
the law, so I agreed to it. But just cause I agreed to it doesn't change
how I feel about it. I'm still against it and would appreciate it if you
would stop thanking me for it at every turn. Every time I hear you
say it, it puts a bad taste in my mouth.

JANE: And here I thought you had committed an act of compassion. Turns
out, you had to be forced into it.

WILSON: You consider this to be an act of compassion? Having a hand
in helping folks gawk at a collection of misery, misfortunes, and
abominations is an act of compassion? Or is it entertainment? Isn't
that what you called it? Misery, misfortune, and abominations here
for your amusement and entertainment.

JANE: I learned early in life to love life's bounty, be it misery, misfortune,
or abominations.

WILSON: You love abominations? Is that what you're saying?

JANE: I don't think you really want me to answer that, do you? I washed
the boy's bed clothes. They're out hanging on the line. When is he
going to be moving into the edifice with the other students?

JANE and WILSON exit.

JOHN (*To Audience*): Sure enough, the next day, a wagon rolled through
town with a washboard jug band on the back. The band played music
announcing to anyone who didn't already know that the circus had
officially come to town. The same day that wagon rolled into town,
Reverend Wilson rolled out of town. Said he had to meet with some
men in Chillicothe, but I thought the real reason was that he didn't

want to be here when the circus arrived. The circus consisted of an assortment of wonderful oddities and delights. There was a man who had six fingers on each hand, a woman who was covered with hair from head to toe, and a boy who could twist himself into all kinds of unnatural-looking shapes. And of course, they had the women who did trick horseback riding, bareback and saddled. They also had an elephant, a lion, a zebra that they called a striped horse, and an ostrich that caused a lot of excitement. I don't think anybody had ever seen a seven-foot bird before. I think a whole lot of folks wanted to eat it. But by far the most popular attraction, the one thing that amazed young and old alike, was Mongo, The Trained Ape. Mongo was an ape who had been trained to perform various tricks. He drank water from a cup. He smoked a cigar. He sat at a table, and when it came time to eat, he used a spoon. This was a particularly remarkable feat, especially when you consider that at least half of the population of town at the time did not use or even own a spoon. But the most disconcerting part of this animal's act was that they had outfitted him with a hat, shirt with a collar, and pair of trousers. Mongo attracted fairly moderate attention for almost a week. But this was nothing like the sensation caused later when, late one night, somebody sneaked into the encampment and defaced the board that stood in front of Mongo's tent. To the shock of some, and to the delight of others, on the board announcing Mongo the Trained Ape, somebody had crossed out the name Mongo and had written, in its place, John Newton Templeton.

JANE enters.

JANE: What you reading?

JOHN: Cicero.

JANE: Can I see?

JOHN: It's in Latin.

JANE: I didn't ask you what language it was in.

JOHN hands JANE the book. She starts to page through it.

JANE: I need you to go into town and pick up a few things.

JOHN: I can drive you if you want to go.

JANE: Did I tell you I needed a ride? Go see Mister Burke. He's going to give you some hog's blood.

JOHN: Hog's blood?

JANE: For the garden. Keep the animals away. That's gonna be one of your
jobs now. Keeping the animals out of the garden.

JOHN: What kind of animals?

JANE: Deer mostly.

JOHN: Reverend said my job was to take care of the horses.

JANE: And take care of the garden. That's now another one of your jobs.
They have deer where you come from in South Carolina?

JOHN: I know about deer.

JANE: Then you know that they have to be kept away or they'll get in and
eat up the fruit of four months of our labor. And what they don't
eat, they'll trample into the ground. From now on, your job will be
keeping them from doing that.

JOHN: With hog's blood?

JANE: You spread it around. Make a big circle around the garden, around
the house. Makes the whole place smell of death. Animals don't like
the smell of death.

JOHN: Some animals. Others might be attracted to it.

JANE: I don't know of any animals that are attracted to the smell of blood.

JOHN: Bobcat. Bear. Coyote.

JANE: You don't know much about the wilderness, do you?

JOHN: I know that the smell of blood will attract vermin.

JANE: Vermin maybe, but not bobcat, bear, and coyote. Bobcat, bear,
and coyote are killers. They're not interested in what's already dead.
They're looking to kill something. They kill, they eat. That means
that they're looking for something alive. The more alive, the better.
Now go do like I told you. The man's name is Mister Burke.

JOHN: May I have my book back, please?

JANE: You'll get it after you do like I told you.

JOHN: If I took it with me, I could read along the way.

JANE: You can read and ride at the same time?

JOHN: I'm getting fairly good at it.

JANE: Multitalented. You see the newspaper? Your man was appointed
president.

JOHN: My man?

JANE: Adams. Reverend's going to be disappointed when he hears about that.

JOHN: How did Adams get to be my man?

JANE: Weren't you pulling for him?

JOHN: I wasn't pulling for anybody.

JANE: You told Reverend you wanted him to win.

JOHN: I said that if I had to choose, I would choose him.

JANE: Cause he's against slavery?

JOHN: Isn't that good enough reason?

JANE: All I did was ask a question. You'd choose Adams cause he's against slavery?

JOHN: That's right.

JANE: The Reverend and Andrew Jackson went to school together. That means that the three of you are practically kinsmen.

JOHN: Kinsmen?

JANE: They're from North Carolina, you're from South Carolina.

JOHN: Andrew Jackson killed over six hundred Indian men, women, and children. He is not my kinsman.

JANE: But isn't that how men forge their bond-ships? Using pieces of land and boundaries drawn on a map.

JOHN: Some men.

JANE: All men. Everything in this world is about the where of the matter. Look at the men from Kentucky. They are united in the fact that they hate the men from Virginia. The Virginians got their own handshake, their own song. And you, the Reverend, and Andrew Jackson are all from the Carolinas. Seems to me that if you could choose, you would have chosen him, he being your kinsman and all.

JOHN: But I can't choose now and couldn't have chosen then. So who I would have chosen, if I could have chosen, is irrelevant, now isn't it?

JANE: That's why I am so perplexed. Seeing how your opinion on the matter is absolutely irrelevant, I don't understand why you didn't just shuffle yo' feet, nod yo' head and agree with the Reverend.

JOHN: This may come as a shock to you, but I am a free thinker. I don't shuffle my feet or nod my head in sycophantic agreement with any man.

JANE: Sycophantic?

JOHN: That's right. Sycophantic. You know what it means?

JANE: I know what it means. Do you?

JOHN: It means I am not some bent-back slave who stands at the elbow of the master agreeing with everything he says. I am a free man. A free man of color. Now if you would please give me my book back....

JANE: Then how come you didn't pay your bond?

JOHN: My what?

JANE: The law says that every free man of color has to post a bond upon entering the state.

JOHN: I know what the law says.

JANE: Then how come you didn't pay?

JOHN: Reverend says that the university is sovereign. Reverend says as long as I'm here, I'm sovereign.

JANE: Reverend says Reverend says. What do you say?

JOHN: I agree with the Reverend. The university is sovereign. That means as long as I'm here, I'm sovereign.

JANE: If you consider yourself sovereign living here and now, then you must have also considered yourself sovereign when you were a slave living on that plantation back in South Carolina.

JOHN: I think there's a difference.

JANE: Do you? Do you remember your life before liberation?

JOHN: What kind of question is that?

JANE: It must've been hard work for a boy of seven, eight years old, picking all that cotton.

JOHN: I didn't pick cotton.

JANE: Then you were a pickaninny.

JOHN: A pickaninny.

JANE: A slave living on a cotton plantation who didn't pick cotton is called a pickaninny.

JOHN: I know what it's called.

JANE: Cause you didn't pick any. I'm guessing you ran around half-naked, maybe wearing a burlap bag if you were lucky.

JOHN: I didn't wear no burlap bag.

JANE: You had nice clothes.

JOHN: Hand-me-downs.

JANE: Hand-me-downs?

JOHN: From the son of Reverend Master Williamson.

JANE: Nice clothes. Better than what you're wearing now, I'm guessing.

JOHN: Somewhat better.

JANE: What about the beatings? You must've been beaten on a regular basis.

JOHN: May I have my book back, please?

JANE: Answer my question first. Were you beat as a little boy?

JOHN: I was never beaten.

JANE: Where you hungry?

JOHN: We were well taken care of.

JANE: They teach you to read?

JOHN: Like I said. We were well taken care of.

JANE: You didn't pick cotton, you didn't work in the fields, you had nice clothes, at least better than what you're wearing now. Plenty to eat, never mistreated, they even schooled you, boy, taught you how to read. So explain to me the difference between your life then and your life now.

JOHN: That's easy. You see, I have something now that I didn't have back then. Now I'm the one who makes the choices about my life. I control my direction and I control my destiny. I remember the first time I saw my daddy do that. My daddy was a carpenter. Supposed to have been one of the best around. Man came to my master's house one day and wanted to hire my daddy out. He said they were building a new city called Washington, and they were looking for the best masons, the best carpenters they could find. By then, my master, Master Williamson, had found religion. He had received what he called second sight. He was no longer Master Williamson.

He had become Reverend Master Williamson and no longer hired his slaves out to anybody who had a dollar. So Reverend Master Williamson did something he had never done before. He told the man that he would have to ask my daddy and then let my daddy decide if he wanted to go help build this new city or not. My daddy listened to the man talk about the great buildings they were building. A tower, a rotunda, a great house. And then, at the end of it all, my daddy carefully considered, nodded his head, and said if it was that great, that he wanted to go there and be a part of it all. I had never seen my daddy do that before. To consider, nod his head, then decide. I thought it was the most wonderful thing in the world. Now, I have that power, and that's the difference between then and now. Now, I have the power to consider, nod my head, then decide.

JANE: I can't tell if you're mixing up this stew for my benefit or if you actually believe this hog slop you're trying to serve me on a silver platter. You do not have the power to decide anything that happens in your life. You gave up that right when you failed to pay your bond. When you failed to pay your bond, you became a charge of the university. We are responsible for you and everything you do. That means you can nod your head all you want but you're not making any decisions, not around here. That's the reason folks in town wanted you to pay your bond. Ohio is a free state. They don't like the idea of slavery. Neither do they like the idea of indentured servitude.

JOHN: I'm not an indentured servant.

JANE: You work here, you don't get paid, the university is responsible for you. You're indentured, whether you like it or not. That means that the only difference between now and back then is back then you were a little better dressed because back then you got hand-me-downs from your master's son, but that's the only difference. Now go into town and do like I told you. You'll get your book when you get back.

SCENE TWO

JOHN and WILSON.

WILSON: I saw what somebody wrote on that board in front of that monkey cage. When did it happen?

JOHN: Couple weeks ago.

WILSON: It's been like that since I left? Nobody took it down?

JOHN: Not if it's still there.

WILSON: I'm sorry, John. I allowed them to bring their wickedness here. I knew something like this would happen.

JOHN: It's not your fault.

WILSON: I'm gonna go see Miller, and I'm gonna give them twenty-four hours to tear down that tent, pack their wagons and get off of government property. If they're not gone by the morning, I will go out and tear down that tent myself.

JOHN: With all respect, sir, you tear down that tent, all you gonna do is antagonize folks.

WILSON: Folks need to be antagonized. They can't do something like this without expecting retribution. To compare a man to an ape. A man is not an ape.

JOHN: But we don't even know if they're the one's who did it.

WILSON: Who else could have done it?

JOHN: Most folks in town can't even read, much less write, and you saw the sign. That sign was done up in a very nice hand. Most of the folks I met had to have somebody read to them what it said and a lot of them didn't find it funny. The only folks who found it funny were the folks here on campus.

WILSON: What folks?

JOHN: The gentleman from Virginia, Mister Drake. And the gentleman from Kentucky, Mister Ward. They thought it was funny. In fact, Mister Ward was the one who told me about it.

WILSON: You suggesting that Mister Ward did this?

JOHN: I'm suggesting that perhaps we've been too harsh in our judgment of the folks in town. I don't think they had a hand in this.

WILSON: They knew the sign was there. And nobody, not one man stepped forward to remove it. The tent goes the first thing in the morning.

JOHN: What about my papers?

WILSON: What about them?

JOHN: Miller agreed to waive my bond in exchange for the right to put up that tent. If you make them take it down . . .

WILSON: It'll send a message that we are serious about you being here. It'll send a message that we will not tolerate any type of tomfoolery.

JOHN: What happens if they revoke my papers?

WILSON: That's not gonna happen.

JOHN: What if it does?

WILSON: Half the town owes the university money for lands they've leased. If they threaten to revoke your papers, I will be forced to demand full payment for every lease that's now in arrears. And they can't pay, John. They don't have the money to pay. I don't think you have to worry.

JOHN: I don't like this. I don't like being in the middle of this.

WILSON: You're in the middle, John, whether you like it or not. You know who I met with when I was in Chillicothe? I met with members of the ACS. Congress just gave the ACS $100,000, John. They're ready to charter a ship. They're ready to purchase ironworks for a sawmill and a gristmill, tools, muskets, gunpowder, fishing equipment, everything men would need to settle a new land. The only thing they need now is someone to govern that land, and I believe that someone is you.

JOHN: Me?

WILSON: There are three other men in this country, free men of color, who are receiving education and training to undertake this endeavor. There's one at Amherst, one at Bowdoin College, and one at Dartmouth. But you, John, you have something these other men don't. You have a mandate from God. I believe that you are the man God chose to lead his people to a new land.

JOHN: Liberia?

WILSON: Liberia.

JOHN: But I don't know anything about Liberia.

WILSON: The only thing you need to know is the word of God. Look at this area. The men who settled this area didn't know anything about the area before they came here. Twenty-five years ago, this was nothing but wilderness. No human habitation at all. Wild animals, deer, bobcats, and Indians. The men who came here knew nothing but the word of God. But we have blessed this land with civilization, culture, and education. We came here and brought God to a Godless region. And that's what God is asking you to do, John. To lead your people through the wilderness to a new land. To bring God to a Godless land.

JOHN: God is asking me to do this?

WILSON: All you have to do is look at your origins.

JOHN: What origins?

WILSON: The circumstances surrounding your birth, John.

JOHN: The snowfall?

WILSON: After the snowfall. What happened that summer, the summer after you were born?

JOHN: What do you mean?

WILSON: There was a man named Gabriel Prosser. You remember Gabriel Prosser?

JOHN: I remember.

WILSON: Who was he?

JOHN: A blacksmith. A slave.

WILSON: And what did Gabriel Prosser do?

JOHN: They said he tried to organize a revolt.

WILSON: Was the revolt successful?

JOHN: No.

WILSON: What happened?

JOHN: They were discovered.

WILSON: Discovered?

JOHN: He and thirty-five others.

WILSON: What happened after they were discovered, John?

JOHN: They were hanged. Thirty-six of them were hanged in the public square.

WILSON: Then what happened? (*JOHN doesn't answer.*) John? What happened after they hanged the men responsible for planning the revolt?

JOHN: After they hanged the men responsible for planning the revolt, the night riders came. They went from house to house. They took only the boys. The baby boys. All of the black-skinned, the brown-skinned, and the yellow-skinned baby boys.

WILSON: And what did they do with the baby boys?

JOHN: They killed them. They shot them. They drowned them in buckets. They cut their throats. They smashed in their skulls with stones. They ran them through with wooden stakes and stuck them to trees. They left shredded bits of bone and flesh scattered along the roadside that led to and from town.

WILSON: What happened to you?

JOHN: My mother said she tried to hide me, but she couldn't hide me. She tried but my mistress, my mistress found me. She took me in. She hid me until the danger had passed.

WILSON: Your mistress may have been the one who hid you, but she was guided by the hand of God. It was God who saved you out of all the others who died.

JOHN: You think God saved me to go to Liberia?

WILSON: To lead your people to Liberia, John. It couldn't be any clearer if God himself appeared and wrote it on the wall.

JOHN: I always thought that I would be a preacher. Or a teacher. I had always imagined myself standing in front of a classroom full of colored children, little brown and black boys and girls. I always thought that was my purpose, that that was the reason God had saved me. I never imagined this.

WILSON: That's the reason I'm here. To teach you. To guide you. To help you understand the things you could never imagine on your own.

JOHN: Liberia?

WILSON: Liberia.

JOHN: What do I have to do?

WILSON: Keep up with your studies. The officers of the ACS will come here sometime next year. They want to meet you, talk to you, get to know you to decide if indeed you are the man they are looking for.

JOHN: They're not convinced?

WILSON: They don't know. Not like I know. But don't you worry. We'll convince them. In the meantime, I'm going to go get rid of that tent. I think you would agree that we cannot allow the future governor of Liberia to be compared to an ape.

JOHN: Reverend?

WILSON: Yes?

JOHN: One more thing. A small thing.

WILSON: What is it?

JOHN: I'm almost embarrassed to ask, because I don't want to sound like I'm ungrateful. . . .

WILSON: Spit it out, boy. What is it?

JOHN: I would like to be paid.

WILSON: Pardon me?

JOHN: For the work I do around the house. For being the student servant and taking care of the horses, taking care of the garden. I would like to be paid.

WILSON: Our agreement was that you would do it in exchange for your room and board.

JOHN: I understand that, sir.

WILSON: It's an even exchange, John.

JOHN: But I would still like to be paid. Even if it's an even exchange, I want to be paid for the work I do. I want to hold the money in my hand. I want to put the money in my pocket. Even if I give it right back to you after you give it to me, I still want to be paid.

WILSON: All right. I think I understand. Have you thought about how much you would like to be paid?

JOHN: You said it was an even exchange . . .

WILSON: All right, even exchange. How often would you like to be paid?

JOHN: How often do the men in the edifice pay for their room and board?

WILSON: Once a month.

JOHN: Then once a month. You pay me, I'll pay you.

WILSON: Fine, John. I think we can arrange that. Anything else?

JOHN: No, sir. Nothing else. Thank you.

> *WILSON exits.*

JOHN (*To audience*): Over the next few months, I tried to figure out who had defaced that sign and written my name over that of Mongo the Ape's. Later, after I was invited to join the Athenian Literary Society, I got the opportunity to spend time with Mister Ward. He was the president of the society, which gave me ample opportunity to read his handwriting. This is where my suspicions about him turned into certainty.

JANE enters with a shirt, hat, and pair of men's trousers.

JANE: Here. This is for you.

JOHN: What?

JANE: New clothes. Not exactly new. New to you. Shirt, hat, trousers. They're cleaning you up. That's the first thing they do. They clean you up, then they get you fat. After that, ring the dinner bell cause it's suppertime.

She offers him the clothes. He only looks at her.

JANE (*Cont'd*): What you waiting for? Take it. Better than what you're wearing now. You ever wear a collared shirt before?

JOHN: No.

JANE: Better get used to it. It's going to be around your neck for a long time. It'll be your albatross.

JOHN: My what?

JANE: Albatross. From *The Rime of the Ancient Mariner* by Samuel Taylor Coleridge. Ever hear of it?

JOHN: No.

JANE: That's right, I forgot. You've taken up the Reverend's penchant for studying only dead men who wrote in Greek and Latin and Coleridge is very much alive. He's English. But we won't hold that against him, now will we? He's a poet who wrote a poem about a sailor who kills a magical albatross that was trying to help him. For this crime against nature, the sailor was forced to wear the corpse of the bird around his neck.

> *Ah! well a-day! what evil looks*
> *Had I from old and young!*
> *Instead of the cross, the Albatross*
> *About my neck was hung.*

This collared shirt will be your albatross. Go ahead. Take it.

JOHN: If I have done something to disrespect you, I apologize.

JANE: Disrespect?

JOHN: All I've done since I've been here is try to please you. And all you've done in return is show me contempt.

JANE: Perhaps my contempt stems from your incessant attempt to please. You ever think of that? You claim to be a free man of color, a man who is in control of his own destiny, but all I see you doing is running around here, nodding your head and smiling. And the type of head nodding you're doing is not the type your father did. Now if that is who you are, all you have to do is say so, John. All you have to do is tell me that you don't want any trouble. Just tell me that the reason you're here is to make everybody happy, and I will leave you alone, I swear, never again will you ever hear another cross word from me, butter won't melt in my mouth. But if you are the man you say you are, your desire to please makes my stomach turn.

JOHN: What's wrong with trying to please people?

JANE: Nothing. If that's the reason you're here. Is that the reason you're here? To dance for us, maybe sing a lil song every now and then? To make everybody happy?

JOHN: I am here to be educated.

JANE: Educated? Such a big word for such a little boy.

JOHN: I have been chosen. Chosen to be governor of a new nation. Governor of a new world.

JANE: You say that as if it's something I didn't know. Is this news to you? I told you this when you first came here. They're training you. They're getting you ready. They're going to clean you up, get you fat, then prop you up in the window for the entire world to see. And you don't even give a damn. Like a hog gorging itself on slop, you don't care that the sound you hear in the background is that of a blade being sharpened. I have to admit, Robert knew what he was doing when he chose you. Here. Here's your clothes.

JOHN: I wasn't chosen by the Reverend. I was chosen by God.

JANE: Course you were. Here's your clothes.

He takes the clothes.

JANE: And I want to apologize. I apologize for everything I've said to you. I promise, you won't hear anything like that from me again. It's just that, when this moment came, I had hoped that somebody else would be standing where you're standing. But that's not your fault. You can't help who you are. You're just a poor ignorant beast being trained for something that you don't understand, and I have to understand that that's not your fault. I'm sorry. I promise, I'll do better in the future.

She exits. After a moment, JOHN starts to undress and eventually puts on the clothes.

JOHN (*To audience*): I had been called names before. Ignorant. Coon. Beast. Nigger. Of course, a colored man living in this country has seen hatred, sometimes on a daily basis. And any colored man living in this country who says that he has not been the object of hatred is either lying to you, or he hasn't been paying attention. So it was not the name-calling that bothered me. I think it was the pity with which she did it. While I had been, in the past, the object of hatred, I had never before been the object of naked pity.

He has finished putting on the shirt, trousers, and hat.

JOHN (*Cont'd*): Look at this. It fit. The trousers, the hat, the shirt, it all fit like it had been made for me. I had never worn a collared shirt before and expected the collar to be tight around my neck, but the shirt fit fine. In fact, the shirt was very comfortable. Except for one thing. It had an odor, a faint odor that I couldn't quite identify. After I tried on the shirt, the trousers, and the hat, I sat in my room thinking about the pity that the wife of the reverend had heaped upon me. Her pity became my pity, and while I should have been very happy, the only thing I could think about was Mongo the Ape.

Lights fade. End of Act One.

ACT TWO

SCENE ONE

JOHN NEWTON TEMPLETON is alone on stage.

JOHN: The men of the American Colonization Society were an interesting bunch. While the organization claimed members from every state in the union, the ones who came to visit were from parts of Ohio, Pennsylvania, Virginia, Carolina, and Washington, D.C. Counting the good Reverend Wilson, there were twelve in all and as far as I could tell, all were pastors, preachers, ministers, and missionaries. Reverend Wilson had arranged this as the first of what was to be two meetings. It was scheduled during class hiatus so as not to interrupt my very important studies. The men arrived throughout the day on a Monday and stayed for seven days. During those seven days, every morning I would recite for them, in either Latin or Greek, passages from Caesar's Commentaries, Cicero's Orations, and the Greek Testament. Afternoons were set aside for debate, or what they called debate.

They gave me topics such as "Was the conspiracy against Julius Caesar justified?" Or "Should women be allowed to vote?" After stating the topic, they would then ask questions related to that topic, and I would answer their questions. This was their idea of debate. We did this every afternoon from one until six. In the evenings, they had dinner, during which they reviewed the events of the day. Being the student servant, I had the honor of serving them their dinner. During the first few days of this routine, I thought they were trying to see how smart I was, to see how much I knew. After a while, I realized that they were not trying to measure the depth and breadth of my knowledge. They were trying to determine if I was actually thinking for myself, or if I was merely repeating what someone had taught me. When, on or about the fifth day, they realized that I was indeed thinking for myself, they seemed to be both delighted and surprised. Reverend Wilson was beaming like a proud new father, and there I was in my shirt, trousers, and hat, performing for the gentlemen. For some reason, I couldn't get the image of Mongo out of my mind.

JOHN sits and starts to read. WILSON enters.

WILSON: You see what your president did?

JOHN: My president?

WILSON: John Quincy Adams.

JOHN: How did he become my president?

WILSON: If you could vote, you would have voted for him.

JOHN: But I didn't vote for him because I can't vote.

WILSON: But you would have. He would have been your choice. That makes him your president. You see what he did?

JOHN: What did he do?

WILSON: He appointed Henry Clay as Secretary of State.

JOHN: I heard about that.

WILSON: Which proves what I've been saying about the man all along. He is corrupt.

JOHN: Corrupt?

WILSON: Henry Clay ran against Adams for president. When it looked like Clay couldn't win, he had a meeting with Adams, withdrew his candidacy, and then threw his support behind Adams. Adams gets elected and what does he do? He appoints Clay as Secretary of State.

JOHN: That's right. Clay helped him get elected. All Adams did was return the favor.

WILSON: Return the favor?

JOHN: I'd do it. If somebody helped me the way Clay helped Adams, I'd return the favor.

WILSON: Please don't tell me that. Please don't tell me that you would fall into the same trap.

JOHN: What trap?

WILSON: Adams didn't appoint Clay because he was the best man for the job. He didn't appoint him because he believed in what Clay stood for. Adams and Clay can't even agree on the color of the moon. The only reason Adams appointed Clay as Secretary of State was to uphold his end of a corrupt bargain. In Latin it's called quid pro quo. You know what that means?

JOHN: Yes.

WILSON: What?

JOHN: It means something given or received in exchange for something else.

WILSON: That's right. And when applied to politics, what does it imply?

JOHN: It implies a breach.

WILSON: What kind of a breach?

JOHN: A breach in the public trust.

WILSON: That's right. Now I hope you're not telling me that you would do the same. I hope you're not telling me that you would betray your own convictions in order to return a favor that someone did for you because if so, we've made a terrible mistake.

JOHN: I suppose I would have to consider all of the ramifications.

WILSON: What's to consider? If someone asks you to betray your own convictions, you don't do it, John, no matter what that person did for you. Look at what I have here.

    He produces a letter.

It's a letter from Reverend McLain. He talks about how impressed he and the other members of the committee were with your performance.

JOHN: My performance?

WILSON: On your oral examinations. Your performance exceeded everyone's expectations. They have asked me to officially ask you if you will accept their offer to become the first governor of Liberia.

JOHN: I thought we had to have an additional meeting.

WILSON: Apparently they didn't think it was necessary. You know why? Because they believe you to be a man of your convictions, John. They believe you to be a man who thinks for himself. A man who would not find himself in debt to some other man because of some small favor. I hope they're not mistaken. I hope that you are indeed a man of your convictions.

JOHN: I believe I am.

WILSON: I believe you are as well. I'll write the committee and tell them that you've accepted the offer. They'll start the paperwork. In a couple of months, we ought to receive your official charter. Congratulations, Governor.

JOHN: Thank you. Now when do I get to meet the others?

WILSON: The others?

JOHN: The first thing I'm going to have to do is establish a provisional government. I'm going to have to draft a political constitution, and I'm going to have to establish a church. This is going to take years to accomplish, and it's going to take more than just one man.

WILSON: Don't worry. We'll get you the help you need. Did you finish your essay for admission into the Literary Society?

JOHN: I finished.

WILSON: Did you give it to Mister Ward?

JOHN: I did.

WILSON: And?

JOHN: He rejected it.

WILSON: Rejected it?

JOHN: He said he wanted me to prepare a topic for debate instead.

WILSON: That Mister Ward is a rascal, isn't he?

JOHN: That would not be the term I would use.

WILSON: No need to be nasty, John. What topic for debate did they give you?

JOHN: "Why should ex-slaves go back to a land that sent them into slavery in the first place?"

WILSON: Interesting topic.

JOHN: Interesting?

WILSON: I'm sure you'll do just fine.

JOHN: He's baiting me.

WILSON: Probably.

JOHN: He heard about my meetings with the Colonization Society and he's baiting me.

WILSON: He's probably trying to test your mettle. That's all. See what you're made of.

JOHN: If he wants to see what I'm made of, all he has to do is read my essay. "The Claims of Liberia," that's what I'm made of. That's who I am. But he doesn't want to read it.

WILSON: The topic for debate is merely an exercise, John. An exercise in the powers of persuasion.

JOHN: I think they're looking for a reason not to admit me.

WILSON: Don't worry. You'll do fine. You know what today is? The first of the month. Time to settle our account. How's it going with the horses?

JOHN: Going fine.

WILSON: Jane tells me that the palomino looks a little lazy moving off her hind legs.

JOHN: She was dipping a bit under saddle, but her back right hoof needed a little trimming. I've already done it and she's moving just fine.

WILSON: Good work, John, thank you. How many hours do you have for the month?

JOHN: Let's see, three hours a day, six days a week, four weeks, that comes to seventy-two hours.

WILSON: Seventy-two hours at seven cents an hour. . . .

JOHN: Five dollars and four cents.

WILSON pays JOHN.

WILSON: There you are.

JOHN: Thank you.

WILSON: Don't mention it. You earned every bit of it, Governor.

JOHN: I suppose I ought to settle up now as well.

WILSON: If you'd like.

JOHN: How much do I owe you?

WILSON: I'm not sure. Let's see, board is a dollar twenty-five a week.

JOHN: Four weeks.

WILSON: That comes to five dollars, even.

JOHN pays WILSON.

JOHN: There you are, sir.

WILSON: Thank you.

JOHN: My pleasure.

WILSON: Bet you never thought you'd come out ahead on the deal, did you?

JOHN: No, never thought that. By the way, I'll need a receipt.

WILSON: Pardon me?

JOHN: A receipt. For the money I paid you. I'll need a receipt.

WILSON: Yes. Of course. Let me just . . .

WILSON writes out a receipt.

JOHN (*To audience*): Holding true to your convictions may make your life more meaningful, but it was nothing like the thrill I got when payday rolled around and I got paid for the work I did. And then to pay for my own room and board, to pay my own way, to hold the receipts in my hand . . .

WILSON (*Handing the receipt to JOHN*): There you are.

JOHN: Thank you.

WILSON exits.

JOHN (*To audience*): It was the sweetest honey, nothing like it in the world.

I prepared for my debate to enter into the Literary Society. Or at least I tried to prepare. "Why should ex-slaves go back to a land that sent them into slavery in the first place?" I could answer the first part of that question: Why should ex-slaves go back to Africa? That part of the question, I had no problem with. But why go back to a land that had sent them into slavery in the first place? Try as I might, I couldn't formulate a logical argument to that part of the question and this bothered me. If I was going to go to Liberia, I needed to be able to answer the second part of that question.

JANE enters.

JANE: I saw that Maybell was dipping a bit under saddle.

JOHN: She needed a little farrier work on her hind hooves. I've already taken care of it.

JANE: You sure she didn't pull a muscle?

JOHN: Pretty sure.

JANE: If she pulled a muscle, she's going to need some attention.

JOHN: You want me to take her out so you can inspect her?

JANE: No, John, I trust you. I'm just concerned, that's all.

JOHN: I wouldn't let anything happen to that horse. I treat her as if she were my own.

JANE: I know that. And I appreciate it. Thank you.

JOHN: No need to thank me. Just doing my job. Just doing what I'm getting paid to do.

JANE: You know that she belongs to me.

JOHN: I know that, ma'am. It was just a figure of speech, that I treat her as if she were my own. I know she belongs to you.

JANE: No. I meant that Maybell used to be mine. Robert bought her when she was a filly and gave her to me as a present. He knew I always wanted a horse. He knew I wanted to learn to ride. Right after we moved here, my youngest boy David died, and I guess he thought Maybell might lift my spirits a bit, which she did. Used to be my job to go out and groom her every day. Pulling, clipping, trimming. After a while, Reverend said I was paying too much attention to her. Said that if we left her out in the pasture where she could roll around on the ground, she wouldn't need to be groomed everyday. But she liked it when I would come out and spend time with her. Seems like she knew when I was supposed to be there, and if I was late, she'd let me know about it. If I was late, I'd see her hanging her head over the door. She'd see me and then start bumping the side of the stall with her hoof.

JOHN: She does that with me.

JANE: Seems like you can tell what she's thinking.

JOHN: She's a smart horse.

JANE: Yes, she is.

JOHN: How'd your boy die?

JANE: I had three boys. Matthew, Mark, and David. The oldest, Matthew, died of the cholera when he was eleven. Mark died of the yellow vomit when he was fourteen. And my baby, David, he lived to be nineteen years old. He wanted to be a preacher like his father. He wanted to prove to his father that he was good enough to march into the wilderness and spread the word of God. He thought that all you needed to go into the wilderness was the word of God. That armed with the word of God, the savages would fall to their knees and pray. But you need more than the word of God. You need to have a gun, and you need to have the heart to use it. But David didn't understand that. They found what was left of his body near what used to be a Shawnee encampment. Animals had gotten to it. And the Shawnee, they had striped his body of everything they could use. Boots, belt, everything except his Bible.

JOHN: I'm sorry.

JANE: No need to be sorry. I'm done with my grieving. I have no more tears to shed.

JOHN: I'm taking Maybell into town. I'll make sure to pay attention to how she's riding. If anything's not right, I'll be sure to take care of it.

JANE: What you going into town for?

JOHN: Mister Morgan ordered some iron leg-traps for me.

JANE: Iron leg-traps?

JOHN: Deer got into the garden again. I figured if we can't scare them away, we'll trap 'em. Maybe have ourselves a little venison.

JANE: I don't want iron leg-traps in my garden.

JOHN: I'm not putting them in the garden. I'm going to put them in the deer run along the edge of the woodline.

JANE: Do you have to?

JOHN: Don't know of any other way. Hog's blood doesn't work.

JANE: It'll work.

JOHN: Didn't work over the last two springs. Didn't work over the summer.

JANE: Just can't use it all the time. First time a deer smells blood, it scares 'em. Makes 'em think death is near. But if they smell old blood, they get used to it.

JOHN: You want me to go out there and sprinkle blood around the house and garden every day?

JANE: What you got to do is figure out when the herd is going to come, then spread the blood right before they get here. That way, it'll be fresh.

JOHN: How am I supposed to figure out when a herd of deer is going to come?

JANE: Used to be easy. They used to come every four to eight weeks. And there was a tribe of Miami that used to follow them. Small tribe. Peaceful. Maybe ten men. Twelve, maybe fifteen women. A brood of small children. You'd see them up on the north ridge. You'd see the Indians and know that the deer herd was somewhere near. But you don't see them anymore. Not around here.

JOHN: I saw some.

JANE: You saw some what?

JOHN: Indians. Three of them. Don't know what kind. Brave, squaw, and a child. I was coming back from Albany. The lower plain was flooded, so I was following the ridges on the way back. I had gotten lost, a little twisted around, and that's when I rode up on the child, maybe three, four years old. He was just laying there, sleeping on a bed of pine needles. I got off the horse for a better look, and that's when the brave appeared. I don't know who was more scared, me or him. Then the mother appeared, snatched up the baby, and the three were gone, just like that.

JANE: You tell anybody?

JOHN: No.

JANE: Don't. Don't tell anyone.

JOHN: Why not?

JANE: They're probably Miami. They're peaceful. No need to say anything. Just keep it to yourself.

JOHN: You think the deer herd is near?

JANE: I don't know.

JOHN: You said they follow the herd.

JANE: I want you to figure out another way to keep the deer out.

JOHN: I don't know of any other way.

JANE: There's always another way.

JOHN: You said my job was to keep the deer out of the garden. If that's my job, you should let me do my job the best way I see fit.

JANE: All right. You're right. Make sure you keep the horses away. I don't want to see my Maybell get torn up by one of those devices.

JOHN: I'll keep her away.

JANE: Thank you, John.

> *He moves to exit, stops.*

JOHN: Ma'am?

JANE: Yes?

JOHN: Why don't you come out and ride with me one afternoon? I'll get Maybell ready and I'll take one of the other horses and we can go up around the north ridge if you want. It's real pretty this time of the year. Or if you want, I'll get Maybell ready and you can just go off on your own. Whatever you prefer.

JANE: Whatever I prefer. You know what I would prefer? I would prefer that you did just that. I would prefer that you went out right now and put a saddle on Maybell and I would get on her and I would ride her into town. I would prefer to get on her and ride her to someplace far away from here. But that's not going to happen, is it?

JOHN: I could get her ready if you want.

JANE: Are you trying to be mean to me or are you just stupid?

JOHN: Ma'am?

JANE: I've been treating you with a civil tongue and would prefer if you did the same.

JOHN: I'm not trying to be mean to you.

JANE: Then you're just stupid.

JOHN: I'm sorry if I said something to offend you.

JANE: Men ride horses, John.

JOHN: What do you mean?

JANE: Men ride horses, and I am not a man.

JOHN: I've seen women ride horses.

JANE: Sidesaddle. But you can't climb a hill sidesaddle. You can't ford a stream sidesaddle.

JOHN: What about the women in the town? Miss Clark? Miss Thompson? And the women in the circus. They don't ride sidesaddle.

JANE: Miss Clark, Miss Thompson, and the women in the circus are not considered to be women. They look like women. They got the parts of a woman but they smoke tobacco. They spit. They're unmarried. They have no home, they have no God. These are not women, John. They're freaks. Aberrations. Abominations.

JOHN: Abominations?

JANE: A woman would never ride with her legs splayed open astride a beast, and I am a woman. I'm not supposed to ride with my legs splayed open. I have to ride in the buckboard or in a wagon. I have to have a man drive me to anyplace I want to go. But you, you can ride. An ex-slave gets on my horse and rides, but I can't ride. I'm not allowed. I'm not allowed because I'm a woman.

JOHN: I didn't know that.

JANE: What do you know other than Latin and Greek?

JOHN: I'm sorry.

JANE: Nothing in the Bible says a woman can't ride a horse. At least, I don't think there is, but I don't know for sure cause I can't read Hebrew. Least, I can't read it well enough to tell. And the English Bible, the King James Bible, they say that's not God's word. They say it's what King James said the Bible says. So until I learn how to read Hebrew, I won't know whether the Bible is against it or not.

JOHN: Would you like to learn?

JANE: Learn what?

JOHN: Learn how to read Hebrew.

JANE: You going to teach me?

JOHN: I could.

JANE: That's very sweet of you.

JOHN: I could do it.

JANE: You think that would change things? You think teaching me how to read Hebrew or teaching me how to read Greek is going to stop this awful, hateful thing from growing inside of me? They brought you here and they let you go to school but they won't let me go to school. My husband is president of the university, and I can't even step foot inside the door. Not unless I'm looking to do laundry. Wash the sheets. Clean the floors. Each time I found out I was going to have a child, I would to pray to God and ask God to please, God, please don't let it be a girl. I would rather it be born dead and I'd feed it to the hogs than it be born a girl. Cause I wouldn't know how to explain to a girl that the hunger she had inside would never be satisfied. I wouldn't know how to teach a girl to never look to the stars but to keep her head bowed down in subservient submission to some man. So I asked God to please, God, give me boys, and God answered my prayers. One by one, he gave me three beautiful, healthy boys. And then, one by one, he took those boys away. I grieved for them, one by one, and then I stopped grieving. Then you came. You could teach me how to read Hebrew and you could teach me how to read Greek, but that isn't going to change anything. I still can't step foot inside the door. I am still forced to stand here and watch while they let you in over me. They let you in. They welcome you with open arms. They give you this gift, and what do you do? You squander it.

JOHN: I'm sorry you feel that way.

JANE: Why be sorry? If you're going to be a houseboy for the slave owners of this world, don't be sorry about it. Stand up and be proud that you're their houseboy.

JOHN: I'm nobody's houseboy.

JANE: You go to Liberia, you're going to be the houseboy for every man that has ever bought, sold, or traded in human flesh in this world. "Yes, sir, Master, you got some niggers you done using? Ah'll take ker of 'em fer ya."

JOHN: Sometimes the limitations of your comprehension are downright embarrassing.

JANE: The limitations of my comprehension?

JOHN: I am truly sorry that you feel the way you do. However, ultimately, what you think, how you feel, your opinion on what I'm about to do is of absolutely no consequence to me. You want me to stand up for what I believe in? I am standing. You want me to be proud of the choice I've made? I am proud, I am happy, and I am humbled to be able to carry out the will of our Lord God Jesus Christ.

JANE: Typical nigger. Don't know the difference between the will of God and the will of a slave owner.

JOHN: I don't know any slave owners. The only slave owner I know died a long time ago.

JANE: Who do you think is running the ACS? They're slave owners, John. All of them. They all either own slaves now or did own slaves at one point in their lives. That's their bond-ship. That's the thing that binds them together. And you're too stupid to see that you're doing exactly what they want you to do. You go to Liberia and take all of the free men of color with you, who will that leave here in this country? Only the slaves, John. Only the slaves. And what will happen if they ever let a woman get anything other than an elementary school education? Will she have to leave the country as well? Is that the price we have to pay for challenging what they believe, for challenging their dogma? Banishment? I can't go to school. I can't ride a horse. Maybell is my horse. Reverend gave her to me. He said she was mine. But all I can do is look at her. All I can do is stand there and watch while somebody else rides. They're giving you your own country. Will you be able to ride?

JANE exits.

JOHN (*To audience*): The Indians I saw, I saw as I was on my way back from Albany. I had ridden out there because I heard rumors about a free man who had opened a school and since it was only about ten, twelve miles out, I wanted to go see for myself. The man's name was Jonathan Goodman, and when I got there, all I saw was one room that also served as his living quarters. In that room he had three books. One Bible, the English King James version, a very elementary book on world geography, and a book called "The Life of Gustavus Vassa, the African." There was not one volume of Latin verses, not one volume of Greek philosophy, and after talking to him, I found out that he didn't even have any students. Hardly the ingredients of what I would call a school. I asked him, I said, "Where are the students?" Poor man, he looked around the empty room and said, "They are here. They're here." Not wanting to embarrass him by leaving straight away, I picked up "The Life of Gustavus

Vassa" and started to page through it. I found out that Gustavus had been a slave in Africa before being sold to an American slave trader. But his description of what he called African slavery bore no resemblance to the institution we had come to know in America. While he was certainly owned while in Africa, the African sense of ownership was different than ours. Gustavus seemed to be owned by the entire community, and he had a place in that community. He was never required to do any more work than the other members of the community, he was allowed to own his own property, and he was allowed to have a family and that family was kept intact. There was none of the cruelty and inhumanity that permeated American slavery. In fact, the only similarity between African slavery and American slavery was that they were both, for some reason, called slavery. This was not what I had been led to believe about Africa. "Why should ex-slaves go back to a land that was the birthplace of slavery?" Because Africa was not the birthplace of slavery. At least not the type of slavery that had a stranglehold on America. I thought this was the answer. The answer to the only question I had left. Until I realized that I would soon be there in Africa. That I would soon hear all of these different languages and see for myself all of these strange customs. I realized that these were the people that I had been chosen to bring civilization to. That's when I started to have my first real doubts, because from what I read during those couple of hours, it didn't appear as if these people were the ones who needed the civilization.

> *WILSON enters with a leather bag containing a flintlock pistol, powder, ball bag, and horn, all of which he starts to unpack.*

WILSON: John? How about after supper you get the horses ready and you and I go out riding. I want to look around down near the river.

JOHN: Sounds good to me.

WILSON: And I heard back from Reverend McLain. He's found a man he wants you to meet. Another free man of color who could assist you in Liberia. Reverend McLain is going to bring him when he comes for your graduation. You can meet this man, talk to him, and if you like him, he can stay here and begin his training in the fall.

JOHN: Don't you mean his education?

WILSON: I'm sorry?

JOHN: You said he can begin his training in the fall. I think you meant to say his education.

WILSON: Training, education. Same thing.

JOHN: Not quite. Training comes from the Latin, traginare, meaning to draw out and manipulate in order to bring about a desired form. When you train something, you manipulate it to follow, to come after or behind. But the word educate, it comes from the Latin, educare, meaning to develop the power of reasoning and judgment. Manipulate to follow, come after or behind. Autonomy, power, reasoning, and judgment. Two words. Two very different meanings.

WILSON: My my, aren't we the scholar?

JOHN: Just pointing out the difference. That's all.

WILSON: All right. He can come for your graduation, and if you like him, he can begin his education in the fall. Is that better?

JOHN: Thank you.

WILSON: And that essay you wrote for Mister Ward? "The Claims of Liberia?" I want you to use that as your graduation speech.

JOHN: I had thought about doing a Latin oration.

WILSON: Latin?

JOHN: Something from Plato's "Symposium."

WILSON: All of your classmates will be doing Latin orations, John.

JOHN: That's the reason I would like to do one.

WILSON: There's nothing special about a Latin oration. And the trustees are already questioning the value of a liberal arts education. We need to show them that we're doing more than simply studying Latin and Greek. We need to show them that we are actively engaged in shaping the face of America, engaged in shaping the future of the world. "The Claims of Liberia" will do that for us. Forget about doing a Latin oration. I think nine Latin orations will be quite enough, thank you.

You ever load and fire a Kentucky flintlock pistol before?

JOHN: No, sir.

WILSON: You ever load and fire any type of pistol before?

JOHN: No.

WILSON: You must always remember to make sure that the ball is seated firmly up against the powder charge. If you try to fire with the ball off the charge, the thing'll blow up in your face. Here, look at this. She's a beauty, isn't she?

He hands the pistol to JOHN.

WILSON (*Cont'd*): First thing you do is check to make sure the barrel is clear. Go ahead. Check.

JOHN: You want me to carry a pistol to the next meeting of the Literary Society?

WILSON: Why would I want you to do something like that?

JOHN: Because of Mister Ward.

WILSON: Mister Ward?

JOHN: He fired a pistol at Mister McCoy. During debate. I thought you knew.

WILSON: No.

JOHN: They were debating the merits of religious devotion and Mister Ward was losing the debate. When somebody started to laugh, Mister Ward pulled out a pistol and fired it at Mister McCoy. Mister McCoy fell to the floor. We all thought he was dead.

WILSON: Was he hit?

JOHN: He had fainted. Which of course meant that Mister Ward won the debate.

WILSON: Nobody told me anything about this.

JOHN: I thought that was the reason ...

WILSON: Somebody spotted some Indians not far from here. That's the reason for the pistol.

JOHN: Indians?

WILSON: Every now and then you come across a couple of stragglers. That's what these probably are. Stragglers living in the caves in the outlying regions. Nothing to worry about. The government's going to send out some riders to track them down. They'll find them, relocate them. Send them to live with the rest of their people.

JOHN: If there's nothing to worry about, why do you need a pistol?

WILSON: You never can be too safe. Besides, you're going to need to know how to fire a pistol once you get to Liberia. Now, check to make sure that the barrel is clear. Once you're sure that the barrel is clear, you add your powder charge.

JOHN: What do I do about the people who are already there?

WILSON: Already where? What people?

JOHN: In Liberia. When I get there, what do I do about the people already there?

WILSON: It's a wilderness, John. There are no people there.

JOHN: Natives. What do I do about the natives?

WILSON: That's up to you. You offer them the word and if they refuse that word . . .

    Beat.

JOHN: If they refuse?

WILSON: I suggest that you give them the option of determining their own fate. If they refuse the word then one option would be to relocate them. Not you, personally, of course. You'll have men to do that for you. Now check your barrel. Make sure it's clear.

JOHN: Where does it stop?

WILSON: Where does what stop?

JOHN: I relocate the people who are there, they relocate someone else. Where does it stop?

WILSON: Relocation is only an option, John. They don't have to be relocated. They can accept the gift of civilization.

JOHN: I'm not quite sure it's a gift.

WILSON: What're you talking about?

JOHN: We seem to be caught in this vicious circle. The English came to Ireland, the Irish came to America, now you're sending me to Liberia. Where do the Liberians go?

WILSON: I'm sure you'll be able to find a place for them.

JOHN: The way Andrew Jackson found a place for the Shawnee?

WILSON: Are you trying to be insolent?

JOHN: I don't think I'm the right man for this.

WILSON: Course you are, John.

JOHN: I feel like I'm giving up without even trying. You said your father fought against the English. But he fought. He didn't give up when somebody asked him to move. He fought, he struggled, he tried to keep his home before striking out to find a new home. And even then, he didn't abandon that fight until after it became clear that he couldn't win that fight. Here I am, I haven't even tried.

WILSON: Tried what?

JOHN: Tried to make this my home. I've given up without even trying.

WILSON: But this is not your home, John. Your home is in Africa.

JOHN: My home is here in the United States.

WILSON: But your people are from Africa.

JOHN: And your people are from Ireland, but I don't see you getting on a boat to go back. My family has been in this country for six generations. Five generations longer than your family. My father cut and fitted by hand every single piece of wood in the main library of the White House. But yet, you tell me that I'm the one who has to go? No, I'm sorry, but I can't do it, I won't do it. Not without first trying to make this my home.

WILSON: This will never be your home. Your people will never be able to live in harmony with the white race here in America. And this was not my doing, this was God's design. God made your people black, not me. And unless you can figure out a way to change your color, you will never be able to integrate into this society.

JOHN: You talk as if it's already been determined.

WILSON: It has been determined. Determined by God. God brought your people here as slaves, as savages. Now God has opened the way for you to return to Africa laden with the fruits of civilization.

JOHN: God did not bring my people here.

WILSON: God opened the way.

JOHN: Slave traders brought my people here.

WILSON: They were the instruments guided by the hand of God.

JOHN: Are you saying that slavery was part of God's design?

WILSON: I am saying that everything in this world is part of God's design. We may not always understand the reasons why God does what he does, but if we have faith and do not question his word, in time, he will reveal the truth and he will reveal the way. Now, I'm going to try to forget everything you just said. I'm going to try to forgive you, but I never want to hear anything like that from you again. You're nervous. I understand that. You have concerns. But you're also educated, John. You should know better. Now, you know what today is? First of the month. Time to settle our accounts. How many hours do you have for the month?

> *Beat.*

John? How many hours?

JOHN: Seventy-two.

WILSON: Same as always. Seventy-two hours at seven cents an hour. That's five dollars and four cents for the month.

> *WILSON pays JOHN.*

WILSON (*Cont'd*): There you are.

JOHN: Thank you.

WILSON: Don't mention it. You earned every bit of it. Governor.

JOHN: I have work to do.

> *JOHN moves to exit.*

WILSON: John?

> *JOHN stops.*

WILSON (*Cont'd*): Aren't you forgetting something? Don't you think you should settle your account as well?

JOHN: Who founded the ACS?

WILSON: Pardon me?

JOHN: I want to know who founded the ACS.

WILSON: You know who founded the ACS.

JOHN: Tell me again.

WILSON: You know them. You met them. Many of them. Reverend Jacobs. Reverend McLain.

JOHN: Who else?

WILSON: Andrew Jackson.

JOHN: Andrew Jackson.

WILSON: Francis Scott Key.

JOHN: Slave owners.

WILSON: Maybe, at one point in their lives.

JOHN: What about you?

WILSON: What about me?

JOHN: Are you a former slave owner?

WILSON: What I used to do or who I used to be is none of your concern.

JOHN: Only by studying the origins of a thing—

WILSON: Language, John. I was talking about language.

JOHN: But language is not the end. Our goal is not to understand the words. Our goal is to understand all of the things the words represent, and if I am being asked to leave my country, to leave the land of my birth, I have the right to know who's doing the asking.

WILSON: God is doing the asking.

JOHN: Slave owners and former slave owners are doing the asking.

WILSON: You're named after a slave owner. Did you know that? You're named after John Newton who bought and sold hundreds of slaves. But he received second sight. God allowed him to see the wickedness of his ways and then God inspired him to write a song of praise about it. "Amazing Grace." You ever hear it? (*He sings.*)

> *Amazing grace, how sweet the sound,*
> *That saved a wretch like me,*
> *I once was lost, but now am found,*
> *Was blind but now I see.*

You should be grateful for former slave owners, because they are the only friends you have. The abolitionists are not your friends. The only thing the abolitionists are doing is exacerbating the problem. But the former slave owners have seen the problem firsthand, they have sat at the table and dined with misery, they have had intercourse with suffering, they have conducted commerce with the devil himself, and now they have second sight. They see a world that they've never seen before, and that world looks different, John. Like the morning you were born. The entire world looks different.

JOHN: A world that looks white. Is that how they see the world with their second sight? A white world cleansed of all of their sins? Is that the reason they want to ship all of the niggers back to Africa? So that they won't have to be reminded of their sins?

WILSON: How dare you speak to me that way.

JOHN: I won't do it, Reverend. I refuse to take a part in the whitewashing of this country.

WILSON: You don't have any choice in the matter.

JOHN: I've always had a choice.

WILSON: You never had a choice. Never. From the day you were born, this was your destiny. This is the reason God saved you. This is what God has chosen you for.

JOHN: Then why doesn't God tell me that? Why doesn't God speak to me and tell me this?

WILSON: Have you been listening? Have you been open to receive the word of God?

JOHN: I've been listening, all right. But the only voice I hear is a voice telling me that if I go to Liberia, the only thing I will do is contribute to more bloodshed and more death.

WILSON: Bloodshed and death are parts of life, John. Life is blood and there could be no life without death. Civilization grinds on. Men who refuse to be a part of civilization's progress are crushed under her slow-moving weight. You try to back out of this now and you will be crushed. I will not let you graduate, the entire time you spent here will be wasted, and you will leave here as a failure. Your failure will confirm many people's suspicions that your people don't have the discipline, nor the intelligence, for higher education. You back out of this now and you will be the last free man of color to attend university here or anywhere else in this country, I guarantee it. There are a lot of eyes upon you, John. And you've been doing well. Don't falter. Now, I think it's time to settle your account.

JOHN: I'll settle my account when I get ready.

JOHN exits.

SCENE TWO

JANE on stage. JOHN enters.

JANE: You find it?

JOHN: I found it.

JANE: What was it?

JOHN: I don't know.

JANE: You don't know?

JOHN: By the time I got there, there was nothing left. Nothing but blood. Pieces of bone. Small pieces of flesh.

JANE: The coyotes got to it.

JOHN: I didn't see any coyotes.

JANE: I saw them. They were feeding on it.

JOHN: I didn't see any coyotes.

JANE: That's because by the time you got there, there was no reason for them to still be there. There was nothing left. Something got caught in that iron leg-trap of yours, and the coyotes got to it. They killed it. They ripped it apart.

JOHN: It was probably just a deer.

JANE: Wasn't a deer.

JOHN: How do you know?

JANE: I saw it. It was too small to be a deer.

JOHN: Then a fox. It was probably a fox.

JANE: I told you to be careful where you put those iron leg-traps.

JOHN: It was just a fox. That's all it was. There's nothing to worry about. I'll go out and collect up the rest of the traps. Give them back to Mister Morgan.

> *JOHN moves to exit.*

JANE: John? Robert says you've changed your mind about going to Liberia.

JOHN: That's right.

JANE: He also said you plan to give a Latin oration for graduation.

JOHN: If I'm not going to Liberia, I shouldn't give a speech supporting the idea, should I?

JANE: John . . .

JOHN: I guess I should thank you.

JANE: Don't thank me.

JOHN: But you were right, Misses Wilson.

JANE: No, John.

JOHN: You were right about everything.

JANE: The only thing I was concerned about was myself, John. I shouldn't have spoken to you the way I did.

JOHN: I was being trained for something I didn't understand.

JANE: I want you to give your "Claims of Liberia" speech.

JOHN: Why?

JANE: Robert won't tell you this, but the university is in trouble. Financially. The people in town can't pay the money they owe, and we were depending upon that money to stay open but there is no money. And the trustees, the trustees won't release any more money until they have had a look at the graduating class. They want evidence that the work Robert is doing here has an impact on the world outside. I'm not asking you to go to Liberia, John. But I am asking you to give your speech. "The Claims of Liberia" will be the evidence Robert needs to prove that the work he's doing here is important. But if you give a Latin oration, all the trustees will see will be more of the same of what they've seen in the past. They will not give us the money we need, and the university will close.

JOHN: You're asking me to enter into a corrupt bargain.

JANE: You really don't believe that, do you?

JOHN: I don't believe you're asking me to do this.

JANE: I'm asking you to help a man who has treated you like a son.

JOHN: A son?

JANE: He brought you into this house, he protected you. I see the way he looks at you, the way he treats you, he doesn't treat any of the other students that way.

JOHN: False words are not only evil in themselves, but they inflict the soul with evil. That's what you're asking me to do. You're asking me to inflict my soul with evil.

JANE: Is that the only thing you're concerned about? Yourself? Your soul?

JOHN: If I don't look after my soul, no one else will.

JANE: You know what an ape is? An ape is a beast that lives a solitary existence aware of only one thing. Its own needs, itself in the present. That's what you are. A goddamn ape. Oblivious to everything except yourself.

JOHN: I may have been an ape once, but not anymore. Here. Here's your shirt.

> *He takes the shirt off, throws it at her.*

JOHN (*Cont'd*): Stinking ape shirt. Smell of that shirt made me sick. Reminded me of everything I was doing. I'd wash it and wash it but the smell of that shirt wouldn't come out.

JANE: This shirt used to belong to my baby boy, David. Robert tried to make me give you this shirt, but I wouldn't do it. He said I was suffering from female hysteria, but still, I wouldn't do it. Then he took you out riding. The only other person he would go riding with was David. I remember one afternoon looking out the window and seeing you two on horseback, hearing your voices, you riding alongside Robert, and for a moment, I thought that my son had come home. That's when I realized why he wanted me to give you the shirt. So I gave you David's shirt, his hat, his pants.

> *She smells the shirt.*

And that smell is David's smell. His sweat. God, how I used to love that smell.

> *She smells the shirt.*

Only now, his smell has gotten all mixed up with your smell and I don't know whether to embrace it or fall away in utter revulsion.

> *WILSON enters.*

WILSON: They found the Indians. They were Miami. They had to kill the brave.

JOHN: What do you mean they had to kill him?

WILSON: He was a savage, John.

JOHN: But why did they have to kill him?

WILSON: He came out of the woods and charged us. He was on foot and tried to attack six men on horseback. One of the men in the party, he spoke Algonquian. He shouted, "We're not here to hurt you. We want to help you." But the brave, he had a knife. He kept cutting and slashing. If they hadn't killed him, he would have certainly injured or killed one of us.

JOHN: What about the woman?

WILSON: We found her sitting at the foot of an oak tree. We rode up on her and she just sat there. She didn't try to run. She didn't try to fight. She just sat there, staring out, covered with blood. Looked like she had been attacked. Bitten. Probably coyote. She had bites on her arms, her hands. Looks like she had to fight them off.

JOHN: And the child?

WILSON: What child?

JOHN: There was a child. Three, four years old.

WILSON: There was no child.

JOHN: A little boy. I saw him.

WILSON: There was no child. We looked, but there was no child to be found. We found the brave and found the squaw. If there was a child, don't you think we would have found him as well?

JANE: Told you it wasn't a fox. God it wasn't a fox.

JOHN: What are they going to do with the woman?

WILSON: Send her to live with the rest of her people. She'll be happier there. This is your pistol, John. I bought it for you. I was going to teach you how to use it, then give it to you as a gift for graduation. I made that mistake once. You want it?

JOHN: No.

WILSON: You're going to need it, John. Where's your shirt?

JANE: Here.

WILSON: It's midday, man. Why aren't you wearing it?

> *Beat.*

Put it on.

JOHN: No.

WILSON: No?

JOHN: I'm not wearing it anymore.

WILSON: Would somebody please explain to me where I went wrong with you?

> *No one answers.*

WILSON (*Cont'd*): The trustees are going to be here in two weeks. I need to start putting together a program for commencement. Would you like to be included in that program? Have you decided what you're going to do?

JOHN: I told you what I was going to do.

WILSON: Tell me again.

JOHN: You're going to have to find somebody else to go to Liberia.

WILSON: You're turning your back on God?

JOHN: Your God, maybe, but not my God.

WILSON: There's only one God, John.

JOHN: I think I read the Bible a bit differently than you do.

WILSON: And there's only one way to read the Bible.

JOHN: Your God brought slaves here in chains. My God wept while it was happening.

WILSON: That's blasphemy. Not only do you turn your back on God, but you blaspheme while doing it? I think you should collect your things, John. It's time for you to leave this house.

JOHN: And go where?

WILSON: That's up to you. You have your papers, I imagine you can travel anyplace in the state you please, but you have to leave here. The university. The town.

JOHN: What about graduation?

WILSON: You're not graduating.

JANE: You can't do that, Robert.

JOHN: I've completed all of the requirements for graduation.

JANE: You can't do this.

WILSON: If he doesn't go to Liberia, if he fails to recognize the overwhelming facts pointing to him being the one chosen to do this, then he has failed in his education.

JOHN: My education or my training?

WILSON: Your education.

JOHN: I still don't think you understand the difference between the two.

WILSON: And you have no idea of what's at stake here. You want to prove that you're as good as white? Stand up and embrace your destiny, John. You have to become a leader. That's the reason I brought you here, that's what the trustees want to see. They allowed me to bring you here, and now they want to see a man who is on his way to becoming a leader.

JOHN: If I'm going to be a leader, I need to do it how I see fit. Not in the way you think I should. My people don't need to wander through the wilderness to find a new home, they've already been on a journey, and that journey was to come here. Now if you set out to train me, you're right, I have failed in that training, you were unsuccessful in teaching me how to blindly follow orders, I do not sit up and speak on command. But if your goal was to educate me, then I would like to congratulate you, because you did a very good job. You taught me how to think for myself, you taught me about a world I didn't even know existed. But if that was your goal, if your goal was to educate me, then you must now give me the freedom to come to my own conclusions.

JANE: He's right, Robert. You have to let him go.

WILSON: No.

JANE: Let him go, Robert.

WILSON: God sent him here for me. God took away my sons, then He gave me John. Don't you see? You are mine, John. God gave you to me. You belong to me.

JANE: He doesn't belong to you, Robert.

WILSON: God gave him to me.

JANE: He doesn't belong to anyone.

JOHN: Here. This is the five dollars I owe you for the last month's room and board. Thank you for taking me in. I'll get my things.

JANE: Wait, John, no. You don't have to go. You can stay here. Robert? Tell him he doesn't have to go. Robert?

WILSON: Five dollars? After everything I gave you, this is what you give me in return? Five goddamn dollars?

JOHN: If you want me to give "The Claims of Liberia" speech, I'll do it. You know why? Because I have carefully considered and come to the conclusion that it's the right thing to do. You're right, you have done a lot for me, and I would like to return the favor, so I'll give the speech. But don't ask me to go to Liberia. If it means I won't graduate, if it means I have to leave this house today, then I'll leave. But I'm not going to Liberia, Reverend. I'm not going to do it.

WILSON: I'll add your name to the program.

WILSON exits.

JANE: John? Would you like to have your shirt back?

JOHN: Thank you.

She hands him the shirt, then exits.

JOHN (*To audience*): I gave the speech, but never did go to Liberia. And I did graduate with nine other men. We all received diplomas which were, by the way, at the time, real sheepskin.

After graduation I moved around a bit and eventually ended up in Wheeling, Virginia, now called West Virginia, where I started a school. I had a little money. I had saved four cents a month for almost four years. That gave me exactly one dollar and twenty-two cents, which I used to purchase three books for my new school. I purchased an English King James version of the Bible, an elementary book on world geography, and a copy of "The Life of Gustavus Vassa, the African." Two weeks after opening my school, I was arrested and jailed for teaching colored folks how to read. But that didn't stop me. I taught in parts of Ohio, Virginia, and Pennsylvania.

And I was not the last free man of color to go to school at Ohio University. Four years after I graduated, Edward Roye was admitted. I imagine that his life here was much like mine, except for one small difference. He eventually became president of Liberia, where he reigned for a year and a half, until the day that the captain of his army walked into his office and arrested him on charges of embezzlement. Corruption. So it began.

For a long time I was worried about my soul. I worried that I had failed to live up to God's plan, that I had failed to fulfill my destiny. But I now realize I didn't have to go to Liberia to start a new life, to work my way through the wilderness, to discover a new frontier. I had worked my way through the wilderness and had discovered a new frontier, and that new frontier was inside of me.

WILSON enters.

WILSON: Ladies and gentlemen, most distinguished assembled guests, at this point in the program, I present to you John Newton Templeton.

All lights fade except one light on JOHN.

Gradually, the other light fades.

END OF PLAY

THE GOSPEL ACCORDING TO JAMES

PRODUCTION HISTORY

The Gospel According to James was commissioned in 2006 and produced March 22 to April 10, 2011, by the Indiana Repertory Theatre, Janet Allen, artistic director, Steven Stolen, managing director. The production was directed by Chuck Smith. Set design was by Linda Buchanan, costume design by Rachel Anne Healy, lighting design by Kathy A. Perkins, and sound design and original composition by Ray Nardelli. The stage managers were Nathan Garrison and Joel Grynheim.

James	André De Shields
Marie	Linda Kimbrough
Tommy Shipp	Marcus Davis Hendricks
Abe Smith	Tyler Jacob Rollinson
Apples	Anthony Peeples
Claude	Keith D. Gallagher
Mary	Kelsey Brennan
Hoot Ball	Christopher Jon Martin
Bea Ball	Diane Kondrat

The Gospel According to James was produced May 14 to June 12, 2011, by the Victory Gardens Theater, Chicago, Illinois, Dennis Začek, artistic director, Jan Kallish, managing director. The production was directed by Chuck Smith. Set design was by Linda Buchanan, costume design by Rachel Anne Healy, lighting design by Kathy A. Perkins, and sound design and original composition by Ray Nardelli. The production stage manager was Tina M. Jach.

James	André De Shields
Marie	Linda Kimbrough

Tommy Shipp	Wardell Julius Clark
Abe Smith	Tyler Jacob Rollinson
Apples	Anthony Peeples
Claude	Zach Kenney
Mary	Kelsey Brennan
Hoot Ball	Christopher Jon Martin
Bea Ball	Diane Kondrat

Kelsey Brennan as Mary and Tyler Jacob Rollinson as Abe Smith in the Indiana Repertory Theatre's production of *The Gospel According to James. Photo by Julie Curry.*

Marcus Davis Hendricks as Tommy Shipp, Linda Kimbrough as Marie, Keith D. Gallagher as Claude, André De Shields as James, and Kelsey Brennan as Mary in the Indiana Repertory Theatre's production of *The Gospel According to James. Photo by Julie Curry.*

André De Shields as James and Linda Kimbrough as Marie in the Victory Gardens Theater production of *The Gospel According to James. Photo by Liz Lauren.*

(*above*) Christopher
Jon Martin as Hoot
Ball, Linda Kimbrough
as Marie, and Diane
Kondrat as Bea Ball in
the Victory Gardens
Theater production of
*The Gospel According
to James. Photo by
Liz Lauren.*

(*right*) Anthony
Peeples as Apples,
Tyler Jacob Rollinson
as Abe Smith, and
Wardell Julius Clark
as Tommy Shipp in
the Victory Gardens
Theater production
of *The Gospel
According to James.
Photo by Liz Lauren.*

Characters

Marie
Caucasian woman, in her late sixties. She's jumpy, skittish, and doesn't trust anyone.

Mary
Marie as a young, somewhat hardened but still trusting twenty-year-old.

James
African American man on a mission, midsixties.

Apples
James as a sixteen-year-old youngster who thinks he wants to be a gangster.

Abe Smith
Nineteen-year-old African American male. More of a lover than a fighter, Abe is well on his way to becoming a man.

Tommy Shipp
Eighteen-year-old African American male, wannabe gangster.

Claude
Twenty-one-year-old Caucasian male. He appears to be an all-American boy who likes being a big fish in a small pond. Some believe that he's Mary's fiancé.

Hoot Ball
Mary's father, who works at the foundry. As he appears in Mary's memory, he's forty years old. He's a working-class man with working-class values.

Bea Ball
Mary's mother. As she appears in Mary's memory, she's in her late thirties.

Note on character ages: It is important that Claude is the oldest of the "River Road Gang," Tommy, Abe, Claude, and Mary. He is the most mature, the leader, the one calling the shots.

Time: 1930 and the early 1980s.

Place: Various locations in and around Marion, Indiana.

This play is a fictional account inspired by actual events.

THE GOSPEL ACCORDING TO JAMES

A play in two acts

For Anna Lee and Sunshine

ACT ONE

The setting is a FUNERAL PARLOR. In the FUNERAL PARLOR, there are a couple of chairs and an urn sitting on a small table.

At various points throughout the play, other locations emanate from the FUNERAL PARLOR. The first is RIVER ROAD, an outdoor area near the river sometimes used as a lovers' lane. RIVER ROAD includes a partially concealed area where folks can confer in private.

Another area emanating from the FUNERAL PARLOR is the home of HOOT and BEA BALL. A jail cell is also in the mix.

At rise, MARIE is in the FUNERAL PARLOR. After a moment, JAMES enters carrying a metal ammunition case.

JAMES: Mary?

James. James Cameron.

MARIE: I know who you are.

JAMES: I heard about your father and wanted to stop by to pay my respects.

MARIE: You heard?

JAMES: I read. In the newspaper. This morning. His obituary.

MARIE: You live here?

JAMES: Milwaukee. But I try to get back once, twice a year to visit. For some reason, I can't seem to stay away from the place. Funny, huh?

MARIE: Funny?

JAMES: Well, maybe not funny . . .

What about you?

MARIE: What about me?

JAMES: You still live in the area?

MARIE: Are you kidding me?

JAMES: Moved away?

MARIE: Ran away.

JAMES: Of course. And is this your first time back?

MARIE: First time back.

JAMES: Well, I'm sorry we had to meet again under such circumstances.
So where is he?

MARIE: Where is who?

JAMES: Your father.

MARIE: He's in the jar.

JAMES: You had him cremated?

MARIE: That's right.

JAMES: Is that what he wanted?

MARIE: No. But I did it anyway.

JAMES: Well, I'm sorry for your loss.

MARIE: What're you doing here, convict?

JAMES: Convict?

MARIE: I'm sorry. I guess I should say ex-con.

JAMES: That was a long time ago.

MARIE: Fifty years, if memory serves.

JAMES: A lot has changed since then.

MARIE: Some things, but not a lot. So what're you doing here, convict? What kinda scam are you running?

JAMES: All I wanted to do was stop by and pay my respects.

MARIE: Is that right?

JAMES: That's right. That's all I wanted to do.

MARIE: Some people were here earlier looking for you. A man and a woman. The man had an accent and the woman was carrying camera equipment. I told them I hadn't seen you in . . . what? Had to be fifty years. Then guess what? They asked me about Mary Ball.

JAMES: I'm sorry.

MARIE: I told them that Mary Ball was dead. They asked if I was sure and I told them I was pretty sure, I was right there with her when she died. They looked very disappointed and then asked me to tell you if I saw you that they'd be at the Denny's out on the highway. So let's try this again. What're you doing here, convict?

JAMES: The governor's gonna give me a pardon and there's this big todo tomorrow at the Sheraton. And this English fella, a filmmaker, he's been following the case for the past few years. He wants to make a documentary and he figured now would be a good time to come over and look around town and maybe interview a few people.

MARIE: So what were they doing here?

JAMES: I told him there was a chance I might see you. I didn't know for sure and I certainly didn't think he would show up with camera equipment. I am sorry. I'll make sure he won't bother you again.

MARIE: Thank you. Now if you're done paying your respects, you can go join your friends out at the Denny's.

JAMES: Mary, listen . . .

MARIE: I told you, Mary Ball is dead. She died a long time ago.

My name is Williams. Katherine Marie Williams.

JAMES: And what do people call you? Katherine? Kat?

MARIE: Marie. People call me Marie.

JAMES: Okay, Marie. Listen. This thing tomorrow at the Sheraton is at two. I know this has been a difficult time for you, but I would be honored if you could attend.

MARIE: For what?

JAMES: I'd like to introduce you to folks.

MARIE: You want to introduce me? Or you want to introduce Mary?

JAMES: They're gonna give me a pardon and an apology. I think they owe you an apology as well.

MARIE: I show up at this thing tomorrow, and you will not be happy cause I will tell everybody I meet that everything you told them is a lie. And you don't want me to do that, do you? You don't want me to piss all over your nice clean pardon.

JAMES: What do you think I lied about?

MARIE: What have you not lied about? That's the question. I mean, I couldn't believe it. Years go by and there was nothing. And then suddenly, one day, I turn on the television and there you are. At first, I didn't even recognize you. I listened to your story and even that didn't register. And then, they said your name and I thought, "Wait a minute, I know this guy. And not only do I know him, he's talking about something that happened to me. He's talking about what happened the night I was there." But the story you were telling was nothing like the way I remembered it.

JAMES: So we remember it differently.

MARIE: This is more than just different details. There are huge parts of the story that you left out. And other parts you changed.

JAMES: Abe was lynched in front of the courthouse in the middle of the town square. Tommy was lynched. Those facts are not in dispute.

MARIE: I'm not talking about that. I'm talking about everything that led up to the lynchings.

JAMES: So what did I lie about?

MARIE: You said I was raped.

JAMES: I never said that.

MARIE: I saw you on the television, James. And I read your book. Did you think that I wouldn't read it?

JAMES: I never said you were assaulted. I didn't know if you were assaulted or not cause I wasn't there when it happened.

MARIE: Another lie.

JAMES: I was not there, Marie. Remember? I left. I ran away.

MARIE: Convenient, how you changed just enough of the story . . .

JAMES: I didn't change one word.

MARIE: What story did you tell the people in the movie you made?

JAMES: What movie?

MARIE: How many movies did you make?

JAMES: I took part in one documentary other than this one, but that was years ago.

MARIE: In your one documentary other than this one years ago, what story did you tell?

JAMES: I told the truth.

MARIE: The truth?

JAMES: The gospel truth.

MARIE: The gospel according to James. So let's hear it. Tell it the way you told it in your documentary, the way you told it in your book, the way you told it over and over . . .

JAMES: I said that we had been pitching horseshoes in Ogden Weaver's backyard and that was the truth.

It was August and it was hot. Around nine o'clock, the horseshoe game broke up.

APPLES enters followed by TOMMY and ABE.

I was on my way home when Tommy and Abe asked me if I would like to go for a ride.

TOMMY: Come on, Apples. You wanna get in on this or not?

JAMES: They used to call me Apples. It was a name I kinda gave myself.

ABE: Come on. We gonna let you ride with the big boys tonight.

JAMES: Tommy had a 1926 Ford Roadster. Wasn't much to look at but as soon as they started driving, Abe said . . .

ABE: I got an idea. Let's hold up somebody and get some money and buy another car.

JAMES: And I said . . .

APPLES: No, I don't wanna do that.

JAMES: I said . . .

APPLES: Let me outta here.

JAMES: And Tommy said . . .

TOMMY: Aww, ain't nothing to it. All you got to do is take a gun and put it on the people and say stick 'em up and if they don't stick 'em up, you just shoot 'em, that's all.

JAMES: I wanted to get outta the car but they wouldn't stop. They just kept driving. They drove out past the Thirty-Eighth Street Bridge until we got to River Road.

Lights up on CLAUDE and MARY inside a new 1930 Chevrolet.

A car was parked there. As we walked towards that car, something kept telling me go back, go back, go back . . .

TOMMY: Here, take the gun.

> TOMMY hands APPLES the gun.

All you got to do is say, "Stick 'em up." Then you let the roscoe do the talking.

JAMES: So I go up to the car and I open the car door and I held the gun up and I said . . .

APPLES: Stick 'em up!

> CLAUDE and MARY get out of the car. APPLES points the gun at them.

JAMES: And this man and this lady got out of the car. When the guy got out of the car I looked at him and you know what? He was a friend of mine.

CLAUDE: James? That you?

JAMES: He was a nice white fella. He used to come down to the place where I used to shine shoes and he would always tip me and we'd laugh and talk.

CLAUDE: What're you doing, James?

JAMES: And when I looked at you, I saw a face I'll never forget as long as I live. A face so pale and lovely and frightened.

MARY: Please don't shoot.

APPLES: Here, you guys take this gun, I'm not gonna have anything to do with you guys.

> APPLES hands the gun to TOMMY, then exits.

JAMES: And I ran. I left them out there at the scene of the crime.

CLAUDE: You boys oughta follow his lead and get on outta here. Ain't nothing here for you. And you already in enough trouble as it is. No use making it worse.

ABE: She's pretty.

TOMMY: Very pretty.

ABE: Bet ya she knows how to shake that thang . . .

CLAUDE: Now looka here, fellas . . .

TOMMY: Shut up before I put a hole in ya.

ABE: Hey there, sweetheart, you know how to dance? You know how to shake that thang?

CLAUDE: I'm not goine allow you to talk to my fiancée that way.

TOMMY: And I told you to shut up. Gimme your watch. And empty your pockets.

ABE: Come on, baby, lemme see ya shake that thing.

CLAUDE: I'm warning you.

JAMES: I ran as hard as I could. And as I was running, I heard a gunshot.

> *TOMMY fires the pistol, hitting CLAUDE in the stomach.*

> *MARY screams.*

> *TOMMY fires twice more. CLAUDE falls. TOMMY and ABE move toward a frightened MARY as lights fade on them.*

JAMES: I don't know who shot who and I didn't want to know.

MARIE: You know who shot who.

JAMES: I could guess. I could speculate, but I don't know for a fact so I'm not gonna speculate. I ran and I kept on running until I got home.

When I got home, I was wringing wet. My mother asked me what was wrong and I lied to her. I told her I had been playing football. But that was the only lie I told.

Later that night, the sheriff came to the house with a lotta other men in cars and trucks. They said I had killed a white man and raped a white woman. I told him I didn't have anything to do with any killing or raping. And I didn't. And you know I didn't. My mother was crying. She begged them to take her instead of me.

At the jailhouse, they beat me and they made me sign a confession. By morning, a mob had started to form outside the jail and by sunset, the mob numbered in the thousands.

About an hour after it got dark, the mob demanded that the sheriff turn over the keys to the jail and when he refused, the mob tore the doors off the jail. Took them less than an hour. They came inside. First they got Tommy.

MARIE: All right. That's enough.

JAMES: Now you tell me what I lied about.

MARIE: Nothing, James. Happened just the way you said it did.

JAMES: I was sixteen years old, and while I admit to getting into more than my fair share of trouble, I got nothing to hide and no reason to lie about anything.

MARIE: I apologize.

JAMES: I accept your apology. Now will you accept my invitation?

MARIE: I'm not going to your little soirée, so stop asking.

JAMES: Then maybe you can do something else for me.

Would you consider meeting with the Englishman?

MARIE: For what?

JAMES: It's still there, Marie. The jailhouse in which Tommy and Abe spent the last night of their lives is still there. It's been empty for years cause nobody knows what to do with it. The bricks in the front are still scarred from where the mob ripped the doors off. And you can still see the bars on the second-floor window that they hanged Tommy from. I drove by there today. Kids were playing in the weeds out front, and I hear that some developer wants to turn it into a condominium.

MARIE: So what?

JAMES: That's like building a playground on top of a graveyard.

MARIE: That has nothing to do with me.

JAMES: I wanna turn it into a museum. A memorial to honor Tommy and Abe and all the other victims of lynching in this country. But I need your help to do it. And all it would take is an hour of your time. You sit down with the Englishman, they turn on the camera, he'll ask you a couple of questions, and you tell him what you remember.

MARIE: Is that the reason you came here on the day of my father's funeral? The reason you brought that man here with a camera?

JAMES: Folks hear you talking and the idea of turning that jail into a museum won't scare 'em so much.

MARIE: You buzzard.

JAMES: I thought that you would want to help set the record straight.

MARIE: I spent my life trying to forget what happened that night. I'm not about to go sloshing through that shit again for you or anybody else.

JAMES: Then why'd you come back, if not to set the record straight?

MARIE: My father died, in case you forgot. I came back to bury my father.

JAMES: You could've just picked up the phone for that. You didn't have to travel all the way from wherever you come from just to have him cremated. But you decided to come back yourself after all these years. I'm guessing you had to get on at least one plane to get here. Rent a car. Had to be a reason. I'm guessing perhaps you came for closure. To grieve. For condolence, perhaps.

MARIE: You're a real piece of work, you know that?

JAMES: You're the only person who knows for sure what happened after I ran away that night. And I think if you took a few minutes to sit down and talk to the Englishman, tell him what you remember, you might find it to be not quite as painful as you think it would be. In fact, you might even feel better afterwards.

MARIE: I wish I could help you, but the fact is, I don't remember what happened that night.

JAMES: You don't have to remember every detail. Just tell him whether or not you were assaulted. Talk to him about that.

MARIE: I just told you I don't remember.

JAMES: You don't remember whether or not you were assaulted?

MARIE: It was a very traumatic event in my life. And those memories, they're like bones made of sand. Every time I try to pick one up, it crumbles.

JAMES: Then maybe you could talk to him about your father.

MARIE: It's time for my father to rest in peace.

JAMES: Was he a member of the Klan?

MARIE: What did I just tell you?

JAMES: Then talk to him about Claude. I always thought you and Claude were the perfect couple.

MARIE: The only thing I remember about Claude is his name.

JAMES: Come on, Marie . . .

MARIE: I'm sorry, but that's the way it is.

JAMES: A whole lotta folks from this town wish me dead, did you know that? They think that when I die, everything that they don't wanna think about, including the past, is gonna die with me. Other folks, they send me notes asking to meet with me, always in private, cause they wanna talk. They wanna tell me what they remember. They need to confess. And once they start talking, all sorts of things start to come to light. Sometimes you discover things you can actually touch, things you can hold. A little piece of something somebody kept as a souvenir. Small piece of bloodstained cloth. A button. Artifacts. Evidence that can transform a memory into reality.

JAMES picks up the ammunition case and opens it.

I have some of it here if you'd like to see.

MARIE: No thank you.

JAMES: They're just things. Nothing to be afraid of. Nothing that could hurt you.

He takes a piece of rope out of the case.

See this piece of rope? This is part of the rope that was used to hang Abe. The woman who gave it to me denied having it at first. She denied knowing anything about it. After I was able to convince her that I came in peace, she took me into her attic and there behind stacks of old furniture and boxes was a suitcase. And inside that suitcase was a quilt. And wrapped inside that quilt was this piece of rope. She said she had been trying to get rid of it for years but didn't quite know how. When I agreed to take it, she cried.

He removes a piece of cloth from the case.

And this, this is a piece of the shirt that Tommy was wearing that night. The blood on this shirt, that's Tommy's blood. The man who had it, kept it in his barn. He didn't want to part with it at first, not till I told him about the museum.

He takes out a piece of tree bark.

This is a piece of bark from the maple from which Abe was hanged.

He takes out a photograph.

And you know what this is. This is the Beitler photograph. There's Tommy on the left and Abe's there on the right.

MARIE: You carry this stuff around with you?

JAMES: This case contains evidence of sin and misdeed. The contents are far too valuable to ever be left unattended. I would chain it to my wrist and throw away the key if I could.

MARIE: That's sick, carrying that stuff around with you like that.

JAMES: For a long time, I hated the people in this town. I hated them for what they did to Tommy and Abe, and for what they did to me. They put me in prison for a crime I didn't commit, but even worse than that, they made me feel ashamed. They made me feel ashamed for what they did to me. I spent years trying to outrun that shame. Until one day, I found myself in Israel. I visited a museum, Yad Vashem. This living memorial. And I saw photographs, evidence of tragedy and horror. I saw artifacts: eyeglasses, pieces of cloth, a room full of nothing but shoes. And there had to be thousands of people there, scores of old men and women, young couples, and children. Hundreds of schoolchildren all learning about the lives of the people who perished.

But something was wrong, off-kilter, and I couldn't figure out what it was until I realized that the people there, they were not ashamed. And I started to grieve for my soul and I asked myself, where was our Yad Vashem? Where was our living memorial? And that's when I knew why God had saved me that night.

MARIE: You think God saved you?

JAMES: He saved me to make sure that no matter how much time passes, we never forget.

MARIE: Typical convict. You go to jail and then you find God.

JAMES: I stood under that maple tree with a rope around my neck surrounded by thousands of people, all of them laughing and cursing. Abe's bleeding corpse was hanging to the left of me. Tommy's ripped and torn corpse was hanging to the right. I prayed to God, I said, "Lord have mercy, forgive me my sins." And that's when a voice came down from heaven. It was the voice of an angel that said, "Take this boy back, he didn't have anything to do with any killing or raping." And those people, that mob, they obeyed.

MARIE: You ever read the Bible?

JAMES: I am somewhat familiar.

MARIE: Remember when the angels came to Sodom and Gomorrah? Unable to find ten good men, the Lord decided to destroy the city. He told Lot and his wife to flee and then warned them, no matter what happens, do not look back.

Lot's wife disobeyed. She looked back and you know what happened? She was turned into a pillar of salt and was never seen nor heard from again. That's why I never look back. Never, no matter what.

JAMES: This is not the same.

MARIE: Back then, this city, this town was just like Sodom and Gomorrah. Bet you couldn't find ten good men with a whole flock of angels. And to continue to look back like this, all you're doing is disturbing a well-buried grave.

JAMES: That's why you're afraid to talk about Claude? Cause you're afraid you're gonna be turned into a pillar of salt?

MARIE: Told you I don't remember anything about Claude.

JAMES: Your memory seems to fail you when it's convenient.

MARIE: You wanna know what I remember about Claude? I'll tell you what I remember about Claude. I remember that Claude was a cruel sonavabitch, that's what I remember about Claude. He was mean. Not to anybody who was bigger than him, smarter than him, or stronger than him. Oh no, those folks he was nice to. But to most women, children, and animals, he was cruel. I remember this one time, there was this cat that used to come around. Big ole black and grey striped tabby. I used to feed it every now and then, give it scraps. Claude didn't like that, the thought that I was showing a lil affection to anybody except him. So one day, I come home and Claude is sitting on my front porch and he's got this big ole grin on his face and I know then and there that something's wrong. Then I see that he's holding the tabby in his arms. And the tabby was trusting, he'd make friends with anybody who'd pet him. And before I could ask him what he was doing, I see that he's taken five or six empty soup cans. And he's punched a hole in 'em, and he's tied them together with some fishing line and he's tied the other end of that line around the cat's neck. And before you can say Blackjack, he tosses the tabby into the air. It lands in the middle of the road and when its feet hit the ground, it heard them cans hit the ground right behind him, and he took off like a rocket. Claude laughed, thought it was funny to see that cat trying to outrun those cans.

The cat took off and I took off after the cat. I figured if I could catch him, I could take the cans off. So I chased that cat for hours, but couldn't even get close. Few days later, I saw him, or what was left of him. He was lying off to the side of the road near a neighbor's house.

All he had to do was stop running. If he had stopped running, I could've untied them cans from around his neck, but he wouldn't stop running. He run himself to death thinking he could outrun them cans, but no matter how fast he ran, them cans were always right there behind him. Claude thought that was funny as hell. That's what I remember about Claude.

JAMES: What about your father? What d'you remember about him?

MARIE: I told you, I am not talking about my father.

JAMES: Then tell me this: Was he a good man?

MARIE: He was a very good man.

He was a good man who lived his whole life upside-down.

> HOOT *enters in dirty khaki work clothes. His shoes are polished to a spit shine.*

He worked the graveyard shift and when most folks were getting ready for bed at night, he was getting ready for work.

HOOT: Bea!

MARIE: When most folks were sitting down for breakfast, he was sitting down for dinner. And while the rest of the world was engaged in their daily hustle and bustle, he slept in a darkened room.

HOOT: Bea? Where you at? Bea!

> BEA *enters.*

BEA: I'm sorry, I must've overslept. I went to see Mother and it took a lot outta me. I'll get your dinner started.

HOOT: How's the old bird doing?

BEA: Doctor says he thinks she's goine make it. She's sitting up by herself. Almost. Still don't know if she knows who I am.

HOOT: Well . . . Guinea says to tell you hello.

BEA: I'm really not in the mood, Hoot.

HOOT: I'm just telling you what Guinea told me. Guinea told me to tell you hello.

BEA: Hello, Guinea.

HOOT: Mary drive you out to see your momma?

BEA: I ain't seen Mary.

HOOT: She said she was goine drive you.

BEA: I waited for Mary for three hours and she never showed up.

HOOT: Then how you get there?

BEA: I walked.

HOOT: You walked?

BEA: How else was I supposed to get there?

HOOT: Mary said she was goine come get ya.

BEA: Mother be dead and in the ground, sitting around waiting for Mary to show up.

HOOT: You walked all the way to Gas City?

BEA: What I just tell ya?

HOOT: Jesus, Bea. Why didn't you say something?

BEA: I told you. I been telling you. Mother had a stroke and I had to find a way to go see her.

HOOT: You didn't tell me you was goine walk. Anything could've happened to you. There are robbers out on that road.

BEA: I ain't got nothing to steal.

HOOT: Robbers don't know that. They go to rob you and you ain't got nothing to steal, that just make 'em mad. You know they killed that boy, Billy Connors.

BEA: I heard he drank himself to death.

HOOT: Highway robbers got him. Robbed him, killed him, and left his body in a ditch by the side of the road.

BEA: I thought he got hold to a bad bottle of bootleg.

HOOT: It was the highway robbers, Bea. It was Friday. He just got paid, and when they found him, he didn't have a dime on him.

BEA: That's cause he spent it all on gin.

HOOT: I'm trying to tell you what happened if you'd listen. Billy Connors got robbed and killed. But you ain't got to worry about that. Roy Cox and a couple other fellas been patrolling that part of the highway. We goine catch the boys what done this but until we do, you need to stay off that part of the road. And you need to do something about Mary.

BEA: Something like what?

HOOT: You need to clamp down on that girl. Straighten her out before she gets herself into trouble.

BEA: She don't listen to me.

HOOT: That's cause you not using the right language. Put some hurting on her. Bet she'll listen to that.

BEA: I already put some hurting on her.

HOOT: Apparently you didn't put enough. You want me to do it? I'll make her listen. I get done with her, bet she won't have no trouble listening.

BEA: I'll talk to her.

HOOT: I ain't talking about talking to her, Bea. I'm talking about making her listen.

BEA: I said I'd do it.

HOOT: How long it take you to walk to Gas City?

BEA: Not long.

HOOT: How long is not long?

BEA: Couple of hours.

HOOT: Promise me you won't try something like that again.

BEA: I wouldn't have to be out there if we bought an automobile.

HOOT: We'll get an automobile soon as we get money for an automobile.

BEA: We don't need all the money, Hoot. Not up front.

HOOT: I ain't buying nothing on nobody's installments. I buy something, I pay for it. I ain't going to no man begging with my hat in my hand.

BEA: It ain't begging.

HOOT: My daddy never bought an automobile on installments.

BEA: That's cause they didn't have automobiles back then. If they had 'em, I'm sure he would've bought one on installments.

HOOT: I ain't doing it. You want an automobile, we'll save up till we get enough. We'll start saving money today. We get enough, we go down, talk to the man, look him in the eye. We give him the money, he gives us the automobile. That's how that work. Till then, I want you to stay off that road.

BEA: You ain't got to worry about that. The way I'm hurting, my knee swole up, my hip hurts. All my regular aches and pains left me. Wasn't enough room for old pain after all this new hurt set in.

HOOT: How 'bout you take a break from cooking and we go to the diner and get something to eat?

BEA: Diner open this early?

HOOT: Opens at five AM. Come on. You spent enough time on your feet.

BEA: Still got to walk to get there. Bad as I'm hurting, I ain't walking nowhere for nobody. House catch fire? Might as well mix up a batch of barbeque sauce cause I ain't moving.

HOOT: Come on, Bea. I'm trying to do something nice for you.

BEA: Thought we was goine start saving money?

HOOT: First thing tomorrow.

BEA: That mean you ain't goine stop off and get a shine?

HOOT: You want me to give up my shine?

BEA: If we goine start saving money.

HOOT: Man shouldn't have to give up his shine, Bea.

BEA: Don't have to give up every day. Maybe every other day.

HOOT: I don't go to work every other day. Why should I have to get a shine every other day?

BEA: I'm just saying, if we goine start saving money . . .

HOOT: The first thing people look at when they see you, they look at your shoes. That's how you judge a man, by how he keeps his shoes. Man who keeps his shoes clean, keeps a shine on, that's the type of man I wanna do business with. Man who can't take care of his shoes, I wouldn't trust him to take care of nothing for me.

BEA: Then maybe you can pick up another shift at work.

HOOT: Everything's starting to slow down. And even if they had another shift to give somebody, they wouldn't give it to me. Not since I quit the Klavern.

BEA: Then maybe you oughta consider joining back up.

HOOT: Won't matter if the plant closes. Plant closes, everybody goine be outta work.

BEA: That plant ain't never goine close.

HOOT: You don't know that, Bea.

BEA: Foundry been there forever.

HOOT: But I ain't never seen it like this before. They talking about laying off more men. You know they laid off Claude Deeter . . .

BEA: Then that's all the more reason for you to join back up with the Klavern.

HOOT: Why you keep asking me to get back with those hypocrites? Cause that's all they are, a bunch of hypocrites. They talk about God, they talk about country, and then the main one, the Grand Wizard, he raped that girl, then killed her. And what the government goine do about it? Nothing. Slap on the wrist. I ain't hitching my wagon to folks like that. I sooner associate with the jigs or the Jews than associate with white men like that. At least the jigs and the Jews, they straight with you. With them, you know where you stand. And some of 'em are smart. Smarter than some white men I know. This one boy at the foundry, he saved my ass the other day. I'm working on the punch press and the stop keeps coming loose. And I'm starting to fall behind. Way behind. So I tell Hank, I say, "Hank, I need somebody to get over here and fix this machine." Hank says they ain't got nobody to fix the machine. I tell him, "I'm not goine be able to hit my quota with this machine the way it is," and Hank tells me if I don't hit my quota, I'm done for. So I'm thinking, what the hell, he's gearing up to fire me. So I go looking for Archie or Bill or anybody who knows how to fix the stop and I can't find anybody. I'm thinking, it's over, I'm getting ready to lose my job. And I get back and there's this colored boy standing there. I say, "What the hell you doing at my machine?" And he says, "I hope you don't mind but I fixed it for you." And I look at the machine and it's running as smooth as a top. I'm telling ya, I got to put my hand on it to make sure it's switched on. Not only that, this boy, he's already run two full loads and I'm all caught up with my work.

So I ask him, I say, "Who sent you over here? Hank send you over here?" And he say, "Nawsir." And I say, "Then who sent you over here? Who told you to fix my machine?" And he said, "Nobody." So I say, "Why you do it, then? Why you come over here to help me this way?" And he says, "Cause it look like you needed help."

Now that's the kinda man I wanna be associated with. To hell with these other yahoos who go to church on Sunday after spending their Saturday nights drinking bootleg, gambling, and dancing to filthy music. Looked like you needed help. Now that's what you call character.

BEA: Colored boy?

HOOT: Black as the ace of spades.

BEA: What was his name?

HOOT: You know what? You right. I oughta figure out his name, find out who he is.

BEA: If you could talk to Hank about giving you another shift . . .

HOOT: I already told ya, Bea, he ain't goine do it. I'll figure out a way to get you back and forth to see your momma. Don't worry. I said I was goine do it and I plan to keep my word.

Lights fade on HOOT and BEA. Lights up on MARIE and JAMES.

MARIE: You know where I was, don't you? While my ma was sitting there waiting for me? I was with you.

JAMES: With me?

MARIE: Don't act like you don't know what I'm talking about.

Lights up on a 1926 Ford Roadster on RIVER ROAD. Inside the Roadster are CLAUDE and MARY.

You and I were there together and you know it.

ABE, TOMMY, and APPLES enter. TOMMY hands the gun to APPLES.

TOMMY: Here, take the gun. All you got to do is say, "Stick 'em up." Then you let the roscoe do the talking.

APPLES: Stick 'em up!

CLAUDE and MARY get out of the car.

CLAUDE: What the hell is this supposed to be?

TOMMY: Man said stick 'em up.

CLAUDE: Stick 'em up?

APPLES: Stick 'em up, Mister.

CLAUDE: And what happens if I don't?

TOMMY: If you don't, he'll shoot ya.

APPLES: That's right. Stick 'em up or I'll shoot ya. Come on. Get 'em up there.

CLAUDE: You know what? I don't think you got the nerve.

TOMMY: Question his ruthlessness at your own peril.

APPLES: That's right.

TOMMY: This man is a killer.

CLAUDE: You talking about this shine? This lil shine is a killer? Where's your shine box, boy?

APPLES: At home, now stick 'em up.

CLAUDE: What happens if somebody needs a shine?

TOMMY: That's their tough luck. Now stick 'em up.

CLAUDE: My goodness, would ya look at this? Looks like I stepped in something nasty. Why don't you gimme that gun, take your ass home, get your shine box, then come back here and clean me up? Can't nobody put a smile on these gators the way you can.

APPLES nervously glances at TOMMY.

TOMMY: Don't give him the gun, goddamn it. Stick him up.

APPLES: Stick 'em up.

CLAUDE: Give me the gun before I kick off in your ass.

APPLES hands CLAUDE the gun.

TOMMY: Damn, Apples. What did I tell ya?

APPLES: What was I supposed to do?

TOMMY: Anything 'cept give him the gun.

CLAUDE (*To TOMMY*): What you bring him out here for?

TOMMY: He's looking for work.

CLAUDE: And who the hell am I supposed to be? Employment agency?

TOMMY: He can be our third man.

CLAUDE: What you tell him?

TOMMY: I ain't told him nothing.

CLAUDE: What he tell you, boy?

APPLES: Just said I could make some money.

CLAUDE: You need to keep your goddamn mouth shut, Tommy. You talk too much.

MARY: Ya'll still talking about trying to hit The Pig?

CLAUDE: This was an A & B conversation, Mary.

MARY: Better leave those gangsters alone.

CLAUDE: A & B, Mary. That means see your way out.

TOMMY: I was there. I was in it. And you know how much money we're talking? We're talking hundreds of dollars. Two, maybe three hundred. Three hundred, split three ways. You know how much money that is?

A whole lot.

MARY: I ain't having nothing to do with it.

TOMMY: You ain't got to have nothing to do with it. That's the reason we got Apples, here.

ABE: Since when you start calling yourself Apples?

APPLES: Since I gave myself that name. That's when.

CLAUDE: You think I'm goine trust this boy to have my back?

TOMMY: All he got to do is hold the gun and stand by the door.

CLAUDE: He let me take the gun away from him, Tommy.

APPLES: That's cause I know you. What was I supposed to do? Shoot ya?

CLAUDE: Listen to me, boy. Don't you ever, for the rest of your life, never point a gun at anybody unless you willing to use it. You unnerstand me?

APPLES: But you and me, we friends.

CLAUDE: I ain't your friend.

APPLES: I shine your shoes all the time.

CLAUDE: That don't make us friends, you lil fool.

APPLES: It means I ain't gonna shoot ya.

CLAUDE: What happens if we bust in on this game and you see somebody else whose shoes you shine? You goine give them the gun too? Run home and get your shine box? Jesus.

TOMMY: So who we goine get to work the door?

CLAUDE: We don't need nobody to work the door.

TOMMY: We need three people.

CLAUDE: Only need one.

TOMMY: We need one person at the front door, one person at the back, and somebody in the game, incognito. That way, nobody tries nothing and nobody gets hurt. Nobody gets hurt, no reason for the law to get involved.

CLAUDE: We ain't talking about Fort Knox. It's a crap game at The Pig, Tommy. Blind man with one arm could take care of this.

ABE: Gonna need at least one other person to clean up the mess that's gonna be left after those gangsters find out who you are and smear your ass between here and Indianapolis.

CLAUDE: I knew you'd come crawling back.

ABE: I ain't crawling back to nothing.

CLAUDE: Then what you doing here?

ABE: I'm supposed to be conking Tommy's hair.

CLAUDE: Damn, Tommy, why you gotta do that shit out here?

TOMMY: Best place for it. Got the river right there.

CLAUDE: But that shit stinks.

TOMMY: You ain't got to smell it.

CLAUDE: Can't help but to smell it. Colored women like it when you do your hair thataway?

TOMMY: All the womens like it when I do my hair thataway. Ain't that right, Mary?

MARY: Oh yeah. I loves me a man that smells like an outhouse.

TOMMY: To hell with you.

ABE: You ready for me to do this?

TOMMY: In a minute.

ABE: I ain't got all day, Tommy.

CLAUDE: Listen to you, like you got someplace better to be.

ABE: Matter of fact, I do.

CLAUDE: Where you got to be that's better than here?

ABE: I gotta appointment with a man called none of your damn business, that's where.

TOMMY: Go on and start mixing it up and I'll be ready in a minute.

ABE: Come on, Tommy.

TOMMY: All I need is a couple minutes, man, damn. Claude?

CLAUDE: Come on.

CLAUDE and TOMMY move away from MARY, ABE, and APPLES.

ABE: I knew I shouldn't be messing around with him.

> *Abe opens the bag and takes out a jar, a potato, a couple of eggs, and a can of Red Devil Lye. He then takes out a knife and starts to slice the potato into the jar while APPLES looks on.*

ABE: What you doing out here?

MARY: Waiting for Claude to drive me and my momma out to see my grandma.

ABE: Why you got to ask Claude to drive you?

MARY: He's the one with the automobile.

ABE: That ain't his automobile. That's Tommy's automobile.

MARY: He drives it all the time.

ABE: Still, why you got to ask him?

MARY: Who was I supposed to ask? You? You ain't got no automobile.

ABE: Not now but I'm gonna get one. I'm buying Tommy's. Looka here. He gave me a key to it and everything.

MARY: You gonna buy that old bucket of bolts?

ABE: I don't know what you talking about. That's a good machine. Checked it out myself. Motor's good. Tires good.

MARY: Still a bucket of bolts.

ABE: That bucket of bolts take you anyplace you need to go. Wanna go to Kokomo? It'll get you there. Wanna go to Muncie? Fort Wayne? Indianapolis? All you got to do is keep water in the radiator.

APPLES: Yeah, but looks like a piece of shit.

ABE: You wasn't complaining when you wanted to ride.

MARY: Since when you plan on going to Indianapolis?

ABE: Who knows where I might end up going.

Hey, Tommy! Come on, boy. I ain't got all day.

ABE (*To MARY*): Mr. Hobbs is paying me eight dollars to fix the motor in his automobile.

APPLES: How much you charge Tommy to conk his hair?

ABE: Why you need to know that?

APPLES: Just trying to figure out how much I should be charging folks.

ABE: You thinking about trying to conk somebody's hair?

APPLES: Don't look like it's that hard to do. I watch my stepdaddy do it all the time. Only, I ain't never seen him put potatoes in his.

ABE: Then either you ain't been paying attention or your stepdaddy's a fool. You gotta put something in it to cut the heat.

APPLES: I thought that's what the eggs was for.

ABE: Eggs help it stick to the hair. It's the potatoes that cut the heat. You don't cut the heat, it'll burn a hole in your head the size of Mississippi. See this?

ABE holds up the can of lye.

ABE: You know what this is?

APPLES: Lye.

ABE: That's right. And this lye is dangerous. Folks try to handle this lye without knowing what they doing, they end up getting it all over themselves and other folks and everybody ends up in a whole world of hurt.

APPLES: The only thing I asked you was how much you charging Tommy. That's all I asked you.

ABE: You need to take your lil young ass home. That's what you need to do.

APPLES: And you need to find yourself some business other than mine.

APPLES moves away from ABE and MARY.

ABE: I saw you at the band concert the other day.

MARY: I didn't see you.

ABE: Cause I didn't want you to see me. But I saw you, plain as day. You were sitting on a quilt with your momma. Ya'll had some potato salad and chicken. Halfway through the concert, you went and bought yourself some cotton candy.

MARY: You know how much I like cotton candy.

ABE: I know. Cotton candy and cotton dresses.

What else you like to wear that's made of cotton?

MARY: Behave yourself, Abe.

ABE: I'm gonna start calling myself Eli. Eli Whitney. Cause I'm looking to pick myself some cotton.

MARY: You a mess, you know that?

ABE: I know, but I can't help it. No matter what I do, I think about you. The other day, I'm working on the motor in Mr. Hobbs' automobile. I smell the oil, the grease, and the gasoline and it reminded me of Joe Johnson who works at Mister Mackie's filling station. Joe lives next door to Myrtle whose sister married Bill Bailey. And every Saturday night, you know that Bill Bailey's got a new picture show playing on the side of his barn. The Baileys, they grow apples and pears, but also berries and cherries, and that rhymes with Mary and that brings me back to you.

MARY: You a bona fide fool, you know that?

ABE: Fool for you. I'm going to Chicago and I want you to go with me. Tommy's gonna sell me his Roadster for fifty-two dollars. I already got forty-five saved. Mr. Hobbs's gonna pay me eight for fixing his motor. That'll be enough to buy Tommy's Roadster. I'm gonna buy that Roadster, then take two weeks pay, get in that Roadster and drive to Chicago. It'll make it, too. All I got to do is make sure I keep water in the radiator.

MARY: What you gonna do in Chicago?

ABE: Live my life. Things are different in Chicago than they are around here. They got colored policemen in Chicago. They got colored banks, colored newspapers, colored grocery stores.

MARY: They got that stuff in Indiana.

ABE: Indianapolis, maybe, but not here. You can go cradle to grave in Chicago and see only colored if you wanted.

MARY: Sounds nice, for you.

ABE: For you too, if you want. Colored folks ain't like white in that respect. Colored folks accept everybody. Black folks, jet black, blue black, all the way to goddamn-you-got-to-be-kidding-me-who-turned-out-the-lights-black. You got your brown folks, light brown, dark brown, cocoa mocha, and chocolate brown. You got your high yella, your strawberry freckled, your creamy tan, your light bright all the way to albino white, which, by the way, is whiter than you are. Why you think they call 'em colored? Cause they come in all different sizes, shapes, and colors. I heard they even got a China man living in Chicago who got himself a colored wife. He say he's colored. And you know what? Ain't nobody gonna argue with him.

MARY: What you gonna do for work, you get to Chicago?

ABE: My cousin's gotta garage there. He always looking for somebody who knows how to fix an engine.

MARY: But times are getting tight, Abe. Banks are closing. People losing their money, losing their jobs.

ABE: Banks are closing in New York, not Chicago. And there's jobs all over Chicago. All you got to do is walk down the street, stop, bend down and pick up one. You wanna work, you'll find something.

MARY: Something better than you got now?

ABE: What I got now ain't so special. Especially if the plant close down. Plant closes, everybody gonna be outta work and I won't miss it one bit.

MARY: I thought you liked working there.

ABE: Used to like it. Back when I thought that things might change but ain't nothing around here gonna change. The way folks treat me. They treat me like I'm a criminal.

MARY: That's cause you been stealing automobiles.

ABE: Ain't no reason for them to treat me like I'm a criminal. 'Sides, I changed. Turned over a new leaf. I no longer involve myself in unlawful enterprises. Here.

ABE hands MARY a ring.

MARY: What's this?

ABE: Used to belong to my daddy. He was a Freemason from the Prince Hall lodge and that was his ring. He gave it to me, now I'm giving it to you. I want you to put it on a chain and wear it around your neck. I want folks to know.

MARY: I'm not going to Chicago with you, Abe.

ABE: You rather stay here with Claude?

MARY: You know that ain't it.

ABE: Claude don't care about you. He don't care whether you live or die.

MARY: Maybe not.

ABE: But you'd rather stay here with him and be used as bait so that he and Tommy can rob old men?

MARY: You wasn't complaining about it when you was doing the robbing.

ABE: You know I never liked you doing that. Why you think I quit doing it? It ain't right, leading men on that way, making them think they gonna have relations with you. Letting them touch you.

MARY: They don't touch me.

ABE: They try.

MARY: I'm not gonna argue with you about this, Abe.

ABE: Did Claude and Tommy kill that boy Billy Connors?

MARY: What're you talking about?

ABE: They found him alongside the road. Pockets empty. Pants down around his ankles. Did you lead him on? Make him think he was gonna get lucky? Take him to a spot where you knew Claude and Tommy were waiting?

> CLAUDE and TOMMY rejoin ABE and MARY.

CLAUDE: What you two talking about?

MARY: None of your business.

CLAUDE: Don't you know by now that everything's my business?

MARY: Everything ain't about you.

CLAUDE: When you find something that ain't about me, you let me know, all right?

Apples? Tommy tells me that you're a sneaky lil sonavabitch, but I say you still got mother's milk on your breath. What you got to say about that?

APPLES: What you want me to say?

TOMMY: See? This is the way he operates. He appears to be all innocent and shit, but that's what makes him dangerous. I'm telling ya, this boy could steal your grandmaw's draws while she was walking down the street.

> CLAUDE produces a Mason jar, half-filled with clear liquid. He unscrews the lid and offers the jar to APPLES.

CLAUDE: Wanna hit?

APPLES: What is it?

CLAUDE: Some of the best bootleg this side of Kokomo.

> APPLES takes the jar, then takes a swig of the gin. Once he recovers:

APPLES: That's some good shit.

*CLAUDE and TOMMY laugh. CLAUDE takes the jar, takes a
swig, then passes it to TOMMY, who takes a swig. TOMMY offers it
to ABE, who declines.*

CLAUDE: You ever been with a woman before?

APPLES: Lots of times.

CLAUDE: He may be sneaky but he can't lie worth shit.

APPLES: I ain't lying.

TOMMY: We can teach him how to lie.

APPLES: I been with lots of girls.

CLAUDE: Girls?

APPLES: Women.

CLAUDE: You know sumthin'? If you was in Africa, you'd probably be
dead by now, you know that? Somebody would've thrown your ass
into a volcano. See, them Africans, being godless sons of bitches, got
no idea of how the world works. Their crops fail or the buffalo go
away, you know what they do? They find themselves a virgin, and
then they have themselves a sacrifice.

ABE: Ain't no damn buffalo in Africa.

CLAUDE: You know what I mean. Flood comes or a drought, or any other
natural disaster that they don't understand, they all get together,
dance around in a circle and chant, then they sacrifice a virgin to try
to make things better.

APPLES: I ain't no virgin.

CLAUDE: The only pussy you ever seen in your life was the pussy you saw
when you was born.

APPLES: I've seen plenty.

CLAUDE: Plenty what?

APPLES: You know.

CLAUDE: He can't even say it.

APPLES: Pussy. I've seen plenty pussy.

CLAUDE: In that case, you probably wouldn't mind seeing a lil more,
would ya?

APPLES: I wouldn't mind.

CLAUDE: Mary? Come here.

MARY: What for?

CLAUDE: Get over here and find out, that's what for.

MARY: What you want, Claude?

CLAUDE: Give him some.

MARY: Give him some what?

CLAUDE: Some of the only thing you got that anybody's interested in, that's what.

MARY: Kiss my ass.

CLAUDE: I would if you'd wash it more often. Now come on. I'm giving you an opportunity to save this boy's life.

MARY: He can die as far as I'm concerned.

CLAUDE: Don't say that. What happens if heathens show up looking for a virgin to sacrifice?

MARY: He'd be one lil burnt up sonovabitch, that's what.

CLAUDE: Come on, now. You want me to take you to Gas City to see your grandma, don't you?

MARY: You supposed to be doing that anyway.

CLAUDE: Things have come up and I've had a change of plans.

MARY: Come on, Claude. You know I'm not feeling good.

CLAUDE: Do this for me and I'll take you.

MARY: I'm not doing nothing with him.

CLAUDE: Then I guess we ain't going to Gas City then.

MARY: I told my momma we'd pick her up an hour ago.

ABE: I'll take ya.

TOMMY: On what? Your back?

ABE: I figured you'd let me use the Roadster.

TOMMY: You mean my Roadster? Is that the Roadster to which you're referring to?

ABE: You ain't using it.

TOMMY: And when did me-not-using-it come to mean you-can-take-it?

ABE: You let Claude use it. Why can't I use it?

TOMMY: I'm paying you to conk my hair, not to drive to Gas City. In fact, gimme back my key. Come on, gimme the key and mix 'em up.

MARY: Come on, Claude.

CLAUDE: Only goine take a minute.

APPLES: She don't have to do it if she don't want.

CLAUDE: And I say she does. I mean, you a man, ain't you?

APPLES: Course I'm a man.

CLAUDE: All right then. Mary? All you doing is wasting time.

MARY: I do this, you gonna drive me for real?

CLAUDE: I'll drive you.

MARY: After stopping to pick up my momma?

CLAUDE: After stopping to pick up your momma.

MARY: You'll drive us there and then wait while she visits with my grandma?

CLAUDE: That wasn't part of the deal.

MARY: It's part of the deal if I'm goine do what you asking. You'll wait while my mother visits with my grandma.

CLAUDE: How long?

MARY: Two hours.

CLAUDE: Half hour.

MARY: Two hours or no deal.

CLAUDE: All right, two hours.

MARY: Say it. All of it.

CLAUDE: I'll pick up your momma then drive both of ya to Gas City and wait for two hours while she visits with her mother.

MARY: Then drive us home.

CLAUDE: Then drive ya home.

MARY: Come on boy. Damn.

    APPLES follows MARY to the secluded area. ABE watches.

CLAUDE: What you looking at? You perverted or something? You like to watch? Can't get none on your own so you wanna watch while somebody else gets it?

TOMMY: Yeah. Thought you was ready with that conk. Come on. I ain't got all day. Mix 'em up. And you better not burn me.

> *ABE puts on rubber gloves, then shakes some of the potatoes out of the jar. He then adds a half can of the lye and stirs with a wooden spoon.*

CLAUDE: Whaddya think? You think it's really his first time?

TOMMY: Course it is. (*To ABE*) Ain't that a lotta lye?

ABE: You need a lotta lye to get that mess to lay straight.

TOMMY: And why you take the potatoes out?

ABE: Cut too many. Don't need all that.

TOMMY: Didn't look like too many to me.

ABE: This is a new technique I'm using.

TOMMY: What kinda technique?

ABE: Special technique I learned in Chicago.

TOMMY: Special technique that don't use potatoes?

ABE: It's gonna be all right. Don't worry. You in good hands. You ready?

CLAUDE: Hold up. Lemme check it out.

> *CLAUDE touches the Mason jar.*

CLAUDE: Goddamn! That's hot.

ABE: The hotter, the better.

TOMMY: You burn me, I'm goine kick your ass.

ABE: Duly noted, my friend. Duly noted.

> *ABE starts to comb the jelly-like mixture into TOMMY's hair. It starts to burn immediately.*

APPLES: You know the reason I gave myself the name Apples? My step-daddy took me down south to visit on his family's farm. They got sheep and goats and lambs. Some of them had names and some didn't. This one lil lamb, cute lil fella, I was gonna call him Charlie cause he was so cute and my step-daddy said, "Naw, you don't wanna name that one." And I said, "Why not?" And he said, "That's a meat lamb, and you don't give names to the ones you gonna slaughter." Ain't that something? You don't give names to the ones you gonna slaughter. So I figured, I better give myself a name. And quick. So I come up with Apples cause . . . cause I like apples.

Don't you think maybe we oughta get started?

MARY: You come near me, I'll break your arm, you understand me?

TOMMY: Hey Abe, man, it's getting hot.

ABE: Supposed to be hot.

TOMMY: I mean really hot. It ain't never been this hot before.

ABE: It's always been like this. You just forgot. Now keep still.

MARY: He don't really expect us to do it, you lil fool. He's just testing you. He's testing you and he's testing me to see how far we'd go. Now, I'm testing him back to see how far he's goine let us go. My money says, he's not goine let us go very far. He's goine find some excuse to come over here and interrupt, you mark my words.

CLAUDE: You think they going at it by now?

TOMMY: Who gives a damn? Man this shit is hot.

CLAUDE: If it's his first time, he ain't goine last long. I figure they gotta be going at it by now. First time, that means he's probably goine last for another three, two, one, he's done.

TOMMY: Goddamn!

TOMMY screams, jumps up and runs off.

ABE: Perhaps I should have added more potato. Whadda you think?

CLAUDE: I think he's goine come back here and kick your ass, that's what I think.

ABE: He can try. That is his God-given right. He is certainly entitled to try.

APPLES: I like shining shoes. If a man's shoes look good, he looks good, and that's my job, making men look good. Man could have nothing. He could have nothing, be nothing. He comes to me, I clean him up, make him look good, put a shine on, next thing you know, folks are calling him mister. Abe thinks he's something cause he knows how to use lye to make men look good but that don't make him better than me. The way I see it, he uses lye, I use polish, but we both doing the same thing.

MARY: Will you please shut the hell up.

I don't believe it. He ain't gonna stop us. That sonavabitch. Come on.

No, wait. When he ask, you tell him we did it. Okay? You tell him . . . tell him it was good to ya.

As MARY and APPLES move to CLAUDE and ABE.

CLAUDE: What the hell is taking 'em so long? It's been fifteen, twenty minutes. I mean, how long can he possibly go at it for?

ABE: You so concerned about it, why don't you go look see?

MARY and APPLES join CLAUDE and ABE.

CLAUDE: Well? How was it?

APPLES: I've had better.

CLAUDE: My man. You wan' another hit?

CLAUDE offers him the gin.

APPLES: Don't mind if I do.

APPLES takes a swig.

MARY: Come on, Claude. I did what you wanted me to do. Now let's go.

CLAUDE: In a minute. Hey, Tommy!

TOMMY enters. His face, head, and shoulders are wet and he has a towel wrapped around his head. He opens the towel.

TOMMY: How's it look? Look good?

ABE: Looks good.

CLAUDE: Looks straight.

APPLES: Just like a white man's.

TOMMY: Still burns like hell though. Burns like hell.

MARY: Can we go now?

CLAUDE: When I get ready and right now, I'm not ready. Tommy, Apples, step into my office.

CLAUDE, TOMMY, and APPLES move to the secluded area.

MARY: You really think you can find work in Chicago?

ABE: Told you my cousin's got a garage there.

MARY: Maybe I could find something too. Housekeeping or something.

ABE: That mean you're gonna go?

MARY: I don't know . . .

ABE: You go with me, you won't have to worry about work. You won't have to worry about a thing. I'll take care of you. Treat you right, like you never been treated before. See these arms? These arms are like a mighty oak tree. I wrap these oak tree arms around you and you'll be safe. Protected. These arms will keep anything or anybody from ever hurting you again.

Lights down on ABE and MARY, up on JAMES and MARIE.

JAMES: It take you long to think up all of that or did you just make it up right here on the spot?

MARIE: You wanted to know what I remembered. I just told you what I remember.

JAMES: How come I don't remember any of it?

MARIE: I don't know how your mind works. After everything you've been through, there's no telling what's going on up there.

JAMES: I'll tell you why I don't remember. I don't remember because it never happened.

MARIE: And I remember it as if it were yesterday.

JAMES: You sure you're actually remembering and you didn't just imagine it all?

MARIE: Depends on what day it is. Some days, the memories are strong. So strong, I can smell the honeysuckle that was in the air that night. Other days, I believe I must've imagined it all. Especially on days when I see you on the television working your magic, I start to doubt everything I remember. But when that happens, I touch one hand to my heart and I know that I did not imagine it all. I know that what I remember is true and that what you have done is constructed a lie so massive and unwieldy that you've lost all control. Your lie has taken on a life of its own.

JAMES: Touching a hand to your heart tells you all that?

MARIE: Me checking to make sure this is here tells me all that.

She shows him a chain that hangs around her neck. On the end of the chain is a ring.

It's the ring that Abe gave me that night. It's my lighthouse, my beacon. It's the one thing that keeps me sane when everything around me starts to crumble. And it's the one thing that proves beyond a doubt that you sir, are a goddamn liar.

How much they pay you to talk on television and do those interviews?

JAMES: They don't pay me.

MARIE: The Englishman. Is he paying you?

JAMES: I don't see how that's any of your concern.

MARIE: You know what? You were right. Talking about it wasn't nearly as painful as I thought it was gonna be. I do feel better.

JAMES: I'm glad to be of assistance. I'm sorry for your loss and I'll make sure that the Englishman won't bother you again.

He begins to collect his things to exit.

MARIE: One last thing. I want you to stop telling your lies. I don't want to ever hear you tell your story again. No more television, no more newspaper articles, no more public appearances.

JAMES: You can't stop me from talking about what happened.

MARIE: No, but I can tell folks what I remember. I can talk to your Englishman. I think he'll find it interesting to see how different my story is from your story. And I wonder if the governor would still be interested in granting you a pardon once he realizes that you're not quite as innocent as he thought you were?

JAMES: Nobody's gonna believe you, Marie.

MARIE: You willing to bet your pardon on it?

JAMES: You've been under a lotta stress lately. Losing your father and all. This has been a very difficult time for you. Anyone could understand it if you were a bit confused.

MARIE: Don't you try to patronize me.

JAMES: Look at you, the way you're sweating. Beads of sweat running down your neck. You've clearly been under a lotta pressure.

MARIE: Not as much pressure as you're gonna be under once folks realize that you've been scamming them all of these years. So I suggest you think about it very carefully. And while you're thinking, I'm going out to the Denny's and meet your Englishman. I'm not gonna say anything. Not just yet. I just wanna let him know that Mary Ball is back from the dead. And then, I'm gonna go back to my hotel and get a change of clothes cause these, look at that, these clothes are ruined. It's not so much the sweat that ruins them, it's the salt. It gets into the fabric and breaks down the fiber. I mean, look at that. The salt is starting to crystallize on my hands and my arms. It's starting to crystallize over every inch of my body.

She examines her hands and her arms as lights fade.

End of Act One.

ACT TWO

The next day.

MARIE and JAMES at the funeral parlor. JAMES enters with the ammo case.

JAMES: I thought I'd find you here.

MARIE: You're a regular Sherlock Holmes.

JAMES: Hotel said you had checked out.

MARIE: And you thought you got lucky and I had left town.

JAMES: I didn't know.

MARIE: Actually, I should be on my way to the airport right about now, but . . . my old man, he wanted to be buried here in town. I figured, to hell with that. I put him in the ground, that means there's a grave, a marker, a place to come back to. And I had planned to never come back to this place again as long as I live. So I had him cremated. Then last night I get a call from the funeral director saying I forgot to take the ashes. I told him I don't want the damn ashes. There's a dumpster out back. Toss them.

Sonavabitch starts to lecture me about state regulations but I don't give a shit about state regulations. So, here I am. And I figure, as long as I'm here I might as well go to your little soirée this afternoon. I mean, I was invited, wasn't I?

JAMES: I think perhaps we got off on the wrong foot yesterday.

MARIE: You think? I met with your Englishman. Interesting fella. He wants to do a story about me. A documentary.

JAMES: I know. He called me. He asked if you were who you said you were.

MARIE: What you tell him?

JAMES: I told him the truth. What did you expect me to tell him?

MARIE: I stopped trying to figure you out a long time ago. I used to listen to you talk and try to figure out why you told one lie as opposed to another. I know why you lied about Claude. Hell, I would've lied too. Claude got killed and you were looking to save yourself. So you described him as a nice white fella cause if you said he was a cruel, crooked sonavabitch who deserved to die, you would have hanged right alongside Tommy and Abe. And I know why you continued to lie. I mean, why walk away from a golden goose? But the one thing that still stumps me today is why you didn't tell anybody who killed Claude. If it were me, that's the first thing I would have told. I would have told who shot him and I would have told anybody who'd listen.

JAMES: He's willing to pay you, Marie. The Englishman is willing to pay you for your story.

MARIE: How much?

JAMES: A flat fee up front and then a percentage of whatever the documentary makes after it's released. But you have to tell the truth about what you remember. Not that bullshit you told me yesterday.

MARIE: That bullshit is what I remember.

JAMES: Then why don't you see if you can remember something different.

MARIE: Is that the deal? You pay me and then suddenly, I remember things the way you remember?

JAMES: The only thing I've done is try to recall the events of that night to the best of my ability.

MARIE: You're a scam artist, James. A scam artist who has spent years profiting off the deaths of Tommy and Abe. But I'm putting an end to all that.

JAMES: I'm not making any money doing this.

MARIE: You mean, you're not making a lot.

JAMES: I'm not making any.

MARIE: You're gonna get a pardon. That's gotta be worth something.

JAMES: They're giving me a pardon because I spent five years of my life in prison for a crime I didn't commit.

MARIE: You were convicted of being an accessory to murder.

JAMES: That's right. But I didn't do anything.

MARIE: What the hell do you think being an accessory means? You didn't have to do anything except be there and you were there, my friend. The way you tell it, you were there, you held the gun, that means you were guilty, convict. The verdict was just, and the only reason they're giving you a pardon is because of what happened to Tommy and what happened to Abe.

JAMES: Nothing good could come out of you telling a different story. Not at this point in time. The dead don't care about justice or revenge. The dead only want to be remembered and that's what I'm doing. Yad Vashem. Remembering.

MARIE: Your gravy train has come to an end.

JAMES: Your story will not stand, Marie.

MARIE: Is that why you came here this morning looking for me? To tell me that my story will not stand?

JAMES: Why'd you come here this morning? Who are you waiting for?

MARIE: I'm not waiting for anyone.

JAMES: You could have just walked away from those ashes. Instead, you arranged to have a service, you ran an obituary, you had to think that somebody would see it and show up.

MARIE: But nobody did, did they? Nobody saw it and if they did, nobody showed up.

JAMES: I saw it. I showed up.

MARIE: Yeah, like a buzzard.

JAMES: Lemme see the ring. The ring that you said Abe gave you.

MARIE: For what?

JAMES: Abe's father was not a Freemason. Abe's father worked alongside his father running the racetrack outside of Weaver.

MARIE: That's what you say.

JAMES: If Abe's father was a Freemason and if that was his ring, then it should have an onyx face and engraved on that face should be a compass and a square.

MARIE: Some of them.

JAMES: All of them. At least all of the ones I've seen. So let's have a look. Let's see what the one you have looks like.

MARIE: Why can't you just let this die? It happened fifty years ago. You're the only one who cares about it. You're the only one keeping it alive. All you have to do is stop talking about it. Stop talking about it and people will start to forget.

JAMES: That's the mistake, thinking that if you don't talk about it, it'll all go away, but it will not go away. The past will always be right here with us. Some people try to ignore it, some try to deny it, some despise it, but it'll always be here, like blood pumping in your veins, you may not be able to see it but it's there. Now let me see the ring.

MARIE: There's nothing to see. It's just a plain gold ring. No markings, no etchings. And I know you think that means something.

JAMES: Your memory cannot be trusted, Marie. You can't even deal with the memory of your own father. If it were up to you, his ashes would be in the dumpster out back.

MARIE: That's what he deserves.

JAMES: Nobody deserves that.

MARIE: You don't know what he did.

JAMES: You told me he was a good man.

MARIE: He was a good man. But he did some things . . .

JAMES: All the more reason for us to remember.

If you don't want the ashes, give them to me.

MARIE: For what? Your museum?

JAMES: Better that than some landfill.

MARIE: I'm not giving you my father's ashes.

JAMES: Then bury him.

MARIE: I'm not putting him into the ground.

JAMES: Isn't your mother in the ground?

MARIE: I don't know where my mother is. I don't even know if she's dead. I guess she's dead, but I don't know. Not for sure. Nobody seems to know what happened to her. And my father, he didn't know. Hell, he couldn't even tell you his own name. She might have left him, but maybe not. The only thing I can tell you for sure is that she lived a difficult life.

Lights up on BEA as MARY enters.

BEA: Before you say anything, I want you to tell me where the hell you been for the past two days.

MARY: I'm sorry, Momma.

BEA: Sorry means I'll bite you in the ass. That's what your sorry means. Why'd you tell me you goine do something if you ain't goine do it, Mary?

MARY: I thought I could get a ride . . .

BEA: You thought?

MARY: But it didn't work out.

BEA: Then it's a good thing you don't get paid for thinking.

MARY: I said I was sorry. What else you want?

BEA: I want you to stop promising to do things you can't do, sitting up in here waiting for you.

MARY: All right. I won't promise you anything anymore.

BEA: I can't depend on you for nothing.

MARY: I said I was sorry.

> *Beat.*

BEA: You still sick? You want something to eat?

> *MARY shrugs.*

BEA: You been gone for two days. You hungry or not?

MARY: I dunno.

BEA: Guess that mean not, cause if you were hungry, you'd know it.

MARY: Something I got to tell you.

BEA: What?

MARY: You not gonna like it.

BEA: What?

MARY: You gonna be mad.

BEA: You better not be pregnant.

> *MARY looks away.*

Goddamn it. I knew this was goine happen. Bound to happen sooner or later the way you were out there carrying on. I'm not goine say

I told you so . . . but goddamn it, I told you so. Didn't I tell you something like this was goine happen?

So what you plan on doing now? You thought about that? You so quick to jump in the skillet, how you goine get out?

MARY: I don't know.

BEA: Course you don't. All you can think about is running around, having yourself a good time. Damn.

What Claude say about it?

MARY: He ain't said nothing.

BEA: You tell him yet?

MARY: Ain't no reason to tell him.

BEA: Boy's goine be a daddy. You goine have to tell him sooner or later.

MARY: Claude didn't have nothing to do with it, Momma.

BEA: Claude didn't have nothing to do with it, then who did?

MARY: You really ain't goine like this one.

BEA: Better not be what I'm thinking.

MARY: Depends on what you thinking.

BEA: Don't play with me, Mary.

MARY: I'm not playing with you, Momma. You want me to tell you, I'll tell you, but you not gonna like it.

BEA: Then keep it to yourself. I've already heard enough I don't like to last me a lifetime.

Goddamn you, Mary. Goddamn your soul. Your daddy goine kill you, you know that, don't you? He goine kill the both of us.

MARY: He got no reason to be mad at you for something I did.

BEA: Since when did reason figure into any of this?

You tell anybody else about this?

MARY: Nobody but you.

BEA: At least you did something right.

I know a lady. Miss Betty. I'll take you to see her. She'll be able to fix this.

MARY: I don't wanna go see Miss Betty.

BEA: Then who you wanna go see?

MARY: I don't wanna go see anybody.

BEA: You wait too long, it'll be too late.

MARY: I been thinking about going to Indianapolis or maybe Chicago.

BEA: And do what?

MARY: Start a new life.

BEA: You gotta have an old life before you can start a new life. And you can't even take care of yourself here. How you think you goine take care of yourself in a place like Indianapolis or Chicago? What you goine do for money? How you supposed to feed yourself?

MARY: Get a job.

BEA: Ain't nobody goine hire you to do nothing for them.

MARY: I can get a job housekeeping. I could take in laundry.

BEA: You can't even wash your own drawers. How you goine get a job washing somebody else's?

MARY: I could get a job in one of the factories, sewing and making hats and stuff like that.

BEA: Don't be stupid. Ain't nobody goine hire you.

MARY: You don't know that, Momma.

BEA: Men are out there standing in soup lines. Strong, able-bodied men who would do anything for work. And here you come, po' lil dumb thing, thinking if a job opens up, they goine hire you over some able-bodied man?

MARY: Abe's cousin gotta garage in Chicago. And Abe knows how to fix engines. I can stay with him till I find something.

BEA: Why you got to tell me that? Didn't I tell you I didn't wanna know? I swear, you ain't got the sense God gave a grape.

Go in there and sit down while I fix you something to eat. Then we'll go see Miss Betty, get this taken care of before anybody finds out.

MARY: I'm not gonna go see Miss Betty.

BEA: Don't mess with me, Mary. I am not in a mood to be messed with.

MARY: I'm going to Chicago, Momma.

BEA: You not going any damn where.

MARY: You can't stop me.

BEA: I can put you in the ground. That's what I can do. That'll stop you. Stop you dead in your tracks. I'll drop you quicker than a hot cake. Now take your ass in there and sit down before I hurt you.

> MARY starts to back away from BEA.

BEA: Don't you even think about leavin' outta here. I'm not playing with you, Mary. You walk out that door, don't come back. You hear me?

> MARY exits.

BEA (Cont'd): Mary!

> Lights fade on BEA and up on TOMMY and APPLES. TOMMY is wearing a hat that covers his new do.

TOMMY: Now Grandpa Johnson grabbed Sister Kate. She shook just like you shake jelly on a plate.

APPLES: I don't get it.

TOMMY: What don't you get?

APPLES: Why he grab her? She do something she wasn't supposed to be doing?

TOMMY: He just grabbed her. That's all.

APPLES: And why they put jelly on a plate? That don't make no sense.

TOMMY: It's a song, Apples. It's not supposed to make sense. Now try it.

APPLES: What's the girl's name again?

TOMMY: Kate. Girl's name is Kate. Rhymes with plate. I don't know how to make this any easier for you.

> MARY enters.

Mary, help me out, would ya? I'm trying to teach this boy how to shake that thing but he ain't getting it.

MARY: You seen Abe?

TOMMY: Ain't been around here. And if you see him before I do, you tell him that I'm looking for him.

MARY: For what?

TOMMY: He burnt me. I woke up this morning, raised up my head but my hair stayed on the pillow.

But I'm not gonna think about that right now. Right now I'm having myself a good time. Come on. Shake that thing with me.

MARY: I ain't got time for your foolishness.

TOMMY: Since when did you get so damn serious? You used to like having a good time. But now, every time I see you, you either sick, gloomy, or depressed.

MARY: There's more to life than just having a good time, Tommy.

TOMMY: That's what they want you to believe, but I ain't buying it. You don't wanna enjoy yourself, take your dark clouds and go someplace else. Come on, Apples, gimme a count.

APPLES: One and a two and a . . .

TOMMY (*Singing*):

> *HAD A LIL DOG, HIS NAME WAS JACK,*
> *HE GOT HIS LITTLE TAIL CAUGHT IN A CRACK*
> *CAUSE HE WAS SHAKING THAT THING.*

APPLES & TOMMY:

> *HE WAS SHAKING THAT THING.*

TOMMY:

> *HE WAS SHAKING THAT THING.*

APPLES & TOMMY:

> *HE WAS SHAKING THAT THING.*

TOMMY:

> *WE GONNA RAISE THE ROOF UP,*

APPLES & TOMMY:

> *EVERYBODY SHAKE THAT THING.*

APPLES:

> *NOW GRANDPA JOHNSON GRABBED SISTER KATE,*
> *I KNOW THAT'S HER NAME CAUSE IT RHYMES WITH*
>   *PLATE,*
> *AND SHE WAS SHAKING THAT THING.*

APPLES & TOMMY:

 SHE WAS SHAKING THAT THING.

APPLES:

 SHE WAS SHAKING THAT THING.

APPLES & TOMMY:

 SHE WAS SHAKING THAT THING.

APPLES:

 WE GONNA RAISE THE ROOF UP,

APPLES & TOMMY:

 EVERYBODY SHAKE THAT THING.

MARY:

 NOW HERE I COME, THE INDIANA QUEEN,
 GOT A HUMP IN MY BACK FROM SHAKING THAT
  THING,
 YOU GOTTA SHAKE THAT THING.

ALL:

 YOU GOTTA SHAKE THAT THING.

MARY:

 YOU GOTTA SHAKE THAT THING.

ALL:

 YOU GOTTA SHAKE THAT THING.

MARY:

 WE GONNA RAISE THE ROOF UP,

ALL:

 EVERYBODY SHAKE THAT THING.

 TOMMY, APPLES, and MARY laugh.

TOMMY (*To MARY*): Now don't you feel better? I know you do, and if you say you don't, I'm gonna call you a liar.

 ABE enters.

TOMMY: And look who's here. Sonavabitch.

MARY: I gotta talk to you.

ABE: Hold on.

MARY: Something I got to tell you.

ABE: Tommy, I got your money. Fifty-two dollars. That's the deal, right?

TOMMY: You burnt me. That's the deal. Woke up this morning with a pillow full of hair. Look at this.

He raises his hat to show ABE his scalp.

ABE: Damn, that's nasty.

TOMMY: Look like an Injun come at me with a tomahawk.

ABE: I can't predict how it's gonna turn out.

TOMMY: You did this shit on purpose and I ought to kick your ass, that's what I ought to do.

ABE: Don't get stupid, all right? I know you're upset but don't go wading into deep water unless you know how to swim.

TOMMY: You think I'm scared of you? I'm not scared of you, you sonavabitch.

ABE: I'm only gonna be your sonavabitch one more time. Now I'm trying to do business with you. You wanna do business or not?

TOMMY: I told you I'm not selling 'til after I get enough money to buy a new one.

ABE: Didn't you get enough last night?

TOMMY: I didn't get nothing last night.

ABE: I heard you got almost four hundred dollars.

TOMMY: From what?

ABE: Didn't you hit The Pig last night?

TOMMY: Somebody hit The Pig?

ABE: It wasn't you?

TOMMY: Hell naw it wasn't me. Who told you somebody hit the Pig?

ABE: Bunch of fellas pitching horseshoes in Ogden Weaver's backyard. Said somebody came in and cleaned them out.

TOMMY: One man?

ABE: Figured it had to be you. Either you or Claude.

TOMMY: That sonavabitch.

ABE: I didn't say it was him. I said I thought it might have been you or him.

TOMMY: Those fellas still out there?

ABE: They were when I left.

TOMMY: Come on, Apples. Let's go see Ogden Weaver and pitch ourselves a game of horseshoes.

ABE: Gimme the key and I'll drive you. I'll drop you off.

TOMMY: This ain't gonna take long.

ABE: Come on, Tommy, man, I can't sit around here waiting for you to get back. I gotta go.

TOMMY: Where you got to be that's so damn important?

ABE: I'm going to Chicago, man.

TOMMY: When?

ABE: Just as soon as you take this money and give me the key. Now come on. Lemme drive you.

TOMMY: You gonna have my back on this?

ABE: You know I don't mess around like that anymore.

TOMMY: If you gonna come along, you gotta have my back. If you ain't got my back, keep your sorry ass here.

ABE: Let me just drop you off.

TOMMY: Apples? You got my back?

APPLES: You know I got your back.

> *APPLES shows the pistol stuck in his belt.*

TOMMY: You can have the automobile when I'm done. This ain't gonna take long.

> *APPLES and TOMMY exit.*

MARY: Thought you weren't going for another week.

ABE: Changed my mind.

MARY: You not gonna wait till you get paid?

ABE: I'm not gonna let a lil money keep me here. Time to go, so I'm going. Now what you got to tell me?

MARY: Was you gonna say anything?

ABE: Would you have noticed if I didn't?

MARY: Why you even ask me something like that?

ABE: I asked you if you wanted to go, but the way you were all humped up with Apples yesterday I figured you were preoccupied.

MARY: That wasn't nothing.

ABE: Wasn't nothing to you maybe . . .

MARY: You know I didn't do nothing with that boy.

ABE: I saw you, Mary.

MARY: You saw the two of us go off together, that's all you saw.

ABE: That's all I need to see. I don't need to see you do it with my own eyes to know what you did. I can tell you exactly what happened. I see smoke, I don't need to see fire to know something's burning.

MARY: I didn't do nothing with him and you know it. And even if I did, it never bothered you before.

ABE: I thought things between us had changed.

MARY: Then how come you didn't say something yesterday when it happened? Why you wait till today to make such a fuss about it? What changed between then and now that got you all bound up?

ABE: Nothing changed.

MARY: Guess you just decided you didn't need the money, is that it? You a rich man now. You can afford to walk away from two weeks pay.

ABE: There was a fight. Last night at work. Nobody got hurt. Not bad. I don't think.

MARY: What happened?

ABE: A few nights ago, your daddy got into some trouble. The stop on his machine came loose and the foreman wasn't cutting him any slack. I figure, I know how to fix it, so I fixed it for him. He come back, and looked at me like he had never seen me before. We've been working in the same place since I was fifteen years old and still he didn't even know my name. But that didn't bother me. Not so much. But then last night he comes in and he's all buddy buddy. Three years and he don't know my name. I save his ass and now we all buddy buddy. But that's all right. That's good. We talk. We laugh. He's happy. Everything's fine and for the first time in a long time, I get a lil bit of hope. Then, during break, he comes over to me and he wants me to come and sit with him and his friends. I tell him I don't wanna sit with him and his friends. I wanna sit with my friends. The way he looked at me you'd think I spat on his mother's grave.

MARY: He was just trying to be nice to you, Abe, that's all.

ABE: He wants to be nice to me, he can come and sit with me. I shouldn't have to go outta my way cause he wants to be nice to me. So I said no, I don't wanna sit with you and your friends. And he gets hot. And you can tell it. And as he's walking away he says something under his breath. I didn't hear what he said but one of the Italian guys, Antonio, he heard. So Antonio says something under his breath but loud enough for everybody to hear. Next thing you know, the whole place goes up for grabs. Tables upturned, fists flying, somebody fell in the corner and they were getting stomped. All I wanted to do was get the hell outta there.

MARY: You scared to go back?

ABE: I've never seen nothing like that before. It's like folks done lost their mind. One minute, men are working alongside each other, the next minute, man is on the floor in the corner getting his brains stomped out.

MARY: They just scared, that's all.

ABE: Scared of what?

MARY: Scared that the plant might close. That plant closes, it'll be the worst disaster this town has ever seen.

ABE: But what does that have to do with me? I got nothing to do with whether or not that plant closes. This is crazy. I'm not going back there. They can keep my last check. I got enough money. Enough to get me outta here. Enough to buy Tommy's Roadster and if he won't sell it to me today, I'll go find something else. Mr. Mackie got a Ford for sale at his filling station. I'll go buy that. I don't care. Just as long as it gets me to Chicago.

MARY: You change your mind about me going with you?

ABE: I don't know if I can trust you.

MARY: Trust me to do what?

ABE: I'm gonna let you in on a secret. A secret about men. A secret that most women don't know. The weakest point in a man's life is when he's together with a woman in that particular way. Not because he's got his pants down around his ankles or anything silly like that. It's because when a man is with a woman in that way, there comes a point when all of his armor falls away, when all of his defenses come down and if the woman's paying attention, she'll be able to see, just for a moment, inside of his soul. She'll be able to see the boy inside the man. She'll see all of his secrets, all of his fears and all of his weaknesses. That's the reason a man protects a woman so. He's not only protecting her, he's protecting himself. He's protecting his secrets. Men know this. They know that a woman is the most vulnerable part of a man. They also know that if you're able to wound that part of a man, the wound you inflict is the most severe.

MARY: I didn't mean to hurt you, Abe.

ABE: A lotta men keep that part of themselves protected. They keep it hidden inside of a box and they keep that box tucked away in some deep dark place that nobody will ever be able to find. And I can't live like that. I can't live with the most important part of myself hidden away somewhere.

MARY: If you trust me with that part of you, I promise, I will never let that happen again. I will protect it, Abe. Just like you said you would protect me with your oak tree arms? I'll protect you with my oak tree heart. We can protect each other. I swear to you, I will never allow anyone to hurt you through me again.

ABE: What you got to tell me?

MARY: There's a car coming.

ABE: Looks like Tommy coming back.

 TOMMY enters with APPLES.

TOMMY: Sonavabitch did it. Sonavabitch went behind my back. Used my plan.

ABE: Apparently, he didn't need your plan if he was able to do it by himself.

TOMMY: Apparently he did need my plan cause somebody got shot. In my plan, nobody was gonna get hurt. Nobody gets hurt, no need for the law to get involved.

MARY: Who got shot?

TOMMY: Some fella who wasn't even there. Some fella who was just walking along the highway.

MARY: How he get shot if he wasn't even there?

TOMMY: I'm just telling you what folks told me. They said the man was walking home from work. Gunman came outta The Pig and shot him.

MARY: He dead?

TOMMY: Shot him in the foot. Might have trouble walking for a while.

ABE: You ready to do business with me?

TOMMY: Soon as I get this taken care of.

ABE: I'm not waiting for you, Tommy. Either we gonna do this or not. Mr. Mackie got a Ford for sale at his filling station. If you not ready, I'm sure Mr. Mackie would be happy to oblige.

TOMMY: You got the money?

ABE: I've had the money, man. Fifty-two dollars. You got the paperwork?

TOMMY: You got something to write with?

ABE: Right here. Put your scrawl down and we're in business.

TOMMY: You know you gotta keep water in the radiator.

ABE: I know that, man, damn. Sign the paper.

> TOMMY *signs the title.*

MARY: Car coming.

ABE: Anybody you know?

MARY: Driving a new Chev-ro-let? Nobody I know.

> ABE *and* TOMMY *complete the transaction.*

TOMMY: Well I'll be dipped in shit and rolled in crackers.

Would you look at this?

> CLAUDE *enters dressed to the nines.*

CLAUDE: Afternoon, gentlemen. And lady. And I do use the terms loosely.

TOMMY: Look at you. And where'd you get the new struggle buggy?

CLAUDE: Picked it up this afternoon. Like it? Six-cylinder engine. Four-wheel mechanical brakes. Attractive styling. Used to be, first thing you'd see when you looked at a man was his shoes. But that's how it used to be. Nowadays, you judge a man by looking at what he's driving, by looking at his automobile. Like that bucket of bolts you banging around in, Tommy.

TOMMY: Shows how much you know. That ain't mine. That belongs to Abe.

CLAUDE: Abe? So you finally scratched up enough dough?

ABE: I gotta go.

MARY: Abe?

ABE: All I'm gonna do is go home, pick up a few things, and let my momma know I'm leaving. I'll be back.

CLAUDE: Where you off to?

ABE: All these years of living on this earth, the one thing you should've learned by now is that what I do ain't none of your damn business.

ABE exits.

CLAUDE: Where he off to?

APPLES: Chicago.

TOMMY: Where you get the money for the threads and the new struggle buggy, Claude?

CLAUDE: I saved a lil brass before I got laid off from the foundry.

TOMMY: Is that so?

CLAUDE: You know I always was the industrious type.

TOMMY: Somebody hit The Pig last night.

CLAUDE: Is that right?

TOMMY: Made off with almost four hundred dollars.

CLAUDE: Three-man operation?

TOMMY: One man.

CLAUDE: But I thought you said you needed three to make it work.

TOMMY: Don't fuck with me, Claude. You owe me money.

CLAUDE: I owe you money for what?

TOMMY: That was my job, my idea. Just cause you decided to do it on your own don't mean that you get to keep all the money. I still get a cut.

CLAUDE: And if I had done it, I'd give you a cut, but I didn't do it and don't know who did.

TOMMY: I want my money, Claude.

CLAUDE: I ain't got your money.

TOMMY: I want my money and you gonna give it to me.

CLAUDE: Or what? What you goine do? Huh?

TOMMY: Apples?

CLAUDE: Apples? What you think he goine do? Shine my new gators?

TOMMY: Gimme the roscoe.

> *APPLES takes the pistol out of his belt and hands it to TOMMY.*

CLAUDE: You think you got the nerve to talk to me while holding a pistol in your hand?

TOMMY: I want my money, Claude.

CLAUDE: If you point that pistol at me, you better pull the trigger, and if you pull the trigger, you better kill me cause if you don't, I'm goine eat your black ass alive.

> *TOMMY points the pistol at CLAUDE.*

TOMMY: I want my money.

CLAUDE: I ain't got your money. Now put the pistol down.

TOMMY: After you give me my money.

CLAUDE: Put the pistol down before I come over there and smack the hell outta you. I oughta kick your ass anyway, outta general principle, pulling a pistol on me. Who the hell you think I am? I said put it down.

> *TOMMY lowers the pistol.*

TOMMY: This ain't right, Claude, and you know it.

CLAUDE: If you make me say it again, I'm goine come over there and light your ass up like a Christmas tree. Now put it down.

> *TOMMY lays the gun down.*

TOMMY: They gonna get you.

CLAUDE: Who goine get me? Boogie man?

TOMMY: Man you shot knows what you look like.

CLAUDE: I didn't shoot nobody. And even if I did, the man ain't talking cause he himself was involved in illicit activity. He tell on me, he tells on himself and I can guarantee that ain't goine happen.

TOMMY: But the man say he wasn't inside The Pig when he got shot. Man say he was outside walking along the highway.

MARY: Don't matter whether the man was inside or outside. Point is, the man is talking. That means that somebody's going to jail.

CLAUDE: Not for sticking up no damn gin joint. Sheriff don't care about that.

MARY: Maybe not. But a man got shot, Claude.

CLAUDE: In the foot.

MARY: Don't matter. First, Billy Connors got killed . . .

CLAUDE: I didn't have nothing to do with that.

MARY: I'm not saying you did.

CLAUDE: He got hold to some bad bootleg.

MARY: All I'm saying is what might have been a slight breeze on any other day is gonna turn into a tornado.

TOMMY: You going to jail, my friend.

CLAUDE: But I didn't do it.

TOMMY: Then who did?

CLAUDE: Might have been you for all I know. You were the one walking around here talking about it. Hell, I heard you.

TOMMY: You know I didn't have nothing to do with that.

CLAUDE: All I know is what I heard and I heard you talking about sticking up The Pig out on Highway 15. Mary heard you, didn't you, Mary?

MARY: What I look like? Your puppet?

CLAUDE: I'm just asking you to tell the truth, that's all.

MARY: Is that what you really want me to do? Tell the truth?

CLAUDE: When it comes to this here matter here. Did you or did you not hear Tommy talking about sticking up The Pig out on Highway 15?

MARY: I don't know what you're talking about.

CLAUDE: All right. That's good. Have it your way, cause it could have been anybody. Could have been Abe for all I know. I heard Abe talking about sticking up the joint. Then he shows up here today with enough money to buy Tommy's Roadster. Now the question is, where he get all that money?

MARY: You know where he got it.

CLAUDE: All I know is he showed up here with a pocketful of money. He buys Tommy's Roadster and then he takes off for Chicago. What is he running for? If he ain't done something wrong?

MARY: Ain't nobody paying attention to you, Claude.

CLAUDE: Tommy heard him talking about sticking up the joint. Didn't you, Tommy?

TOMMY: I want my money, Claude.

CLAUDE: I ain't got your money.

TOMMY: Then you going to jail.

CLAUDE: All right, Tommy, listen. I got a little bit of brass left from when I was working at the foundry. I'm willing to share it with you, seeing how we such good friends. But first, I need to know, did you or did you not hear Abe talking about sticking up that gin joint?

> *Beat. TOMMY sizes up the situation.*

TOMMY: Yeah, I heard him.

MARY: What the hell are you talking about, Tommy?

TOMMY: I heard Abe talking about sticking up The Pig out on Highway 15.

MARY: You know he didn't have nothing to do with that.

TOMMY: I'm just telling you what I heard.

MARY: You didn't hear a goddamn thing.

CLAUDE: Apples heard him. Didn't you, Apples?

APPLES: I guess I did.

CLAUDE: You gotta do better than that. You gotta say for sure.

TOMMY: I can say for sure, I heard Abe talking about it.

MARY: Abe ain't never done nothing to you, Tommy. Why you wanna lie on him like this?

TOMMY: He burned me.

MARY: So you're goine lie on him?

CLAUDE: Ain't nobody lying. Just telling you what we saw, what we heard, and what we remember.

MARY: Ain't nobody gonna believe you, Claude. Abe don't even fit the description.

CLAUDE: Since when did that ever stop anybody from taking a nigger to jail?

Gentlemen, seeing how we have information that is pertinent to a crime, it is our duty as citizens to report this information to

Sheriff Campbell as soon as possible. Anybody up for a ride in my new automobile?

MARY: Don't do this, Claude.

CLAUDE: You sweet on that lil piece of dark meat, ain't you?

MARY: I'm not goine let you hurt him this way.

CLAUDE: And what you goine do to stop me, huh?

Tommy? Get your roscoe and let's go.

> *TOMMY moves to pick up the pistol but MARY beats him to it. SHE levels the gun at CLAUDE.*

CLAUDE: You little bitch. I oughta come over there and smack the shit outta you. Don't you know that you should never point a pistol at anybody unless you're willing—

> *MARY fires the pistol, hitting CLAUDE in the shoulder.*

CLAUDE: You shot me.

> *MARY fires twice more, hitting CLAUDE both times.*

> *CLAUDE falls to the ground.*

> *TOMMY and APPLES are stunned.*

> *Lights up on JAMES and MARIE*

JAMES: That's not the way it happened.

MARIE: You said you weren't there. You said you ran away.

JAMES: We were pitching horseshoes in Ogden Weaver's backyard. Tommy said let's stick up somebody and get some money. We get to River Road, I recognized Claude and then I saw you for the first time. I handed the gun back to Tommy and ran.

MARIE: You ran after I shot Claude.

JAMES: That's not the way I remember it.

MARIE: My father came home and heard about what happened.

> *Lights up on HOOT and BEA.*

He was pissed off to begin with.

BEA: Where've you been?

HOOT: Guinea says to tell you hello.

BEA: You in a fight?

HOOT: Guinea says—

BEA: Hello, Guinea. Now what happened to you, Hoot? You out there fighting?

HOOT: I try to be nice. I try to extend a hand of friendship. But they don't want your friendship. They say they want to be treated like everybody else . . . if that's true, why they always stay clumped together? They wanna sit together at their own table, they wanna have their own organizations. You'd think if they wanted to be treated like everybody else, they'd make an effort to mingle with folks. But no, they don't wanna be like everybody else.

BEA: Where've you been, Hoot?

HOOT: Where the hell you think I've been? I been at work, that's where I've been. Couple men got fired and they needed folks to fill in so I did a double shift. Ain't that what you wanted me to do? Pick up another shift?

BEA: I wish you would've let me know.

HOOT: And how was I supposed to do that?

BEA: Sheriff came here looking for you.

HOOT: For what?

BEA: Claude Deeter got shot.

HOOT: When?

BEA: Couple hours ago.

HOOT: He dead?

BEA: Sheriff says he thinks he's goine be all right.

HOOT: What happened?

BEA: Somebody tried to rob him.

HOOT: Goddamn it. Folks work hard. And then you got this other element out there . . .

BEA: Sheriff wants you to come down to the hospital.

HOOT: For what?

BEA: He wouldn't tell me. But I think Mary might be mixed up in it.

HOOT: Goddamn it, Bea. Why can't you keep tabs on that girl?

BEA: I try, Hoot.

HOOT: You not trying hard enough.

Now tell me exactly what the sheriff said.

BEA: He said that Claude got shot and he was at the hospital, and he wants you to come there as soon as you got home.

HOOT: Lemme go change my shirt.

BEA: Hoot? I think Mary mighta got herself into trouble.

HOOT: I'ma find out what happened.

BEA: I mean, she mighta got herself into another kind of trouble.

HOOT: What other kinda trouble?

BEA: The worst kind of trouble a girl can herself get into.

HOOT: You think? Or you know?

BEA: She told me.

HOOT: Well, that was just a matter of time, wasn't it?

I'll talk to Claude when I get to the hospital. He's a good boy. He'll know what he has to do.

BEA: I don't know if Claude's the one you should be talking to.

HOOT: This don't concern nobody else except him and her.

BEA: That may not be the case.

HOOT: You mean she been tramping around with somebody else?

BEA: She hasn't been tramping around, Hoot.

HOOT: What's the boy's name?

BEA: I don't know. Not for sure. All I know is that she and this boy are friends. This boy from the south end of town.

HOOT: You talking about a colored boy?

BEA: There's nothing wrong with them being friends.

HOOT: You're talking about more than being friends. You telling me that she got herself into trouble.

BEA: I don't want you to get upset about this, Hoot.

HOOT: You trying to tell me she got herself into trouble with a colored boy?

BEA: I just told you, I don't know for sure.

HOOT: Then why you say such a thing if you don't know for sure?

BEA: Cause I don't know how Mary's involved in all this. And all I'm trying to do is tell what I know before you go running off to that hospital.

HOOT: I blame you for all this, you know that, don't you. You and that goddamn Guinea. I knew I couldn't trust you to raise that girl right.

BEA: His name is not Guinea.

HOOT: It'll always be Guinea as far as I'm concerned.

BEA: His name is Antonio.

HOOT: Oh, that's real nice. Antonio. So tell me . . . you still in love with Antonio?

BEA: I was never in love with him, Hoot.

HOOT: Then what do you call it?

BEA: We went to a picture show together once twenty years ago.

HOOT: I don't care if it was yesterday. What did you do with him when you were at the picture show, sitting in the dark?

BEA: We watched the picture show.

HOOT: Like I'm supposed to believe that. What you think I am, a fool? You wish you had married him instead of me?

BEA: How many times do I have to tell you?

HOOT: Every time I have to ask. Now tell me. Do you wish you had married him instead of me?

BEA: No, Hoot. I do not wish I had married him instead of you.

HOOT: When I see him, I'll tell him you said hello.

> *Lights shift.*

JAMES: I'm gonna tell you the way it really happened. They took me to the jailhouse and started to ask me about the Billy Conners killing and all the other robberies. I told them I didn't know anything about any killing, rape, or robberies. So they beat me and made me sign a confession. Then they put me in a cell with these other fellas. They had already put Tommy in one cell and Abe in another.

From the cell I was in, I could see out onto Third Street. For hours I watched the crowd gather and finally, I laid down and tried to go to sleep but I couldn't sleep. So I cried. I cried until no more tears would come. I guess I drifted off cause I woke up when I heard somebody shout, "They're throwing bricks through the window." So I jumped up, went to the window and looked out and as far as I could see were people. Men, women, children. Most of the men were carrying bats and clubs and pick handles and crowbars. And a lot of them were wearing the robes of the Ku Klux Klan.

MARIE: There was no Klan there that night.

JAMES: Usually they don't want people to know who they are but that night, they were barefaced.

MARIE: There was no Klan there.

JAMES: I could hear Sheriff Campbell talking to the crowd.

MARIE: I'll tell you who was there.

JAMES: And the crowd was not too happy with what he was saying.

MARIE: Frank Neely who worked behind the counter at the drugstore, he was there.

JAMES: I heard Sheriff Campbell threaten to shoot into the crowd—

MARIE: Misses Marley and her two boys, Jeffery and Reginald . . .

JAMES: And that's when I realized that Claude was dead.

MARIE: The manager of the bank, Don Everhart, he was there.

JAMES: I heard men shouting and then I heard a sledgehammer hit the steel doors in the front of the jail.

MARIE: Mildred Daily was there with her thirteen-month-old baby.

JAMES: After almost an hour, I heard a roar go through the crowd and that's when I knew that the doors had come off the front of the jail.

MARIE: But the Klan, the Klan was not there.

JAMES: Once the doors came off, they came into the jail and first they got Tommy.

Lights up on TOMMY.

When they brought him out, I couldn't see him because of the way folks were swarming all around him like ants fighting over a breadcrumb. Two men were dragging him and three or four others were stomping on his head and his chest.

TOMMY: I tried to cover my head but eventually I blacked out.

JAMES: They hanged Tommy from the side of the jail. He was dead before they put the rope around his neck but they continued to kick and stomp his dead body. Then they ran a crowbar through him a couple of times just to make sure.

TOMMY: All of a sudden it got real quiet. I could see people dancing around in circles and it looked like they were chanting. I saw a boy, fourteen or fifteen years old. He looked up at me, then fell to his hands and his knees and vomited.

JAMES: Then they got Abe.

Lights up on ABE.

I could see 'em dragging him down the street towards the courthouse. They were hitting him with clubs, kicking and stomping. Like Tommy, Abe was dead before they put the rope around his neck.

MARIE: He was not dead.

JAMES: They hanged him from the maple in front of the courthouse . . .

MARIE: He was not dead. They got the rope around his neck and then pulled him into the air. I begged them. I said . . .

Lights up on MARY and HOOT.

MARY: No, please. Stop.

MARIE: But they wouldn't listen.

MARY: He didn't do anything!

ABE: I remember choking. So I reached up, grabbed the rope and pulled myself up until I was able to breathe.

MARIE: The crowd did not like this one bit. So they let him down and while holding him prone, they broke both of his arms. Then they pulled him back into the air.

ABE: All of a sudden, it got real quiet and I could see men laughing and shouting. I could see the men from the foundry, men I had worked alongside for years. I saw Mary's father looking up at me. And as he looked up at me, I saw his face change. He recognized me. In that moment, he remembered who I was.

Lights fade on HOOT.

MARIE: I couldn't watch anymore so I turned my eyes to the ground and that's when I saw it . . . there in the dirt, a single spark of light. It was a ring.

MARY: His ring.

JAMES: You found it in the dirt?

MARIE: I had dropped it. There was a lot of confusion that night and in the confusion, I had dropped it. So I bent down to pick it up and that's when I saw Tommy's body fall to the ground. They had cut him down from the side of the jail. Then they dragged his body through the street like a dead horse tearing off most of his clothes. Then they hanged him alongside Abe.

Lights fade on MARY as APPLES enters.

JAMES: And that's when they came and got me. I remember rough hands grabbing my head and stuffing it into a noose. I blacked out and when I came to, I was standing under the maple with Tommy on one side and Abe on the other. My mother brought me up to always pray to God. So in that moment, I prayed, "Lord forgive me my sins and have mercy on me." All of a sudden, it got real quiet. And that's when the voice of an angel rang out from heaven and that voice said:

HOOT: Take this boy back, he had nothing to do with any killing or raping.

JAMES: And everything around me stood perfectly still like I was in a petrified forest.

HOOT: I know this boy. He's my shine. His name is James and I'm telling you, he didn't have nothing to do with it.

JAMES: Then all at once, the hands that had killed became soft and kind and tender. And they removed that rope from around my neck and I was able to stagger back to the jail.

Lights out on APPLES, MARIE and JAMES. Lights up on BEA.

BEA: Where you been?

HOOT: I was at the hospital and then I was at the jail.

They got 'em.

BEA: They got who?

HOOT: The boys who killed Claude.

BEA: Claude is dead?

HOOT: Died yesterday, right after I got to the hospital. Sheriff had put Claude's bloody shirt up in the window to let it dry. Folks saw it, got upset and started to congregate around the jail. Finally they busted in, pulled them boys out and hanged 'em in front of the courthouse.

BEA: They were lynched?

HOOT: Nobody got lynched. This ain't Mississippi, this is Indiana. They were hanged.

Mary come home yet?

BEA: No.

HOOT: You know what? You were right when you said she got herself into trouble. She was assaulted. Claude was trying to defend her when he got shot. Did you know they were goine get married?

BEA: Who was goine get married?

HOOT: Mary and Claude. They would've been the perfect couple. And then this had to happen. It's a tragedy. Makes my heart ache.

BEA: Who told you they were goine get married?

HOOT: Claude told me right before he died. I was right there with him. We talked. Talked about a lotta things. Talked about the plans he and Mary made. I was holding his hand when he passed.

BEA: What did you do to that boy?

HOOT: I didn't do nothing to him. Boy got shot.

BEA: The sheriff said he was goine be all right.

HOOT: Apparently the sheriff was mistaken.

BEA: What did you do, Hoot?

HOOT: I didn't do nothing. The boy was delirious, talking out of his head, saying crazy things about Mary, about what she had done. I sat there and held his hand and he passed away.

BEA: Was this before or after he told you they were goine get married?

HOOT: The boy had been shot and he died from his wounds. They got the boys who did it. Them boys confessed and signed confessions. And the one boy will even tell you exactly what happened. And instead of waiting for the government, folks decided to take matters into their own hands. And that's their right. This is a free country. Folks got the right to make their own law. Majority rules, justice was served, them boys got what they deserve and nobody had to wait for it to happen.

You wanna go see?

BEA: See what?

HOOT: The bodies. They're still out there. And there're more folks out there now than there were when they got strung up.

BEA: Nobody cut them down?

HOOT: There was talk about cutting them down, but if leaving them up there helps folks feel better, might as well leave 'em up, long as they're doing some good.

Wanna go? Lotta folks out there. Folks coming from all around to have a look, to take pictures.

BEA: No, I do not wanna go see.

HOOT: I can drive you if you want.

BEA: How you goine drive me?

HOOT holds up a car key.

HOOT: Got it last night. I wanted to surprise you so I left it parked up the street. Old Ford Roadster. Ain't much to look at and looks like it's got a leak in the radiator. But I'm sure it'll get you back and forth to see your momma as long as you keep putting water in it.

HOOT puts the key into BEA's hand.

BEA: Momma died last night, Hoot. My sister called Miss Myrtle and she came over and told me.

HOOT: Aww, Bea, baby, I'm sorry.

BEA: It's all right. I mean, I knew it was coming. Still . . .

Automobile is a nice surprise. Won't need it to visit Momma but I'll still be able to use it to get around. Maybe I'll be able to drive to Indianapolis every now and then to see my sister.

HOOT: I'd prefer it if you didn't. It's dangerous in Indianapolis. Nothing good ever come outta there.

BEA: I come outta there.

HOOT: Besides you. The only thing they got in Indianapolis is gin mills and whorehouses.

BEA: What about my sister?

HOOT: I don't want you going to Indianapolis. Fact be, now that your momma's gone, ain't no reason for you to cross the county line. Your sister wants to visit, she can come here.

I'm going to bed. Mary gets here, I want you to wake me the minute she walks in the door. All right?

HOOT exits. After a beat, MARY enters.

MARY: Daddy home?

BEA: Don't act like you didn't hear him in here talking.

Thought you were going to Chicago.

MARY shrugs.

You involved in that mess out there tonight?

I can tell by the look on your face that you had something to do with it. Looks like you been through a meat grinder.

Were you out there? You see it happen?

MARY: I don't wanna talk about it.

BEA: Was one of them boys the boy you were involved with?

MARY: If I tell you, you gonna damn my soul again?

BEA: Look, Mary, sometimes I say things. I don't know why I say them. Probably because it's the only thing I know how to say cause that's what somebody said to me. What I'm trying to tell you is, I don't know if you still wanna go to Chicago but if you do . . . here.

BEA hands MARY the car key.

BEA: There's a Ford Roadster parked up the street. That's the key to it. I don't know if it'll get you to Chicago but I'm sure it'll get you close.

MARY: Momma . . .

BEA: Shhh. You don't wanna wake your daddy.

MARY kisses BEA.

MARY: You've been crying?

BEA: What're you talking about?

MARY: I can taste the salt in your tears.

BEA: That happens whenever I start looking back on things.

Promise that when you get to where you're going, you'll let me know that you're all right.

MARY: I promise.

Lights fade on BEA and MARY as lights come up on MARIE and JAMES.

MARIE: I never saw or spoke to her again.

I got to Chicago and gave myself a new name. I stayed there until the baby came. I couldn't find work so I had to survive on handouts. The nuns were nice but after the baby was born, I couldn't bear to stay there without Abe, so I left. And I've been running ever since.

JAMES: Was it a boy or a girl?

MARIE: It was a boy, I think, but I don't know for sure. I had arranged to give him up for adoption. He was born, I heard him cry, then they took him away. I don't know if the hair was curly or straight. I don't know if the skin was black, brown, creamy tan, light bright, or all the way white. Every now and then I imagine I see him walking down the street, but since I don't know what he looks like, it's just a guessing game on my part.

JAMES: You ever try to find him?

MARIE: For what?

JAMES: He's your flesh and blood.

MARIE: He's part of the past. He's part of everything I've spent my life trying to forget.

JAMES: He's also part of the present and a part of the future.

MARIE: Somebody's future, not mine.

JAMES: I was wrong about this, Marie. You should tell your story, just as you told it to me. Would you be willing to do that? Meet with the Englishman and tell him everything that you remember?

MARIE: I remember being in Chicago with Abe after he was lynched. Do you want me to talk about that or do you want me to keep it quiet?

JAMES: What do you mean?

MARIE: I remember Abe and I living together in a small apartment over his cousin's garage. I remember Abe coming home wearing oil-stained coveralls . . . I know it doesn't make sense but that's what I remember. I remember me, running him a bath with the baby balanced on my knee. I remember unbuttoning his shirt, touching his chest, kissing his oak tree arms . . . and that's when I know I must have imagined it all. But I couldn't have imagined everything. I have his ring and his ring is real. I know it's real because I can hold it in my hand. And I know I didn't imagine his arms breaking. His neck stretching . . .

JAMES: Goddamn you.

MARIE: So just tell me which story you want me to tell and I'll tell it. I'll do whatever I have to do to make it all go away.

JAMES: Give me the ring.

MARIE: What?

JAMES: The ring, give it to me. You want it to all go away? Then give me the ring.

MARIE: But this ring is the only thing I have left . . .

JAMES: And once you give it to me, you can stop running and it'll all start to fade away until one day, you won't even be able to remember his name. Now give it to me.

MARIE: I can't.

JAMES: What do you mean, you can't? You won't? Or are you unable to?

MARIE: I can't.

JAMES: All right. This is what I'm gonna do. I'm gonna walk over there. And I'm gonna reach out and I'm gonna take the ring from around your neck.

MARIE: Please don't.

JAMES: All you have to do is stand there.

MARIE: Please.

JAMES: If you don't want me to do it, all you have to do is raise your hand to stop me and I'll stop.

MARIE: Don't.

JAMES: Shhh.

MARIE: No.

JAMES: Shhh. Shhh.

> *JAMES moves to MARIE. MARIE stands still.*
>
> *JAMES removes the chain and the ring from around MARIE's neck.*
>
> *Lights up on HOOT and APPLES.*

HOOT: We goine try to get you outta here before that crowd changes their mind and comes after you again. But you got to help me. Help me help you. You tell me what you remember and I'll tell you whether or not it's the truth.

APPLES: We'd been pitching horseshoes that afternoon in Ogden Weaver's backyard

Lights fade on HOOT.

The horseshoe game broke up and I was on my way home when Tommy and Abe asked me if I would like to go for a ride.

Lights up on TOMMY and ABE.

MARIE: It feels strange.

JAMES: You'll get used to it.

You should go get on your plane.

MARIE: If I found my son, what would I say to him?

JAMES: Tell him what you remember.

MARIE: Yeah. Good-bye, James.

JAMES: Good-bye, Marie.

MARIE picks up the urn containing the ashes and moves to exit.

MARY enters in panic. SHE's out of breath as if she's been running a great distance. SHE screams out in desperation:

MARY: Marieeee!

MARIE stops and listens as if she heard a faint voice from far away.

JAMES: No, Marie. Do not look back.

MARIE pauses, makes the decision, then exits leaving JAMES, APPLES, TOMMY, ABE, and a silently sobbing MARY on stage.

JAMES picks up the ammunition case, opens it, and places the ring and the chain inside the box.

JAMES closes the ammunition case.

Lights fade.

END OF PLAY